BRI

HORIZONS

The Monochrome World of Emma Peel:
The Avengers on film: Volume 1

edited by Rodney Marshall

with a foreword by *Avengers* writer Roger Marshall

©Copyright 2014 Rodney Marshall
(Essays are individually owned by specific writers as indicated in the text)

About the editor

The son of *Avengers* script-writer Roger Marshall, Rodney Marshall has produced four books about this iconic 1960s television drama: *Subversive Champagne*, a study of the Emma Peel era; *Adventure & Comic* Strip, exploring the Tara King season; *Making It New? a* reappraisal of *The New Avengers*; and *Bright Horizons* (editor), a critical exploration of the monochrome Emma Peel season. He lives in Suffolk and South West France.

The Avengers on film collection:
Bright Horizons (Volume 1: Emma Peel monochrome)
Mrs. Peel, We're Needed (Volume 2: Emma Peel colour)
Anticlockwise (Volume 3: Tara King)
Avengerland Regained (Volume 4: *The New Avengers*)

Bright Horizons is dedicated to Roger Marshall and all the other writers, directors, actors, set designers, technicians and post-production crew who helped to make the monochrome filmed season so special. The fact that we are still watching it, never mind writing about it, half a century later confirms what a fantastic job *The Avengers* team did.

My thanks to Jaz Wiseman for designing the cover and for his enormous contribution to preserving *The Avengers*' history: restoring the magical images and capturing the artists' thoughts before they disappeared irretrievably.

"One reason I love *The Avengers* is that such sheer hard sweat, blood and tears went into it and such beautiful humour, wit and sexiness came out of it. In that way – for all its fantasy – it's closer to everyday human feelings than soaps or Shakespeare."
(Frank Shailes)

"We were a bunch of merry men and women, some of the finest craftsmen, creators and curators of a place that existed somewhere in our imaginations...I understood, as I started reading the script for each new episode, that I would be given the key to a new world. Surrounding me was a host of writers, directors, set designers and actors, as well as wardrobe, sound, and lighting people, all with inspired shooting and editing skills. All were at the top of their game, at the right place, and at an extraordinary moment in time. What a privilege it was. What an amazing confluence of good luck, good timing and grace...I leave it to historians to figure out whether *The Avengers* 'mattered', to anthropologists, to experts of every kind. All I know is that we did it."
(Patrick Macnee, *The Avengers: A Celebration*, Titan Books)

"Because film offers you that opportunity to do something very, very different, why not exploit it?"
(Jaz Wiseman)

"The series is always a work in progress and it was evolving."
(Don Leaver)

(*Optimum Classic/Studio Canal* DVD commentary of *The House That Jack Built*)

"There's nothing straight in *The Avengers*"
(Brian Clemens, *Optimum Classic/Studio Canal* DVD commentary of *The Town of No Return*)

RBS: Colour makes you more 'showbusy entertainy'. Black and white *invested*.
JW: There's a real depth in terms of the quality, the contrast, and the lighting has to be great...The black and white Emma Peel is the peak of the show.
RBS: If you are going to film in colour you want to be 'colourful' and you're maybe sometimes drawn into filming locations for location sake.
JW: This retains a certain *noir* quality in terms of the directing and the acting. There are shots where it's very black and then suddenly you get a face coming out. The black and white adds to the storylines and plot. And the enjoyment.
RBS: It adds to the *menace*.

(Jaz Wiseman and Robert Banks Stewart discussing the advantages of filming in black and white on the *Optimum Classic/Studio Canal* DVD commentary of *The Master Minds*)

Avengerland has one foot in the real world but one elsewhere. On the surface it might appear, from the outset, to offer a normal post-war backdrop: a train station, churchyard, City bar or country pub. However, public spaces have been emptied of normality and the mundane. We have entered a parallel universe; a seemingly timeless, two dimensional never-never land.
Sometimes *Avengerland* even promises a romanticised, green-and-pleasant land: an idyllic village, Scottish castle, punting on a lake. This sense of arcadia is never allowed to establish itself, however. It is immediately cut through by unexpected or surreal acts of violence. The emptiness, and/or lack of ordinary people, simply adds to the sense of surrealism, providing an unsettling atmosphere. *Avengerland* becomes more a state of mind than a geographical location.
(Rodney Marshall, *Subversive Champagne*)

FOREWORD

[Roger Marshall "sheds some light" on the inspiration behind and origins of *The Hour That Never Was*]

'Serendipity'. The gift of making fortunate discoveries by accident. The quality that any half-decent writer needs in his toolbag. In 1953 I was doing National Service in Malaya. Living in the same officers' mess was 'Bunny' Rymills. Maybe, out of respect, I should call him Squadron Leader Rymills. A real live war hero and me still in my teens, less than a year out of school.

Bunny was a veteran of 161 Squadron, RAF Special Duties pilots who made hazardous flights into occupied France to bring Special Operations Executive agents and Resistance fighters back to safety in Britain. Bunny completed 65 such missions without a break, twice the usual number, flying without lights and praying that the torch waving him down to some ploughed field was held by a French hand rather than a German. Bunny's obituary in the *Telegraph* described him as "tall, witty, noisy and never at a loss for words". That's a fair assessment and a lot of those words found their way into my bag. Twelve years later came *The Hour That Never Was*. Bunny never realised it, but one of his passengers out of RAF Tangmere was John Steed.

The Avengers moved from videotape (Teddington) to film (Elstree) late in 1964. The first production was Brian Clemens' episode *The Town of No Return*. Brian and I drove up to Norfolk to watch some of the initial shooting and to see how Pat Macnee and Liz Shepherd, his new partner, were making out. While there we chanced on an old RAF wartime air base (RAF Bircham Newton). Driving along the deserted runways, poking into the mess halls, canteens and living quarters we soon realised that here were the ingredients for another episode. Serendipity! The control tower with one or two broken windows was a sanctuary for scores of birds snoozing in the afternoon sun. Hitchcock would have danced. [1] By the end of the day we had a draft sketched out on the back of an envelope. The usual process is to match location to script. In this case we reversed the procedure – marrying script to location.

The next slice of good fortune was the arrival of Gerry O'Hara to direct. Unlike most of his contemporaries, Gerry had not been broken on the wheel of Lew Grade's mid-Atlantic 'schlock operas'. He'd been steadily working his way up the league table of world-class assistants. He came along prepared to make a small budget feature. And that's what he delivered.

As a university student MGM kindly allowed me to spend two weeks watching production at their Borehamwood studios. One of the films on the floor was *Anastasia*, starring Ingrid Bergman, directed by Anatole Litvak, a Russian-born Hollywood heavyweight. At his elbow was his assistant, Gerry O'Hara. We didn't actually speak and it was ten years before Gerry and I worked together. I should have mentioned that sometimes serendipity takes its time.

In *The Hour That Never Was*, Steed has taken Mrs. Peel along to a farewell party at RAF Hamelin. The base is being closed down and the staff sent to various outposts throughout the world. What nobody realises is that the men have been brainwashed and are ready to be activated via the base's PA system. The plot is foiled and yet again Steed has saved the empire. Gerry didn't get to shoot in Norfolk. Too expensive to take a unit there and put them up in local hotels for two weeks. But he did get to see the deserted base and found an equivalent close to Elstree. [2]

© Roger Marshall
February 2014

1. I have always thought that this would have added yet another wonderfully surreal, disturbing image to *The Hour That Never Was*.
2. On receiving this foreword I asked Roger why he thinks this episode is still so popular, arguably the most iconic *Avengers* hour of the season or series. Is it the bleakly atmospheric location; those surreal, avengerish details such as the rattling chains, spinning wheel and whining milk float; or the fact that Steed and Mrs. Peel are alone for so long on screen? His succinct response was: "Maybe people like the idea of two against the world."

CONTENTS

Preface (pages 15-21)

Introduction (22-26)

The Town of No Return by Rodney Marshall (27-37)

The Murder Market by Sam Denham (38-53)

The Master Minds by Rodney Marshall (54-60)

Dial A Deadly Number by Margaret J Gordon (61-70)

Death at Bargain Prices by Margaret J Gordon (71-80)

Too Many Christmas Trees by Bernard Ginez (81-94)

The Cybernauts by Richard Cogzell (95-102)

The Gravediggers by Dan O'Shea (103-110)

Room Without A View by Rodney Marshall (111-119)

A Surfeit of H$_2$0 by Rodney Marshall (120-126)

Two's A Crowd by Frank Shailes (127-141)

Man-Eater of Surrey Green by Rodney Marshall (142-149)

Silent Dust by Denis Chauvet (150-165)

The Hour That Never Was by Jaz Wiseman (166-173)

CONTENTS (continued)

Castle De'ath by Rodney Marshall (174-180)

The Thirteenth Hole by JZ Ferguson (181-189)

Small Game for Big Hunters by Frank Shailes (190-200)

The Girl From Auntie by Margaret J Gordon (201-212)

Quick-Quick Slow Death by JZ Ferguson (213-221)

The Danger Makers by Dan O'Shea (222-230)

A Touch of Brimstone by Piers Johnson/James Speirs (231-251)

What the Butler Saw by Rodney Marshall (252-262)

The House That Jack Built by Rodney Marshall (263-269)

A Sense of History by Darren Burch (270-279)

How to Succeed...at Murder by Frank Hui (280-288)

Honey for the Prince by Rodney Marshall (289-296)

Afterword (297-304)

Contributors (305-308)

Production Timeframe (309-310)

Bibliography (311)

PREFACE

In *Subversive Champagne* I focused on a selection of monochrome Emma Peel episodes, adding a handful of Peel colour ones in a second edition. I was trying to define what makes this genre-defying series both creatively innovative and culturally important. I described the monochrome filmed season as representing the artistic pinnacle of the extraordinary, 'cult' television drama, *The Avengers*. Since then I have explored the final season of the original 1960s series, the Tara King era, and the 1970s *The New Avengers*. In many ways, every new season of this series was the 'new' *Avengers*, as the show constantly evolved, partly voluntarily, in order to reflect the changing social/cultural climate, partly due to necessity as actors, directors, producers and writers moved on, and others were invited in.

Despite some wonderful material in both the videotape era and the colour seasons, I remain convinced that it was at this crossroads between the limitations of 'live' videotape and the cartoonish or comic strip colourful world of *The Avengers* on film, that the series created something – in the words of Ponsonby Hopkirk – 'quite-quite-fantastic'. As Marcus Hearn suggests: "*The Avengers* peaked with the black-and-white Emma Peel episodes" (*The Avengers: A Celebration*, p. 105). I decided to return to that wonderful single season in an attempt to re-explore and capture the essence of the show's greatest achievement (in terms of seasons as 'collective bodies').

This time I wanted to offer a close analysis of every single one of the twenty-six episodes. However, I also wanted to offer a 'plurality of voices', drawing on the opinions and observations of a broad range of *Avengers* experts/fans. This seemed appropriate, given the equally wide range of writers and directors who worked on this magical season. There is a fittingly global feel to *Bright Horizons*, with contributions from the UK, France, Australia, the United States and Canada, matching *The Avengers*' unique worldwide appeal. The contributors come from an equally wide range of professional backgrounds: psychiatrist, hairdresser/chiropodist, actor, molecular biologist, researchers, website designers, horse breeder, youth worker, teachers etc. We even have an *Avengers* script writer.

This project began as a 'creative idea' thrown out to members of the *Avengers Declassified*'s fan forum. No one working on the monochrome filmed season of *The Avengers* in the mid-1960s could have imagined that nearly fifty years later a global 'virtual community' of fans would be discussing the series in infinite detail, sending instant messages across the world in a split second from their own computers. Not even Philip Levene would have thought up such an unlikely science fiction/technology plot. Online forums are sometimes portrayed in the media as shady places where strange people lurk behind pseudonyms. However, *Bright Horizons* is proof that such a community can work together to create something 'real'.

Each contributor was encouraged to employ his/her own approach and style. I simply asked writers to contemplate the following question: what is it about this single season which sets it apart from the rest? *Bright Horizons* attempts to answer this, while reflecting that *The Avengers* was quite unlike any other television drama produced before or since. Most of the chapters offer a 'critical commentary' of a specific episode which obviously involves a certain amount of re-telling the plot or storyline but adding analysis to the mix. Are they aimed at people who have already watched the series? Yes, probably. Hopefully, though, they do not alienate would-be *Avengers* fans and will entice newcomers to explore the magical, unique world of *Avengerland*. I envy anyone setting out on this voyage of discovery for the very first time.

Margaret J Gordon's Freudian analysis of *Dial A Deadly Number*, *Death at Bargain Prices* and *The Girl From Auntie* is provocatively bold. Is Fitch "a killer henchman with a homoerotic perversion for rich men's hearts"? Do Steed and Emma really 'castrate' Horatio Kane's department store, preventing it from 'climaxing'? Do Auntie's knitting-needles offer a disconcerting 'phallic' threat? It is fascinating to consider these potential psychoanalytical layers of the written/visual texts. If, for example, the gun is the ultimate phallic power symbol, does the fact that Steed carries one less frequently in this filmed season tie in with Margaret's belief that Emma Peel is beginning to control her partner's 'wandering eye'?

James Speirs' controversial and *risqué* exploration of *A Touch of Brimstone* asks us to question whether we actually enjoy the 'spectacle' of Emma Peel tied up or exhibited as a sexual object of desire. If so, what does this say about us as viewers? Piers Johnson's essay on the same episode sparkles with his spell-bounding knowledge and insights. No *Avengers* critic responds better in terms of the visual and aural appeal of the series. Piers' commitment went as far as sitting down to *listen* to the episode – without images – in his experimental research. I don't share Piers and James' fascination with this in/famous episode, but that is what makes the season (and series) so fascinating: we each react to an individual *Avengers* 'hour' in a different way. *A Touch of Brimstone* is the one episode covered by two writers. There is, naturally, overlapping material in these essays but the contrasting approaches counterbalance this.

JZ Ferguson's chapter on *The Thirteenth Hole* demonstrates her unrivalled ability to explore the characters of John Steed and Emma Peel; it is a truly remarkable essay. If there is a more astute observer of *The Avengers*, I have yet to encounter him/her. Her analysis of *Quick-Quick Slow Death* explores the episode's hidden depths in a story seemingly 'played for laughs'.

Dan O'Shea's study of *The Danger Makers* offers further insights into the characters of Steed and Mrs. Peel, while reminding us how important an ingredient strong guest characters/actors is in the show's success. I wholeheartedly agree with his claim that Nigel Davenport's portrayal of Major Robertson represents the pinnacle of guest performances in Season 4. Both the complexity of the character and the actor's interpretation are outstanding. Dan's chapter on *The Gravediggers* highlights the fine balance which exists between eccentric and cartoon caricature in terms of guest characters/actors.

Darren Burch's detailed approach allows him to connect *A Sense of History* to the show's videotape past as he views the episode as almost an antidote to Clemens' arguably less subtle vision of *Avengerland*. Talking of subtlety, Richard Cogzell's careful, thorough analysis of *The Cybernauts* reminds us how cleverly constructed and subtle Philip Levene's iconic episode is. It is an 'hour' close to Richard's heart and that love shines through in his words.

Bernard Ginez and Denis Chauvet's chapters are expanded versions of their online reviews to be found on the wonderful French website *Le Monde des Avengers*. They appear here both in translation and in the original French. Both critics shed light on intriguing possible influences for the writers/directors of the episodes they examine. Both are equally keen to emphasise the rich intertextuality of the episodes in a period when *The Avengers* drew on Britain's historical/cultural heritage. This is particularly relevant in *Too Many Christmas Trees* and *Silent Dust*. No doubt some of the finer points will have been blurred or lost in my translations so French-speakers are encouraged to read the original versions.

Frank Hui's description of Brian Clemens offering us "extreme strokes" is a memorable one; a fore-echo of the style of script which regularly followed in the colour world of *Avengerland*. His analysis of *How to Succeed...at Murder* explores this schizophrenic episode's "incongruous mix of tones", a story which "ends up denigrating feminism as much as it sheds a spotlight on it."

Sam Denham's exploration of *The Murder Market* places Diana Rigg's first ever episode within its *Avengers* context while examining both the series' new style of "elegant escapism" and the episode's daring "Freudian deconstruction". He even finds time to add some diabolical puns to his text. Like the show itself, underneath his champagne there is plenty of (textual) subversion. In many ways we get 'two for the price of one' here as Sam's essay offers an excellent introduction to the groundbreaking videotape-to-film transition *and* an exploration of *The Murder Market* itself.

Frank Shailes' exploration of the Kalayan 'jungle' in *Small Game for Big Hunters* reminds us how significant the variety (of sets and locations) is in making our journeys to *Avengerland* so thrilling: "We are planted in the midst of the action, bewildered and grasping for clues...the same glorious confusion every week. No escape now – we find ourselves concentrating on another world." This is central to the show's unique visual appeal. Frank's analysis of *Two's A Crowd* reflects the structural subtlety of *The Avengers* in Season 4.

Jaz Wiseman has done more than most to capture, restore and preserve *The Avengers*' history. His moderated commentaries with the likes of the late Roy Ward Baker have enabled key *Avengers* figures to add to the series' collective history. His chapter here on *The Hour That Never Was* explores and celebrates this iconic episode's visual appeal; it is an episode in which the Macnee/Rigg rapport is matched by the writer/director's shared vision.

My own chapters were written specifically for *Bright Horizons* but can also now be found in the 2014 version of *Subversive Champagne*. My return to a number of supposedly unglamorous episodes reminded me how consistently excellent the season is. My sole use (or abuse) of editor's privilege was in 'reserving' the chapter on *The Town of No Return* which I remain convinced is the best episode of the season/series. While I tend to concentrate on the visual texts themselves, many of the writers here place the episodes within the social/cultural context, correctly shattering the illusion that *The Avengers* was a 'timeless' show; it was a product of the exciting, revolutionary times in which it was produced.

I originally placed my editor's notes within the main body of each chapter's text but, on proof-reading the book, realised how irritating this would be for reader and writer alike. The numbered notes now appear at the end of each chapter.

Each chapter is prefaced by a 'factual' double page covering fictional locations/sets and characters. Neither list is exhaustive; they are simply meant to provide rough guides. Some minor characters have been left out and I have no doubt that a number of the locations were actually studio sets and vice versa.

I have taken a different approach in terms of an introduction. Rather than placing Season 4 within the context of *The Avengers'* overall history – as I did in *Subversive Champagne* – I have used Brian Clemens and Roy Ward Baker's excellent commentary on *The Town of No Return* (*Optimum Classic/Studio Canal*, 2010) as a launching pad to explore the new adventure as *The Avengers* embraced film for the very first time. Each citation in the introduction is taken from the same source, a historically important commentary moderated by Jaz Wiseman, one of the many writers who have contributed to this book. The first part of Sam Denham's essay on *The Murder Market* offers an alternative, contextualised introduction.

Of course this wonderful season owes a great debt to the videotape era. The magic recipe was being created from the moment Honor Blackman arrived at the beginning of the second season. The bizarre and the surreal can be found in a number of Cathy Gale episodes, from *Mr. Teddy Bear* through to *Mandrake*, a darkly humorous hour which offers a pre-echo of the Emma Peel era. Without the 'Gale force' we would never have enjoyed the 'appeal' of Emma.

With 2014 representing the 50th anniversary of *The Avengers* on film there is no better moment to celebrate the show.

© Rodney Marshall
Suffolk, UK
March 2014

INTRODUCTION

Laurie Johnson's musical score for the opening and closing credits on the filmed *Avengers* is the one which people tend to remember, rather than the earlier, jazzy composition of Johnny Dankworth for the videotape era. As writer Brian Clemens comments: "It suddenly got bigger and more important. We wanted to score each one like a movie." Clemens' remark is an important one. *The Avengers* on film (in Season 4) was not simply a series of twenty-six 'episodes', in the way of many other 1960s television dramas. Each one was treated as an individual, one-off 'cinematic' event, with music and fashions created specifically for that particular episode. Clemens goes on to suggest:

"Each episode was treated like a small movie...We [even] 'cast' the clothes for each episode."

Writer Brian Clemens and director Roy Ward Baker are both keen to point out the extent to which attention to every detail was vital, part of the new "opportunity" which film provided. Location hunting, visits to Parisian fashion shows, the casting of guest characters, and post-production were all intrinsic elements. However, as Baker observes, it always began with a well-researched script:

"The director is basing everything he does on the writer. It's the writer that's the fundamental genius at the bottom of the enterprise and everybody starts to build on that foundation."

The monochrome filmed season was able to draw on writers who already knew the *Avengers* style and product: Brian Clemens, Roger Marshall, John Lucarotti, Martin Woodhouse, and Malcolm Hulke; in addition, there were exciting newcomers such as Tony

Williamson and Philip Levene who would serve the series faithfully and innovatively until the end of the Tara King era.

Writers were given certain guidelines. In Season 4 the show had a formula, or structure: a teaser; a series of strange events; the Avengers' investigation; a fight finale; and a 'tag' scene in which the co-leads headed off, 'receding towards a bright horizon'. This obligatory happy ending added to the sense of fantasy and light entertainment, despite the brooding presence earlier on of a darker, dramatic undercurrent. In addition, writers were aware that – as Clemens observes – "we never wrote an ordinary scene… there's nothing straight in *The Avengers*." Realism is shot through with quirky and surreal details and events; the constant interplay between contrasting styles and genres is part of the disconcertingly clever mix, or what I term 'subversive champagne'.

Film changed things: it liberated the series, allowing the writers and directors the freedom to explore strange locations and, in the words of Jaz Wiseman, "give it that *film noir* feel and cinematic quality". [1] Baker refers to the importance of "the strangeness of the location itself", while Clemens stresses the importance of an *Avengerland* of "deserted areas" which "enabled us to keep to…a world uninhabited except by the people themselves." *Avengerland* can be a field, graveyard, abandoned airbase, warehouse, laboratory, department store, club, pub, country house, city street, country lane, or golf course. It can be a potentially banal or mundane place, but all it takes is a strange detail to stir up the surreal magic: a nodding toy, a spinning bicycle wheel, the whine of a milk float and an atmospheric, unsettling sense of 'otherness' has been created and unleashed. It is a state of mind as much as a geographical space.

The decision to film in monochrome (35 mm) was solely a question of budget. Brian Clemens wanted the extra £4,000 an episode to film in colour but that additional money was not granted. The financial risk was avoided. Ironically, this represents a wonderful moment of serendipity. Baker refers to his fondness for black and white while, with the benefit of hindsight, Clemens suggests that "it's funny; it's more real than colour." Monochrome allows a visual purity which is (arguably) lost in colour, regardless of the advantages which 'Technicolor' brought to the subsequent seasons.

Of course *The Avengers* by now was a 'cult', fashionable product, one which Baker claims that "half the actors of London wanted to be in". 'What was wrong with the other half?', I'm tempted to ask. This desire to participate was helped by the attractive roles of classy, urbane villains/diabolical masterminds on offer, as Clemens acknowledges:

"In Hitchcockian style we always wanted our villains not to look villainous but to look gracious, and mannered, and, if possible, handsome."

As both director and writer observe, part of the viewers' appeal was the dyadic structure of the Avengers themselves. Baker suggests that "a two-handed show is always better than a single", adding that Diana Rigg's arrival was crucial to the success:

"She had intelligence and wit, and that's something which the whole programme had the whole way through...She plays on a level with Patrick [Macnee/John Steed]. They are equally witty and amusing."

As Wiseman observes, the chemistry between the lead actors/characters is central to both the storylines and the season's success. Unlike the Gale/Steed relationship which was frequently volatile or icy, something had changed on both sides of the gender divide.

Clemens offers a creative suggestion, which may or may not have been passed on to his fellow writers at the time:

"They've had a torrid affair and it's over and now they're very comfortable with each other. They can get on with the job in hand without that sexual tension."

It is an intriguing idea or theory, albeit an impossible one to prove. Certainly, Emma Peel is a protagonist who manages to resist labelling: feminine, fashionable and sexy, witty and charming, cool but rarely cold, cerebral and yet also a deadly, trained fighter. Like Cathy Gale, she is physically and intellectually stronger than her male counterpart, something unheard of in the mid-1960s world of television drama. *The Avengers* both celebrates her attributes but also teases her/us for her 'perfection', adding new (impossible) skills virtually each week. What is equally intriguing is the fashion polarity which sees John Steed and Emma Peel on opposing sides of a divide, as Rigg/Peel wore the latest fashions, unlike Macnee/Steed:

"We were reflecting the times...although there's still a feeling of anachronism about *The Avengers* because what Steed's wearing he could have been wearing in 1922."

As Wiseman observes, Steed would be equally at home on a present day commuter train. There is a sense in which Steed is 'timeless', while the co-lead is a woman of the mid to late-1960s, part of a countercultural, revolutionary decade.

Bright Horizons – as a title – acknowledges the formulaic structure of the season/series, the insistence that any (dramatic) unease is lost or packed away before the tag scene. It also reflects the dazzling visual appeal of *The Avengers* on film.

Perhaps the most important observation about the 'new' *Avengers* in Season 4 is made towards the end of the commentary by Clemens as he observes that "the images were so strong". This is thanks to the whole *Avengers* artistic/technological structure or 'food-chain', from writer, set-designer, director, cast, through to post-production and publicity. The filmic nature of each *Avengers* 'hour' meant that there was an extraordinary individuality to the episodes. This is reflected in the following twenty-six chapters as we explore the magnificent monochrome world of Emma Peel and John Steed.

Spy-fi, sci-fi, spoof-fi, fantasy, wit, quirkiness, surrealism and a darker drama; Season 4 defies classification as *The Avengers* stepped beyond traditional genre labels, albeit within a formulaic structure.

© Rodney Marshall

1. *Film noir* is a term used to refer to the monochrome episodes by a number of critics/writers including Jaz and myself. Hitchcock's *Psycho* is often viewed as the ultimate *film noir*. It is easy to see how *The Avengers* makes use of a number of the techniques and styles of this cinematic genre: shadow, low-lighting, quirky camera angles etc. These characteristics give an episode such as *The Town of No Return* a psychological thriller element. Some might even argue that *neo-noir* is a term better suited to *The Avengers* given both the decade and the series' increasingly self-referential approach.

THE TOWN OF NO RETURN

Filmed (with Elizabeth Shepherd): 29th October – 13th November 1964
Re-filmed (with Diana Rigg): 21st – 30th July 1965

Exterior Locations:
Norfolk coastline/beach
Little Bazeley village streets and churchyard
Abandoned airbase
Deserted country lanes

Sets:
Emma Peel's apartment
Train carriage
Little Bazeley railway station
The Inebriated Gremlin pub: bar and guest bedrooms
Parish Church
Smallwood's blacksmith forge
Little Bazeley Primary School
Underground bunkers

THE TOWN OF NO RETURN

Main Character List:
Saul: fisherman/blacksmith in Little Bazeley (imposter)
Mark Brandon: school inspector (imposter)
John Steed
Emma Peel
Smallwood: visiting his brother, Tom, in Little Bazeley
'Piggy' Warren: landlord of The Inebriated Gremlin (imposter)
Jill Manson: headmistress of Primary School (imposter)
Jonathan Amesbury: vicar in Little Bazeley (imposter)
The real Mark Brandon

After the stricture of 'live' videotape, with the necessarily claustrophobic atmosphere of a studio-bound *Avengerland*, the teaser of *The Town of No Return* immediately offers us the exact opposite: seemingly deserted sand dunes, a flat landscape and a vast coastline. The sense of realism is reinforced by a fisherman (Saul) mending his nets, before the sight of a second figure emerging from the sea, in a waterproof covering, undermines it. When Brandon rips himself out, he is dressed immaculately, in a dry jacket, tie, and hat, carrying an umbrella. If the spectacle itself is surreal, then this is reinforced by Saul's lack of surprise. It is as if he has just witnessed a normal event – which in fact he has – and the banal conversation which follows about directions and the weather increases our sense of the surreal, rather than returning us to a knowable realm of normality. Brandon's warning that it "looks like rain" is both mundane yet also an example of pathetic fallacy. Little Bazeley by the sea will represent a heart of darkness for the Avengers. The appearance of the sinister title – *The Town of No Return* – provides us with a sense of foreboding.

Despite the fact that this episode was re-filmed mid-season, it represents the 'introductory' episode for the new Steed/Peel era, a fact which explains the formality of the post-teaser scene. The camera focuses in on Emma Peel's named doorbell, before moving to her Cyclops eye peephole which opens; from the real and traditional, to the surreal and quirky in seconds. As Emma Peel takes off her fencing mask, Steed removes his bowler, a visual mirror to their earlier greeting: "Good morning, Mrs. Peel." "Good morning, Steed."

Nothing Steed says or does in this opening scene can be taken at face value. This begins with his 'statement' that he "happened to be passing by". His subsequent "friendly advice" about Emma Peel's fencing technique is playfully patronising – almost foreplay – tempting her into the physical fencing duel which ensues, a battle which takes place while they verbally 'fence', as Mrs. Peel attempts to extract the truth behind his visit.

This scene offers us a huge amount of information about their relationship and the power games which are involved. Steed is a suave salesman, selling adventures:

"Brisk walks along the seashore, sand beneath your feet. The breeze snatching at your hair."

His reference to sandcastles hints at a childish, playful nature, while her warning that she refuses to carry his bucket and spade tells us (and Steed) that she is not going to be a subservient female partner. Her superior fencing technique allows her to overcome him effortlessly, while his ability to lure her into a trap, caught up in a curtain, reminds us that he is not someone who fights fair, despite his chivalrous/camp removal of ornaments from the fight path of the fencing duel. The fact that Emma somehow senses that Steed has already booked their adventure tells us that she knows him all too well. He is cunning, pretending to play the true 'English gentleman' but with a ruthless, "dirty" streak. The introductory nature of this scene is explained by Brian Clemens, who observes: "she's a face behind a mask. She's shown as a woman of action and when it's over she lifts the mask." (*The Town of No Return* DVD commentary, Optimum Classic/Studio Canal, 2010).

The fact that their conversation about Little Bazeley literally carries on seamlessly from Mrs. Peel's apartment into the train carriage warns us that *The Avengers* on film will both reveal and revel in its artificiality. Nothing can be taken at face value; no scene – as Brian Clemens warns us – is "straight".

This warning is in evidence in the train carriage, as Steed and Emma embark on a swift, witty conversation in which intertwined narratives about tea and missing agents crisscross and merge. Steed pretends to offer choice – adventure or no adventure; milk or lemon – but Mrs. Peel has no options:

Steed: Milk or lemon?
Emma: Lemon.
Steed: It'll have to be milk.

His "condensed" version of events flaunts the *Avengers* formula:

Steed: Then a few weeks later we had to send another agent to look for the first one – and a few weeks after that we had to send in another agent...
In unison: Who was looking for the agent...
Emma: Who was looking for the agent.
Steed: That's the general idea.

Diana Rigg/Emma Peel's "canted eye" – in the words of Roy Ward Baker – reveals her intellectual (viewer's) scepticism, as Steed magics a steaming silver teapot from his bag, alongside china teacups and Marzipan Delights; she is equally unimpressed by his familiar-sounding narrative about missing agents. She has obviously heard it all before. Their reading material, *Primary Education* for Emma, *Great Disappearing Acts* for Steed, shows us two actors/characters attempting to take on new roles. (The seamless visual transition from the steaming teapot to the train's own steam is typical of the episode's clever, playful stylishness.)

As Steed, Emma Peel and Smallwood – the passenger who has joined them – arrive at their destination, the 'Welcome to Little Bazeley' sign is immediately followed by the sight of a hostile-looking Saul, whose mad gaze is in turn replaced by the 'PEACE' sign on a graveyard stone cross, this making way for the pub sign for The Inebriated Gremlin. There are signs everywhere, all asking to be read, digested and analysed.

The quirky name and board of the seaside village pub offer a momentary flicker of hope that it will provide a warm, log fire welcome, in stark contrast to the dismal, windy weather outside, but the haunting music warns us that this is unlikely. We enter before the visitors do, and both the silence and the stern faces set the cold, unfriendly atmosphere. Steed's immediate comment "chilly is the word for it, decidedly chilly" refers to Little Bazeley inside and out.

Initially, landlord 'Piggy' Warren seems to offer the antithesis of his clientele, with his welcoming, childish public-school banter and ridiculous moustache. However, his questioning of Smallwood, Steed and Mrs. Peel borders on interrogation and his explanation of the frosty locals will turn out to be ironically false:

"Oh, they're not as bad as they look. Country folk, you know... suspicious of strangers...basically a fine bunch of chaps."

They are, of course, all strangers – enemy agents – and are acting out their stereotypical roles. The unsettling atmosphere is increased as Mark Brandon – the waterproof figure in the teaser – 'welcomes' Mrs. Peel:

Emma: Well, now I'm here, I think I ought to stay, don't you?

Brandon: Of course you must – now you're here – you must certainly stay.

We are beginning to understand why the title of this episode is *The Town of No Return*. The following scenes alternate between the almost agoraphobic feel of the coastline and the claustrophobic atmosphere of the pub. Steed is discouraged from leaving the pub to post a letter, while the exit of gun-toting locals, soon after Smallwood leaves, is explained away as "a spot of badger hunting. It's more fun at night." The sight and the explanation are ridiculous, yet they increase the dramatic tension rather than undermine it.

In the exterior scenes, the sight of Saul stalking Smallwood as dusk settles offers a series of noirish, chilling images amidst deserted windswept lanes and an empty smithy, despite the fire burning. Meanwhile, the pub bedrooms have nailed-down windows, increasing the sense of the Avengers being trapped. The close-up of an old pilot's mask provides an irrationally disturbing image, one which moves directly onto that of a skull on a parish gravestone. More signs left for us to take in and interpret if we so wish. As Smallwood approaches the church, passing the 'PEACE' sign, the hymn playing is *All Things Bright and Beautiful*, horribly at odds with the images we are viewing. The sense of surrealism peaks as Smallwood opens the church door to find a deserted interior, despite the singing and organ music.

The sand dunes have now become the location for a human hunt, Smallwood's ripped clothing and terrified face offering a sense of realism and surrealism interplaying. The silhouettes of Saul, the hounds and Smallwood on the horizon swap with the sight of Steed and Mrs. Peel eating unenthusiastically in front of the pub's log fire, with the 'soundtrack' of the hunt disturbing them even more than us; at least we can see what is happening, even if we don't as yet understand it. The final close-up of the captured, cornered Smallwood contrasts – as Clemens observes – with the vastness of the landscape.

We are twenty minutes in and yet it is only now that the investigation really gets going, reminding us of the subtlety of *The Avengers* at this stage in the show's history. Up until now, it has been a case of building up the unsettling atmosphere.

The scene in which Steed throws pebbles on the beach is a memorable one. Beginning playfully enough, the sight of a dozen pairs of feet in the sand, coming out of the sea, leads Steed to quote from *Alice in Wonderland*. The storyline, like Lewis Carroll's surreal tale, is becoming "curiouser and curiouser". As he observes, "all is not as it should be":

"I've been surveying the countryside. The tractors all stopped. Ploughs rusting in the furrows."

There is an apocalyptic feeling emerging, as if we have arrived in a post-nuclear-attack landscape, mirroring the Cold War plot which will soon be unveiled. The discovery of Smallwood's body in the sand is disturbingly realistic, his broken glasses returning us to a recurring leitmotif, symbolising, perhaps, the fragility of human life in *Avengerland*. The sense of a depopulated space is at the heart of the dramatic undercurrent, as it would be in *The Hour That Never Was*: "And where have all the people gone?...I haven't seen a solitary soul."

Visually, this episode is impressively noirish and the scenes cleverly, seamlessly move into each other, the fire of the smithy becoming the log fire of the pub, playfully suggesting that both are darkly dangerous locations.

The church appears at first to offer an oasis of normality, the Reverend Jonathan Amesbury a mildly eccentric, gentle country vicar, complaining of bats in the belfry and mice in the organ. Mrs. Peel is certainly charmed, although Smallwood's earlier venture inside has warned us that nothing is as it seems.

Steed's exploration of the abandoned airbase is the episode's central scene in terms of the playful interplay of the real and surreal, the dramatic and the light-hearted, the elegiac and the chilling. Faced with a weed-strewn parade ground, Steed imagines the sounds of soldiers marching, planes flying. He even offers a salute. Next, he moves on to the playground, sitting on the merry-go-round, accompanied by fairground music. The carefree, boyish moment is a fleeting one, giving way to the real/surreal sight of a 33 Squadron door opened to reveal a concrete floor without walls or roof, rusting dormitory beds, and a broken mirror which Steed acknowledges with his bowler. The dramatic undercurrent pulses again as Steed pieces together the bricks of a crude jigsaw which records the loss of 'Piggy' Warren, killed in action in 1942. The constant, theoretical threat of the Cold War is set alongside the historical reality of World War Two. I would go as far as to suggest that this is the most effective scene shot in the entire season, rivalled only, perhaps, by the shaking metal chains/milkfloat in *The Hour That Never Was*.

The strange nature of the disturbing drama is mirrored by Mrs. Peel being held at gunpoint by the vicar, while a taped choir plays a requiem. *The Town of No Return*'s heightened atmosphere is reaching breaking point. Mrs. Peel's ironic smile as she is cornered by the fake fisherman, school inspector and vicar promises us that the tension will be overcome. Eventually.

The final pub scene reveals Steed's ability to instantaneously transform from charming gentleman to cut-throat investigator. His interrogation of the imposter Warren is ruthless and, as Piggy's moustache catches fire, Steed's genuine concern about Mrs. Peel's disappearance is matched by his enjoyment of the landlord's squirming discomfort:

"You're expendable, Piggy. You're dead, remember? Killed in action 1942. Where is she, Piggy? Where is she?"

Once again, the move into the following blacksmith scene is cleverly seamless, the burning moustache replaced by a glowing, hot horseshoe. Steed's fight with Saul begins 'straight' before ending with a stylishly artificial knock-out from the reinforced bowler and the unsaddling of a tied-up Mrs. Peel who he advises needs "to cut down on the oats". Despite the increase in the action as we enter the final few minutes, there is still time for the playful, as 'schoolmistress' Peel offers Steed a lesson about the diabolical master plan while Steed sits attentively behind a child's desk, putting up his hand to make suggestions; even the formulaic explanation scene has a quirky playfulness to it in *The Town of No Return*.

The underground tunnels/bunkers scene lacks the earlier tension. It is as if the discovery of the plot is more important than the foiling of it. The protracted final fight action benefits from the wonderfully theatrical lowering of the metallic portcullis door, allowing Steed to dispose of a handful of armed soldiers before the 'curtain' rises again. It as much a fantasyland as the 'bright horizon' which Steed and Mrs. Peel head towards on a scooter in the tag scene, the country lane every bit as deserted as Little Bazeley was.

The Town of No Return offers an almost faultless starting point for viewers to the adventurous, innovative, playful new world of *The Avengers* on film. Many of the character types, places and leitmotifs which would dominate over the forthcoming seasons are re/introduced. These include: grinning imposters; atmospheric, agoraphobic, deserted locations; claustrophobic, interior traps; graveyards and churches. Subtle wit, light-hearted action-adventure and a darker dramatic undercurrent combine as the plot mixes realism and surrealism, defying any desire to define – or confine – *The Avengers* within a specific genre, blurring the boundaries of traditional television drama classification.

As a postscript, it would be fascinating to unearth the original *The Town of No Return,* filmed with Elizabeth Shepherd in the co-lead role. Parts of this were used when the final version was put together. *The Town of No Return* is historically interesting, given the decision to 'release' the original Emma Peel. We are unlikely to ever see the original; it may not even remain in existence. Nevertheless, the fact that there are/were two different versions of the episode – and that we see fragments of the original embedded in the remake – adds a further layer to this already fascinating introduction to *The Avengers* on film. *The Town of No Return* represents both a defining presence at the beginning of a new era, but also a mysterious absence.

© Rodney Marshall

THE MURDER MARKET

Filmed (with Elizabeth Shepherd): 23rd November – 4th December 1964
Re-filmed (with Diana Rigg): mid-December 1964

Exterior Locations:
Cemetery
Country road

Sets:
Aquarium
Steed's apartment
Beale's photo studio
Stone's house
Togetherness: corridor, reception, Lovejoy's office, Dinsford's office
Henshaw's apartment
Riding stables locker room
Funeral hall
Hearse

THE MURDER MARKET

Main Character List:
Barbara Wakefield: assassin
Jonathan Stone: philanderer, co-owner of Togetherness
John Steed
Emma Peel
Beale: commercial photographer
Jessica Stone: widow of Jonathan, co-owner of Togetherness
Robert Stone: Jonathan's brother
Simmons: Togetherness henchman
Adrian Lovejoy: Togetherness advisor
Walter Dinsford: Togetherness 'Counsellor of True Love'
Henshaw: Togetherness client

In which Miss Wakefield snuffs out an old flame and Lovejoy meets his match...

The second of Season 4's episodes into production - tantalisingly at the second attempt - *The Murder Market* could easily be dismissed as a frothy light-hearted romp in comparison with other more *outré*-flavoured episodes of the same season. This would be a grave mistake, as the episode presents *The Avengers* at its most subtly intoxicating. From a script submitted by Tony Williamson, a new addition to the roster of *Avengers* writers for the fourth season, *The Murder Market* is a pivotal, if not seminal *Avengers* escapade which throws into sharp relief the differences between the film and tape episodes, whilst serving as a blueprint for many of the later film series adventures.

The Avengers was a new departure in television writing for Williamson, whose previous drama credits were for productions far more grounded in reality, among them *Coronation Street, Compact, Z-Cars, No Hiding Place* and *The Plane Makers*. [1] He was, however, an experienced comedy writer, having worked on sketch shows with Season 1 *Avengers* contributor Dennis Spooner after the two men met while serving in the RAF. Williamson readily embraced the world of *The Avengers*, his first script adhering closely to the videotape style of story structure, while displaying a fresh approach to dialogue and characterisation. He would go on to gain two further credits for the fourth season, with the sublime *Too Many Christmas Trees* and the slightly below par *The Thirteenth Hole*. He would later return for the Tara King series after a stint on the avengerish *Adam Adamant Lives*, for which he would revisit the theme of murderous match-making with his script *Death by Appointment Only*. [2]

Exactly how much of Williamson's original script for *The Murder Market* reached the screen unaltered is difficult to know. A final draft screenplay allows us to compare the written page with the on-screen result, but without a copy of the original draft it is impossible to say how much is in fact Williamson. (Julian Wintle and Brian Tesler considered *The Murder Market* one of the best scripts they'd seen at the time it was submitted, their comments presumably based on the original draft.) Largely speaking the final draft script as written is what we see on screen, with only minor changes, and as an early script it also bears witness to how late in the day Steed's new partner became Emma Peel, with several pages still referring to the character as 'Mantha'. The name's aural similarity to 'panther' co-incidentally suggests the cat-like qualities of Steed's new associate, a facet carried through in Diana Rigg's performance.

The final draft script also demonstrates that even at this early stage of the season's production a new approach had been established in the treatment of *The Avengers*' underlying concept. In a strangely ironic about-face, the gritty realism that was so keenly attempted in the confines of the studio has already been abandoned in favour of a mannered, more stylised approach for the less restricted medium of film. In addition, rounded characters have been replaced by larger-than-life caricatures, while the dialogue has also undergone a sea-change, with naturalistic speech being ditched in favour of sharper exchanges and wittier repartee reminiscent of Wilde or Coward, shot through with these writers' particularly British style of blackly comic humour. Scenes and transitions are also more deftly handled, moving the action swiftly along, in marked contrast to the more leisurely pace of the earlier seasons. All this was greatly assisted by the move to Elstree Studios, which could provide technical flexibility on sound stages equipped for feature films and offer the razor-edged editing facilities of celluloid cutting rooms.

This new world of movie magic would serve *The Avengers* magnificently, allowing its creative team to cast a cinematic spell over the series which, combined with the new literary approach, would result in a style of screen presentation more closely resembling a kitsch version of *Kind Hearts and Coronets* rather than gritty 'kitchen sink'. [3]

Initially, the director assigned to *The Murder Market* was Wolf Rilla, an experienced feature film and television director. [4] Rilla began shooting his version of the episode in late November 1964 with Elizabeth Shepherd then cast in the role of Emma Peel, but according to director Peter Graham Scott, ABC supremo Howard Thomas made the decision to abandon filming and replace Shepherd within days of Rilla starting work, after viewing the rough-cut of Scott's *The Town of No Return*. [5] During a two week hiatus in December, Scott screen-tested a number of actresses before a new choice was made, and before Christmas the die was cast for the future of *The Avengers* on film. The new Mrs. Peel would be 28 year old RADA-trained 'Yorkshire lass' Diana Rigg. Production resumed on *The Murder Market*, but now without Rilla - Peter Graham Scott having been retained to oversee the rebirth of the series after its aborted first attempt. An all-round film and television professional with a wide range of credits, including the half-hour incarnation of *Danger Man*, for which Brian Clemens had contributed scripts, Scott's assured and precise direction would give *The Murder Market* a cinematic quality, while retaining the quirky visual style of the videotaped shows. He would also ensure that viewers were thrown in at the deep end with his teaser, which neatly establishes the essence of the series and the episode's macabre plot, while cleverly plumbing richer sub-textual depths.

As *The Murder Market*'s opening frames fade in, viewers are immediately forced into a double take. We see the face of a man, but wait a minute! He's surrounded by darting fish! Our attention is immediately captured. The camera then glides smoothly past the aquatic creatures to reveal that the actor is standing in front of a tank in an aquarium gallery. This neat directional touch is not in the script and serves both as a knowing nod to the famously inventive camera set-ups of the videotaped episodes while acting as a substitute for a theatrical curtain, drawing aside to reveal the on-stage action. Now that we have found our feet, the plot swiftly thickens. Our well-dressed 'fish' is awaiting a mate, who turns up in the glamorous shape of Suzanne Lloyd. But our man is no match for the shark-like Miss Lloyd, who draws a pistol from her purse and callously shoots him. This being *The Avengers*, we see no blood, or any bullet holes, except in the fish tank behind our victim, which immediately drains its contents over his corpse. A simple enough scene, but it repays a second look.

The Murder Market presents us with a script which explores fundamental aspects of life. The relationship between the perennial human concerns of marital union and death is clearly highlighted throughout the episode - but birth too is part of the same equation, and in the watery worlds of aquaria we are reminded of the protozoic aspects of new life - the primordial and sexual nature of fish in their liquid environment providing a suitable visual representation of the process of conception. The scene's air of carnal expectancy, the floral buttonhole, and the silenced gun add to the atmosphere of sexual potency, the latter's presence given a perverse twist, and a hint of the episode's theme of forbidden love, by being held in the hands of what appears to be a seductive woman. In addition to this symbolic reading of the scene, the initial visual image of the tank full of exotic fish appropriately represents the experience of the viewer - we are observing an artificially-created environment inhabited by colourful creatures performing exclusively for our fascination and entertainment. Film buffs might also appreciate the setting as homage to similar aquarium encounters in Hitchcock's *Sabotage* and Welles' *Lady From Shanghai*. A textbook example of cinematic pre-figuration, the scene neatly prepares us for the action that follows. [6]

The newly recruited Mrs. Peel now arrives stage left, looking rather frumpy in a fur coat that does her figure no favours. She is already clearly conversant with Steed's methods. "Your popularity poll?" she asks, observing a graph he is drawing up. In the script this was originally described as a wall chart, but a more convenient drawing-board version has been substituted. The classic *Avengers* investigation scenario is quickly established, variations on which would arguably become a series cliché. There have been a number of unexplained deaths. Somehow their cause must be linked. One common factor provides a clue. While Steed follows this lead, Mrs. Peel must see that no other stone remains unturned.

This time the clue is a photographic portrait, introducing Steed to the David Bailey-esque photographer Beale, a goatee-bearded character whose appearance bares more than a passing resemblance to contemporary photographs of Brian Clemens. The similarity doesn't end there. Like Clemens, Beale is a creator of artifice, his studio being used to sell swinging sixties images in which you can't actually see what's being sold; a contrived world where style appears to matter more than substance and which seems to be populated by empty-headed cipher-like clothes-horses, rather than fully rounded characters. In a subtle change to the script, Beale's model is also no longer bikini-clad, but is more imaginatively attired in just a shirt and tie – a far sexier proposition – which adds to the scene's air of *demi-monde* semi-reality. Having now deconstructed the film-making process, and shown us that what we are watching is completely make-believe, the script then returns us to our fantasy *Avengerland*.

While Emma is met by a stony silence from the latest victim's less than grieving widow, Steed follows the photographer's trail and, in a recurring leitmotif of the Emma Peel seasons, arrives via a corridor in front of a sign displaying the episode's focal concern. This week the target is Togetherness, the word serving doubly as the theme of the episode and as the name of the high-class dating agency whose activities are at the heart of the action. Befitting a story which revolves around a dating agency, *The Murder Market* will abound with references to doubles, couples and mirror images, while the company's motto, 'Where there is always a happy ending', also provides the sign with a nicely ironic coda, given the ensuing action.

Entering Togetherness under a shower of confetti, Steed is immediately confronted with an idealised paradise of heavenly bliss. Love is all around in Harry Pottle's flamboyantly over-dressed set of floral arrangements and cherubic cupids. At the heart of the sugary conception we see the mannequins of a married couple, standing in mute testimony to the commercialised convention that marriage has become. In comic contrast, this bubble of homogenised amorous aspiration is punctured when we see the mismatched offspring of the agency's services – a beaming tall girl and a bemused short man. Their departure introduces us to Steed's latest opponent, the deceptively-named Lovejoy, played with scene-stealing relish by Patrick Cargill. Inviting Steed into his inner sanctum, Lovejoy's initially angelic façade of unctuous charm is quickly seen to crack in the face of Steed's implacable superiority during a beautifully scripted exchange. "Work?" purrs Steed. "Tried that once – didn't work out." As Steed wrong-foots Lovejoy at every well-turned line, the two snakes in the grass face each other with slithery silkiness, Cargill's hooded eyes adding to his sinister presence. It soon becomes clear that all is not sweetness and light in Togetherness, when they are interrupted by prospective client Henshaw, who bursts into the office acting like a nervous chicken. As Lovejoy curtly dismisses him we clearly glimpse the venal beast that lurks behind his thin veneer of smooth civility, and our suspicions are aroused. Having sown the seeds of our story, the scene is now set for a scenario offering the prospect of a bumper crop of sexually-orientated, innuendo-laden imagery, fresh and ripe for the picking.

Returning to Togetherness after dark, and having gone through some laughably perfunctory motions of looking for clues, Steed discovers a florid mural of the eternal lovers. But like Lovejoy's outward demeanor this picture of apparent innocence also cracks in two to reveal a rotten core. On pulling Adam and Eve apart Steed discovers their sinful secret. Behind their joyful representation of the promise of new life lies the cold certainty of death - with Henshaw's name at the top of the list. Alerted by Steed, Emma dashes to the latest sacrificial victim's apartment, but is too late. Instead of a bride in the bath, she discovers Henshaw's submerged body – and catches a fleeting glimpse of his killer. If Lovejoy is the anti-Steed, then the episode's anti-Emma is the far from warm-hearted lover Barbara Wakefield, her barbaric deathly touch the mark of a cold-hearted killer. Like Emma, Barbara is a masculine female – clearly displayed through her handling of lethal weapons, but she also represents sterility, her latest victim's watery death resembling that of a still born child (this subliminally reminding us that we rarely, if ever, see children in *The Avengers* – a factor which adds to the show's childlike air of unreality). [7]

Back at Steed's apartment, Emma's half-hearted anger in response to his belated warning about Henshaw appears to be a legacy from the Cathy Gale era, and the fact that it is almost immediately forgotten shows us that our new arrival's relationship with Steed is going to be quite different. Not so much 'Love – hate' as 'Take it or leave it'; emotions rarely run deep in Emma's episodes. And there certainly isn't the time for sentiment. With Togetherness now clearly implicated in the murderous proceedings, in a familiar film series plot development *The Avengers* move the action along by offering themselves up to the enemy. Steed is first in to bat, revisiting Lovejoy to take part in a beautifully choreographed scene in which the two men circle each other like scorpions in a dance to the death. Having been seemingly hooked, Steed is sent on a date - to the aquarium.

Here, like our earlier victim, we see him down among the fishes. But social chameleon that he is, Steed makes himself quite at home with the pond life, burbling happily along with his newfound fishy friends, while he awaits the arrival of Miss Wakefield. This time the smiling siren is in a less predatory mood, and the pair waste no time getting down to some kinky horseplay in the riding stables. In a setting straight out of a fetish lover's fantasy – all thigh boots and harnesses – the ambiguous sexuality of the assignation is played up by dressing the pair in practically identical outfits, leading us to wonder who is actually wearing the trousers in the relationship. As Barbara teases information from Steed about his imaginary cousin, he offers himself up, in the form of a snugly fitting boot, to her domination before the scene ends with him playfully fondling his riding crop.

Back at Togetherness, Emma is also flirting outrageously, with a gawping Lovejoy, as she requests a date with "stamina", but soon finds herself marked down as the agency's next target on Barbara's return when she is recognized from their encounter at Henshaw's. In a graphic act of visual mutilation not carried through to the on-screen action, the script describes Emma's photograph being decapitated with a pair of scissors to signify her fate. Such scenes of photographic savagery would become a recurring *Avengers* obsession during Clemens' tenure as producer.

In a late addition to the script, the teasing sexual metaphors keep coming as Steed and Emma regroup to compare notes. This scene went through significant changes before the final version was committed to celluloid. Pages in the final draft script indicate that the action was originally to take place around a billiard table, and would have seen Steed and Emma potting shots as they discussed the case with an air of masculine competitiveness, once more redolent of the Cathy Gale era. But in May 1965 script revisions were added which re-envisaged the scene with Steed playing the tuba while Emma practised her golf swings. When the scene was shot however, the roles were switched at Patrick Macnee's suggestion – on the basis of his believing that his co-star should benefit from being the focus of the action. The sexual *frisson* that results from seeing Diana Rigg performing on the instrument, while Patrick plays with his club - which eventually ends up being poked down the aperture of the horn - could hardly be more Freudian. Shot by Roy Ward Baker during his stint with the series (in his book 'The Director's Cut' he describes engaging a professional tuba player to coach Diana Rigg in the correct fingering), the scene is a model of cinematic economy. The entire action, which called for smooth timing from the players and polished camera movement from the crew, is shot in just one continuous take.

With Steed now hooked as a promising catch, Togetherness must reel him in – and what more suitable way to do so than with an invitation to a cake tasting? The centrepiece of the episode, this is the scene in which the villains reveal their true colours, and the programme makers lay the kinky innuendo on even more thickly.

Packed with more fruitiness than a rum punch, the scene oozes decadent debauchery as Lovejoy and his associate initiate Steed into the ways of Togetherness. Gaily savouring the proceedings, the threesome's fraternal *bonhomie*, coupled with Lovejoy's orgiastic lip-smacking delight in sampling the pleasures on offer, lace the scene with sybaritic homo-eroticism, emphasised in perhaps the most impudent shot of the episode. In such heady surroundings it comes as no surprise that the subversive champagne pops up - this time in a row of carefully positioned bottles canted at waist level, behind which the three actors suggestively present themselves. A daringly provocative hint at then illicit sexual practices, this scene demonstrates how easy it is to forget how much attitudes have changed since 1964.

Now fully accepted as one of the boys, Steed is sucked further into their dastardly machinations by Lovejoy, now unmasked as a killjoy - an angel not of connubial bliss, but of destruction. This part of the plot is more elaborately detailed in the script than in the finished episode, with Lovejoy referring to Steed's military background and Steed describing how he might hypothetically kill his imaginary cousin by orchestrating an accident with a strategically-positioned bar of soap. A more significant omission is the following scripted scene which sees Lovejoy seal Steed's initiation by awarding him with the tools of their manly trade – a loaded pistol and a complimentary bottle of champagne. This is the 'subversive champagne' referred to by Emma in the original draft of the next scene, and with which Steed toasts her, before aiming his more lethal, newly-acquired weapon in her direction. The sparkling sexual fizz of the lovable Eros is transformed into the cold and deadly agent of Hades.

Mrs. Peel, it seems, is dead. Diana Rigg hasn't completed a single episode and already she's laid out in a coffin - her life as an Avenger cut prematurely short. The camera holds her frozen death mask in shot while Peter Graham Scott directs a continuous take of his own, as we see Steed and Lovejoy appearing to cement their dubious relationship prior to Lovejoy leaving. And exhale! At last we and Emma can breathe a sigh of relief as her eyes flick open, and our Juliet awakens from her pretense of deadly slumber. Life goes on, and Steed clearly still holds a candle for his new partner, the eternal flame burning prominently in shot behind him. Adding to the potent phallic imagery of waxen flame he then produces...guess what? Yes, an even more subversive bottle of champagne. In the spirit of Dionysus, Emma can entertain herself while awaiting her release from purgatory.

Our heroine's ordeal isn't over yet though. Steed has been recognised by Beale as the man who was nosing about in his studio, so Lovejoy returns the favour by paying Steed a visit. Fresh from playing with his soldiers, Steed opens the door to be greeted by his mirror image who, affirming his role as the anti-Steed, will later top off the doppelganger effect by donning a Steed-like bowler, having invited his reflection to attend Mrs. Peel's funeral.

Having toyed with sado-masochism and indulged in homo-eroticism the episode now takes forbidden love one step further, nodding knowingly at necrophilia as our 'corpse' cavorts blithely with a giant candlestick, champagne bottle gripped firmly in hand, before the macabre reverie is rudely interrupted by the arrival of Lovejoy and his pall-bearers. The dead body hastily returns to her casket to be borne away, seemingly tightly-sealed inside. With Emma having already given us a sombre rendition of the Wedding March on the tuba, Laurie Johnson now picks up the musical baton, providing us with a jaunty version of the Funeral March to add to his exemplary contribution to the episode. In the process he reminds us how similar the notes in the two pieces of traditional music are, as the funeral procession makes its way through a gothic graveyard. Ironically, it was during the shooting of this location sequence, one of the first filmed for the episode by Wolf Rilla, that the cast and crew heard the news that Elizabeth Shepherd's contract had been terminated. In tribute, a mordant Patrick Cargill was heard to murmur while gazing into the scene's empty grave, 'Alas poor Beth, I never even knew her you know'.

Our new Mrs. Peel proves to be made of sterner stuff, and having risen miraculously from the dead arrives fighting fit in the Togetherness office to seek further evidence of the organisation's dirty deeds. In a reversal of their earlier encounter she is discovered by Barbara Wakefield, who takes control of her avenging opposite number by out-gunning her. On the return of the funeral party, led by this week's newly revealed diabolical mastermind (it's Mrs. Stone, the first victim's widow – not that we care), Steed's duplicity is realised. But first there are other fish to fry. Orders are issued to eliminate his partner, but having anticipated their move, the civil serpent has already slithered back into their nest. Here, like a vengeful God, he wreaks havoc in their pastiche of paradise, and in a maelstrom of violence the Eden of vipers is laid waste. Concluding this gleeful orgy of wanton destruction, Steed shows he is more of a man than his effete opponents - saying it with flowers by laying out Lovejoy with a bucketful of blooms, while splattering his associate with a well-aimed face-full of cream cake. Emma in the meantime has been fighting her own 'mano a mano' battle with Barbara, her counterpart savagely thrusting at her with a flashing blade before harmlessly ending up throwing herself into Steed's arms.

The avenging pair's work is now done. Having made a mockery of matrimony, casually dismissed death and split Togetherness asunder, they depart together in Togetherness's hearse towards a rosy fun-filled future, leaving us to muse about the moral of the story. We have entered a new world with this incarnation of *The Avengers* - a sharper, wittier and more self-knowing world of elegant escapism. Like the Cathy Gale episodes, the Emma Peel adventures will take us into curious corners of British society and set the action against the backdrop of familiar British institutions, but while Cathy's episodes would draw the line at being critical of institutional short-comings, Emma's indulge in wholesale demolition. This is never more so than in *The Murder Market*, in which the institution of marriage is comprehensively blitzed in a firestorm of Freudian deconstruction, the charade of conventional behaviour shown to conceal seething primitive desires. The episode echoes and anticipates the new era of sexual and social freedom that would reach every strata of society in the 1960s.

Far from being a frothy, inconsequential glass of bubbly, *The Murder Market* is in fact an elaborate confection. A three-tiered wedding cake of an episode which takes us through the stages of birth, life and death. An episode packed with fruitiness and nuttiness, coated with the bitter taste of marzipan, and topped with the elegance of royal icing. As such, it fittingly celebrates the knot being tied between its two newly united leading players. The toast is – "*The Murder Market!*"

© Sam Denham

1. *The Plane Makers* starred Peter Jeffrey; its sequel, *The Power Game*, starred Clifford Evans and Peter Barkworth (eleven *Avengers* guest appearances between them).
2. Williamson also wrote the Season 5 script *The Positive-Negative Man*.
3. A satirical 1949 British 'black comedy' film.
4. Most famous for his critically-acclaimed horror film *Village*

of the Damned (1960).
5. The truth behind Shepherd's departure has never been revealed. All we have is a number of 'unofficial/official' PR versions, such as that she wasn't "avengerish" enough, a strange Clemens comment when you consider that the series itself was only just beginning to re-evaluate *Avengerland*.
6. Intertextual references to Hitchcock abound in this episode. Drawing on *Rear Window*, the photographer Beale's camera turns the female model into an object. The basic premise of Togetherness – clients swapping murders to provide cast-iron alibis – is clearly borrowed by script writer Tony Williamson from *Strangers on a Train*.
7. When we do encounter a child – the precocious Sally in the Tara King episode *Take Me to Your Leader* – she seems ridiculously out of place in *Avengerland*.

THE MASTER MINDS

Filmed: 17th December 1964 – 8th January 1965

Exterior Locations:
Country roads
Sir Clive Todd's house: façade
Houses of Parliament (stock footage)
London street (stock footage)
College for Young Ladies: grounds, archery range
Countryside/security fence

Sets:
Strong room
Sir Clive Todd's house: living room, bedroom, study, hall
Houses of Parliament: lobby, Alan St. Johns' office
School: hall, gym, corridor, staircase, Steed's bedroom

THE MASTER MINDS

Main Character List:
Sir Clive Todd: senior civil servant
Desmond Leeming: senior member of RANSACK
John Steed
Emma Peel
Butler: to Sir Clive
Major Plessy: senior civil servant
Sir Jeremy: senior civil servant, PM's advisor
Dr. Fergus Campbell: service psychiatrist
Davinia Todd: Sir Clive's daughter
Holly Trent: games mistress, mastermind
Professor Spencer: senior member of RANSACK

Steed: There is a kind of fantasy about it all, isn't there?

The Master Minds has a playfully self-referential title, poking fun at the formulaic approach of a series in which Steed and his female partner encounter diabolical masterminds on a weekly basis. The teaser, once again, plunges us immediately into a strange world where the realism of a burglary is undercut by the strange guards' uniforms which the criminals are wearing. The director offers us a daringly effective camera angle as the security gate descends, threatening to squash one of the robbers and the camera itself. The decision to terminate the bungling burglar – the leader of the gang chillingly ordering another man to "Kill him!" – heightens the tension.

The post-teaser scene demonstrates how simply *The Avengers* on film creates an effective sense of atmosphere. Steed's car heads along deserted country lanes against a backdrop of bare winter trees, the fore-grounded milk churns – as much as the blazing headlamps and the half-light – telling us that it is dawn. If a sense of realism has emerged then this is not allowed to establish itself as Sir Clive Todd's elderly butler answers the door in a surgeon's mask. The Sixties interior [1] – with a central, circular brick fireplace – is undermined by the odd sight of the same, 'timeless' uniform we saw in the teaser:

Emma: Steed, you did wake me up a few minutes ago?
Steed: There is a kind of fantasy about it all, isn't there? Toy soldiers, and all that.
Emma: Is it some kind of fancy dress party?

There is a deliciously artificial layer here. The Avengers are talking as much about the series in general as they are about Sir Clive

Todd's odd choice of clothes. As if to emphasise this, the plot pauses while the camera focuses in on Mrs. Peel, taking her in from head to toe as she shows off the glamorous outfit which has remained hidden underneath her coat. As Jaz Wiseman observes on the Optimum DVD commentary, the setting and fashions "encapsulate the whole Swinging Sixties feel"; the scriptwriter Robert Banks Stewart remarking that: "The Swinging Sixties were very, very fully represented by the filmed series of *The Avengers*." This self-consciously staged 'fashion shoot' moment will be playfully echoed later when Sir Clive's daughter Davinia reveals the *Côte d'Azur* bikini underneath her leopard-skin coat, offering an image of the more countercultural, permissive side of the decade with its sexual revolution, something which the cutting-edge, subversively sexy Emma Peel was at the heart of.

The appearance of Campbell, a Service Psychiatrist, brings with it another battle between realism and something more playfully bizarre. Seemingly forgetting that Sir Clive is the patient, he offers a snap judgement of Steed: "Your facetiousness covers an edgy temperament...I'd say your nerves mostly jangle like wires in the wind." The bedside consultation becomes confrontation in the form of verbal jousting, with Steed able to arm himself with the required psycho-babble: "Traces of an incipient inferiority complex. I should watch it!" With his ability to put people down through witty retorts, it is little wonder that Steed rarely carries a gun in this season. These opening ten minutes demonstrate the innovatively daring internal conflict at play in *Avengers* episodes in terms of genre and style.

Despite the slick, stylish opening, *The Master Minds* is best remembered for its 'second half', set at an all-girls' boarding school. Our introduction to the 'college for young ladies' comes immediately after the 'straight' scenes in which Steed tries to understand why the psychiatrist has (reluctantly) murdered Sir Clive. Our first sight of the notice-board breaks the previous dramatic tension, the school motto – 'Defend Thy Honour' – almost tailor-made for Steed, both in terms of his avengering and his pursuit of the opposite sex. The humour continues to dominate as Steed encounters 'eggheads' in the midst of ridiculously cerebral conversations, playfully poking fun at the early 1960s fashion for MENSA's intellectual elitism and perceived snobbery. When Steed encounters Professor Spencer standing on his head in the gymnasium, the absurdity of the image is stylishly increased by the camera work, offering us the Professor's viewpoint, with Steed now (seemingly) upside down. This is a perfect example of the season's desire to disorientate or challenge the viewer, providing us with disconcerting yet excitingly new artful approaches to television drama. Steed – our avengering hero – is reduced to a cheating schoolboy as he crouches over a tiny desk, sitting the RANSACK IQ test, relying on stealth, and the far more intellectual Emma Peel, in order to win favour from the organisation. The playfulness continues as Steed explores his temporary bedroom. Opening the wardrobe, he discovers a girl's gallery of bare-chested musclemen, flexing his own for comparison, before smiling wryly at the sign, 'If you can't sleep, ring for a mistress.'

We sense that the leisured humour or 'champagne' will soon be undercut, in turn, by a darker drama. The strange, eerie music score helps to create the sense of disquieting mystery as Steed watches the other RANSACK members making their way downstairs like zombies. This strange scene will repeat itself, both increasing Steed and our own sense of bewilderment but also adding a further cyclical or labyrinthine feel to the story, as if Steed is caught up in a puzzling intellectual maze. The camera initially provides us with

Steed's eye-view as he watches the hypnotised members staring ahead in the gym, the flickering shadows which appear on their faces telling us and him that they are watching a film. It is this type of stylish shot which provides *The Avengers* with its champagne sparkle.

Robert Banks Stewart's description of the mixture of "thrill and comedy" (Optimum/Studio Canal DVD commentary) in *The Avengers'* plots matches, to a certain extent, my own use of 'subversive champagne' to describe the fascinating interplay between different genres and styles which collide in *The Master Minds*, as elsewhere in Season 4. Jaz Wiseman describes it as "magic dust" which is being "sprinkled" on a 1960s television drama which would otherwise simply have been yet another formulaic espionage series.

The darkest moment of *The Master Minds* occurs as Steed has finally been uncovered as a spy and Mrs. Peel – who we think is still under a hypnotic trance – volunteers to kill him on the moonlit archery range. The scene is superbly structured as we constantly switch between Emma Peel's silhouetted figure in the distance, preparing to fire an arrow at Steed, and the latter's close-up face in front of the target, as uncertainty changes to disbelief and fear. When the camera finally closes in on Emma she fires, and smiles. We are left uncertain as to where her arrow has landed. The scene is stylish, disturbing and beautifully shot.

This begins a playful final ten minutes in which we are teased by the script on a number of levels. The villains are aware that she is no longer in a state of trance and *The Master Minds* finally moves from atmosphere into action. Steed – like an urban Tarzan – swings in on Professor Spencer's rope which we should have guessed would be playfully redeployed. The fight finale is delightfully surreal, as the real tussle takes place directly in front of the mastermind's film which shows military personnel heading into action of their own. The double spectacle acts on a playfully self-referential level before becoming surreal as the silhouettes of Emma Peel and the (still unknown) mastermind fight behind the projection screen. As Wiseman remarks, it is "such an *Avengers* touch". As the villains' film is sent into reverse so are their plans. How fitting that the cliché of the unmasking is countered by the manner, as the games mistress is sent tumbling through the projection canvas, landing at Steed's feet. The diabolical plan, the dramatic action and the surreal image have all been literally ripped apart. [2]

If I have a reservation about *The Master Minds* it is simply that it feels like two episodes, one set at Sir Clive's home, the other at the boarding school, rather than an organic whole. If the first offers us the 1960s feel of the season, the second provides us with a stylish surrealism. However, both parts offer us plenty of subversive champagne as we are encouraged to forget about the weapons plot and simply enjoy the spectacle.

© Rodney Marshall

1. The modern interior is at odds with its middle-aged, conservative owner.
2. *The Master Minds* contains some striking uses of *film noir* techniques; qualities such as the use of shadows, low-lighting and quirky camera angles. However, the projection canvas sequence's self-referential playfulness makes me wonder if this season wasn't as much 1960s *neo-noir* as *film noir*.

DIAL A DEADLY NUMBER

Filmed: 11th – 22nd January 1965

Exterior Locations:
London street (stock footage)

Sets:
City bar
Tod-Hunter boardroom
Boardman bank: Boardman's office, wine cellar, Harvey's office
Undertaker's offices
Warner's answering service offices
Boardman's penthouse apartment
Yuill's apartment
Penthouse underground car park
Fitch's 'workshop of horrors'
Taxi interior

DIAL A DEADLY NUMBER

Main Character List:
Ben Jago: investor
Norman Tod-Hunter: company chairman
Henry Boardman: City merchant banker
Billy: City bar manager
Fitch: 'mechanical genius' working for JP Warner
John Steed
Emma Peel
Quinn: Boardman butler/henchman
John Harvey: Boardman's partner
Frederick Yuill: broker
Undertaker
Suzanne: Yuill's secretary
Myers: Yuill's butler/henchman
Ruth Boardman: Henry's wife
JP Warner: answering service owner
General: wine tasting guest

"As it's now fifty years old it's no surprise that this episode looks somewhat dated. As one of the first filmed episodes it's a paradox that there isn't a single foot of exterior film in the whole shoot. Even the underground car park shoot-out was filmed in the studio. However, the bank's parlour and broker's office lined with cases of mounted fish suggest the sumptuous lifestyle and are beautifully shot in Don Leaver's black and white production.

The murder weapon is a bleeper, the forerunner of today's ubiquitous mobile phone. It 'sounds' in the user's breast pocket but in this case also slips a fatal injection into the heart: a new dimension to the cardiac arrest.

For once Steed does not carry his lethal brolly and, in fact, uses a small pistol, killing one of the henchmen. The third act shoot-out takes place in the bank's extensive wine cellars and ends when Steed fells his opponent with a cork propelled at great velocity from a well-shaken magnum of champagne. As Mrs. Peel later says, "An adaptable little wine."

The lack of exteriors means there is the minimum of action and a lot of dialogue. Following Liz Shepherd's abrupt departure, it's one of Diana Rigg's first completed episodes. Not surprisingly, she carries it off with consummate ease." (Roger Marshall, private letter, January 2014)

Dial A Deadly Number, a very witty, tightly-written episode has subversive tendencies, satire and 'frothy champagne' all in one. Roger Marshall has the right mixture of each here. He transforms this episode into a labyrinth: with a creature as frightening as a Minotaur and a hero as cunning as Theseus.

This is a story high on the perversity scale and off the charts on bizarre. It is much deeper than a story about murderous bankers or killer bleepers. Roger Marshall does a magnificent job of characterising a psychotic, perverse serial killer, as I will describe. I cannot think of another *Avengers* villain with more perversity except, perhaps, the mastermind in *Take-Over*. It also offers a picture of the British hierarchy as utterly without 'class' or scruples. It is hard to find one person who has an ounce of moral fibre: maybe the undertaker and the bleeper distributor are the sole exceptions. In the later episode *How to Succeed...at Murder*, the viewer can actually empathise with some of the businessmen who are being terminated. In contrast, in this episode one has no empathy for any of these poisonous characters. Everyone is as cold as ice, as Mrs. Peel keenly observes.

The wine duel shows us how idle the rich are with their expensive wines and competitive snobbery. Also, metaphorically speaking, it shows us how Boardman (the chairman) wants to 'kill off' his new competitor, Steed, in a wine tasting 'duel'. After all, in Boardman's world, everyone is a competitor. It's an absolutely breathtaking scene, as Steed and Boardman pace to opposite ends of the wine cellar to shoot oenological questions at each other, played deadly seriously. It's Boardman's own wine cellar and, as in any rigged duel, it's seemingly impossible for Steed to hit the bull's eye. Naturally, he does so:

"1908 would...*not* be the year. 1909. From the northern end of the vineyard," Steed declares, making Boardman's monocle pop out, as if he has just been shot. [1]

It is marvellous satire and in this scene the wine cellar seems like one big spittoon. I can imagine the guests wishing to rid themselves not so much of the wine's aftertaste, but rather the poisonous elements that surround them. The fundamental underpinning of this episode is based on the psychodynamics of perversion, with a twist of psychosis thrown in. *Dial A Deadly Number* is another 'post-war era' episode, but this time reminiscent of Nazi Germany. The sadistic banking system presented is in many ways comparable on a much smaller scale to the Nazis, but this time taking place in London. Their mission is to systematically kill off all major company chairmen. As Steed aptly puts it, he's the "sixth company chairman to drop dead in a year. They all have one thing in common, a banker named Boardman." No doubt these bankers would take control of the financial world if their scheme continued. Instead of an outright takeover, they seem to gain perverse pleasure in watching the suffering of their victims' companies and by profiting from their financial instability. To carry out these killings they hire a lecherous henchman named Fitch. The similarities with Nazi Germany are striking: a familiar relationship between a power-hungry establishment and a serial killer/perverted practitioner of sorts.

Just as the Nazis employed Josef Mengele to devise instruments of torture and death, the financiers likewise hire Fitch. Mengele was the SS medical officer who supervised the selection of victims during the Holocaust, determining who was to be killed and who was spared. He is known for performing bizarre and murderous human experiments on his victims. Although clearly the Holocaust was a horror incomparable to any fictional event, I simply use the illustration to compare the psychodynamics of these perverse characters.

Fitch was clearly cut from the same cloth. [2] As he tells us, "For most people, you know, life is ruled by time. I won't accept that. One can rule time." His central problem is that he is insane. He *really* believes he is the supreme ruler, controlling time itself. In his own mind, he achieves this by controlling the precise moments of the deaths of his victims and naming clocks after them. If Fitch commemorates death through clocks, Mengele also exhibited similar behaviours. Fitch's room of clocks is his trophy cabinet, representing his perverse, delusional belief that he is indeed the sadistic ruler of both time and mortality; simply by stopping the clocks, indicating the precise moment of his victim's death, in his mind he controls time. But there's more: the clocks are not just clocks to Fitch. He has a relationship with them. He talks about them with Mrs. Peel as if they are real people that he owns, controls and hates.

Fitch's sadistic pleasure in controlling his scientific specimens as objects clearly gives him libidinal pleasures. There are two kinds of bleeper pens: one used to communicate and the other to kill. Steed discovers that the bleeper pen in Fitch's room is different from the others: it has "a capillary needle straight through the heart".

The poison pen in this episode appears to be a phallic appendage of Fitch that is sexually aroused by controlling the time of death of his victims. Fitch's pen pops out an erect needle at his selected time of erotic arousal. The needle penetrates the victim's endocardium to ejaculate a toxic serum into the chamber of the victim's heart, thus controlling from afar their time of death. Cardiac arrest occurs when the heart goes into ventricular fibrillation, which is defined as the uncontrolled twitching or quivering of muscle fibres of the heart, specifically the ventricles. Of course the victim no doubt experiences horrific pain and an ominous sense of doom; but in Fitch's psychotic and twisted world, he probably finds their cardiac arrest sexually arousing as well. At the time of the victim's 'climax' (cardiac arrest), he likely sees his victims' ventricular fibrillation as a deadly 'orgasm' of sorts. It is as if, in Fitch's twisted brain, he converts the heart of his victim into a sexual organ that is capable of muscular contractions. Fitch would likely perceive the victim's cardiac arrest as an orgasm of the heart. Note the homoerotic nature of this man, as his victims are all men, although he seems delighted to kill Mrs. Peel with "scientific tenderness" as his first female victim. In one of his final scenes, Fitch's graveyard of clocks gives us his correct diagnosis: 'cuckoo, cuckoo' as one of the clocks chimes on the hour. An utterly chilling and brilliant touch of Marshall's indeed.

Roger Marshall makes this character into a lifelike psychopathic criminal with an unusual finesse. Death is arousing for Fitch. In fact, cardiac arrest is an orgasmic event. His victims' suffering elicits perpetual excitement. He is a Jack the Ripper of sorts: a serial killer rapist but with men's hearts.

Once again *The Avengers* has succeeded in making an ordinary object – a bleeper – into something perverted: a sophisticated sex toy of Fitch's. A utilitarian device, made to facilitate communication, is now perversely changed into a device for torture and murder. This is a trademark of *The Avengers*. In *The Girl From Auntie*, the ordinary knitting needle that "brings peace to the home" becomes a perverse murder weapon, and in *Death at Bargain Prices* the seemingly ordinary department store is an atom bomb. This is most arousing for the audience, with no need for explicit signs of sex or nudity in *The Avengers*. The subliminal messages are kinky, perverse and arouse the unconscious mind of the viewer. In addition, the idea of a low tech device, or even an ordinary item, being used to undermine the most high tech device appears to be a trademark of *The Avengers* as well. We see Steed effectively use a pellet gun in *Death at Bargain Prices*. Similarly, in this episode a champagne bottle and flying cork effortlessly undermine all the guns and fancy cutting-edge modern gadgetry.

The villains are obviously obsessed with the control of their plan. But how does one conquer murderous control freaks? Steed finds the perfect solution: instill fear and doubt. Make them feel out of control. He does so by letting Mrs. Boardman replace his pocket watch with one that is a bomb when it is opened. By switching watches on her – mercilessly tossing his watch about – he terrifies both her and Fitch into submission.

The rich portrayed in this episode are unabashed and make no excuses for their bad behaviour. Boardman's wife is portrayed as a woman who will sleep with anyone possessing immense wealth and power. She is having an affair and Steed first meets her chatting intimately with Jago. As an obvious excuse to leave, she tells Steed she has a hair appointment, when her hair is clearly coiffed beautifully. Steed retorts, "Are you sure?"

Steed represents an erotic attraction for Mrs. Boardman. As she walks into his apartment she discloses, "Much as I imagined it." Steed retorts, "The fact that you imagined it at all intrigues me." Steed states he is not being tactful about Mrs. Boardman's affairs, "just optimistic".

Mrs. Boardman: What's optimistic about that?
Steed: The hope that history may repeat itself.

Roger Marshall creates a marvellously witty, sexual repartee between the two. In this episode, filmed shortly after the Gale era, Marshall shows Steed's character evolving. In this scene, with a clever *double entendre*, Steed shows his confrontational nature:

Steed: The whole thing depends on the shares falling in price.
Yuill: What was the name of your friend's company?
Steed: Todd Hunter [the company chairman just murdered]. It was quite a killing. That is the correct term isn't it? [As a stuffed, demonic-looking fish is brilliantly magnified for the audience to view].

Yuill: Do you fish Mr. Steed? You should. You'd find it very relaxing.

Steed is not nearly as aggressive as in the past, and his own moral compass seems to be changing as well. It appears as if Mrs. Peel is having a positive effect on him. He describes Mrs. Boardman as "promiscuous" to her. "A true gentleman doesn't know of a woman's promiscuity", she proclaims. It is as if in these opening episodes she is helping Steed in confronting his own ethics, even if old habits die hard.

Mrs. Peel presents herself at the Boardman's as a rich investor from Barbados. The interaction that Steed has with her is almost reminiscent of the Gale era. "Where is your tan?" he asks. It is as if he is trying to blow her cover by repeatedly, publically doubting that she actually resides there. I suppose another viewpoint could be that he is trying to show the villains that they are not working together. Either way, it is a humorous touch.

A central theme of this episode is ethics, or the lack hereof. The financiers tell us that, in the final analysis, everyone is corruptible; everyone has his price. They will kill for power. Mrs. Boardman clearly will sleep with anyone for/with power. Fitch is a killer henchman with a homoerotic perversion for rich men's hearts. Even Steed struggles a bit with his own moral compass. However, in the end he overcomes any minor transgressions.

The tag scene is brilliant as well, with Mrs. Peel also scoring a bull's eye in wine tasting. However, she has rigged the game herself. "Nose or palate?" Steed asks. "Eyes. I read the label."

This episode is timeless. The theme of power and corruption is as old as time itself. However, the technology was way ahead of its time. Even the murder weapon has similarities to the present day. Dick Cheney, recent US Vice President, felt threatened that terrorists could remotely tamper with his pacemaker in a similar manner; instead of a poisonous needle, he feared his pacemaker could be programmed to elicit a fatal shock to his heart.

Finally, this is a story all about time: when it is time to buy and when it is time to sell. There are more clocks in this episode than I care to count. Everyone is nervously checking the time. The financiers are trying to 'master' time by striking at the precise moment to buy, sell, kill, or all three. That is their solution to this very human predicament. Fitch clearly has a different solution to the problem. No wonder he lets us know that time rules, because in the financial world we are shown that time simply does rule. Clock by clock. In Fitch's crazy mind, as he shows Mrs. Peel, he has found his own grandiose plan to conquer and thus master time. He tells her, "Time controls everyone." He is right, in this deadly world of finance.

However, the man with the best sense of time is Roger Marshall who hits a bull's eye: a most fizzling finale with a high flying champagne bottle cork: complex, bright, refined, elegant and intellectually satisfying. Just like the episode and the writer.

© Margaret J Gordon

1. Just as Mrs. Peel will later cheat in the tag, so too does Steed here. He has no way of knowing which end of the vineyard the wine comes from, yet his bluff works because his charm and confidence bamboozle his opponent.
2. Fitch even brags about his wartime killing 'exploits'.

DEATH AT BARGAIN PRICES

Filmed: 25th January 1965 – 17th February 1965

Exterior Locations:
London street (stock footage)

Sets:
Pinter's department store: departments (toy, hat, china, baby, ladies' underwear, food market, camping), lift, Horatio Kane's penthouse, staff room, entrance hall, staircase, store room, laboratory
Emma Peel's apartment

DEATH AT BARGAIN PRICES

Main Character List:
Moran: agent
John Steed
Farthingale: Pinter's junior manager
Massey: Pinter's employee
Emma Peel
Jarvis: Pinter's 'house detective'
Horatio Kane: 'King Kane', industrialist, mastermind
Major Wentworth: Kane's right hand man
Glynn: Pinter's chief window dresser
Tony Marco: Pinter's chief accountant, sexual predator
Professor Popple: nuclear physicist
Julie Thompson: Pinter's food market

Death at Bargain Prices is a favourite episode of *Avengers* fans. The story is about an elderly businessman who owns a large department store in central London. He is an industrial magnate, but his business has hit the financial buffers. Horatio Kane, confined to a wheelchair, is clearly a man who is in pain, both physically and emotionally. He identifies himself with his line of discontinued automation; he too feels like an obsolete mechanical device. He is an angry man, perhaps enough to be plotting a revenge for his sense of devaluation by London's business society. The story has a familiar feel to it but the added *Avengers* eccentricity makes this episode come alive. Brilliantly directed by Charles Crichton, the black and white filming gives us a sense of darkness and foreboding. The dark shadows and harsh lighting provide us with the feeling that we are in a building which is as grim as the man who resides in it.

Although labelled as pure fantasy, *The Avengers*, at times, could offer a mixture of both fantasy and contemporary reality. This episode has a socio-historic context; it takes place in a once vibrant department store in the central London shopping district. I am not certain about what inspired the writer, but it is reminiscent of the rise and fall of Harry Gordon Selfridge. Selfridge revolutionised the way Britons shopped. His department store was dubbed "one of the great cathedrals of shopping". He was the first to put items for sale on extravagant displays. He turned shopping into theatre. Sound familiar? But Mr. Selfridge was also a flamboyant gambler, who destructively squandered his wealth on mistresses and yachts. He ended his days penniless in a tiny rented flat. At 83, Selfridge was ousted from the business he had created. He was given an ultimatum of retiring and relinquishing executive control of his department store, or providing payment of his debt. His only joys at this point were his daily trips to the store he created, where once he was arrested on suspicion of being a vagrant. Upon his death, his family could not even afford a headstone.

In no way is *Death at Bargain Prices* any sort of defamation of character of any real person. This is pure *Avengers* fantasy. However, one can imagine this episode as the murderous revenge fantasy of one such man: both the rage towards the London society that once admired him, as well as the board members who ousted him, and changed his beloved store's name. And who currently resides at 114 New Oxford St London W1, the address of Pinter's department store? A new industrial magnate of our times: *Starbucks*.

The teaser is set 'after hours' in the department store: a visual feast of dresses, a toy department full of teddy bears, toy cars, bicycles, and even a huge lifelike toy elephant. From the very beginning, there is an air of paranoia and hostility permeating from every corner of this department store. And the familiar beginning: the close-up of a lone man in a deserted building, seemingly knowing that he is about to meet his death. As he climbs the lift-shaft the door opens, only to be met by a man hiding behind a toy Yogi Bear, with a machine-gun. In *The Avengers*, horror can lurk behind the everyday veneer of normality. Post-teaser, we learn that the man who was gunned down in the lift was a secret agent; even stranger is the fact he was shot on a Sunday, when the store was closed.

Mrs. Peel is the most potent of investigative agents. Her apparent feminine vulnerability makes villains underestimate her prowess. The favourite erotically-charged dialogue of this episode occurs when Steed discovers that she has been assigned to work in the women's lingerie department. "I asked the chief predator where to find you, and he said, 'Our Mrs. Peel is in lady's underwear'. I rattled up the stairs three at a time". We certainly can see that/why Steed would love to probe in Mrs. Peel's undergarments; what is also intriguing is how Mrs. Peel is probing in Kane's, our chief predator. Steed's methods are perhaps more confrontational. However, he does learn more about King Kane. As he poses as an efficiency expert who wants to help failing businesses, Kane, played by Andre Morell, gives the most eloquent of speeches:

"'The department of discontinued lines', that's what they call it, relics of a bygone age. A machine was a thing of joy then, built to last a man's lifetime. Now it's out of date before it's left the assembly line. That's what they like to say about me, you know. They say this is where I belong, a discontinued line."

It is ironic that Kane, who is one of the leading original industrialists, almost appears to identify himself as a Luddite. It is as if he wants to control the pace of the industrial revolution he once pioneered. He finishes by saying, "I can't compete anymore. That's what they say. Haven't got the grasp of modern technique. I'll surprise them yet. I'll show them Horatio Kane can...." Steed urges him to finish, but Kane replies, "You are talking to the wrong man. I am just a poor, sick old man." [1]

This is only part of the story for Kane, as he has more power than first appears. Although a subsequent episode, *The Cybernauts*, dealt with a crippled man in a wheelchair, the villain wanted to use automation to take over the world. In this episode, the mastermind plans to use technology to *destroy* the world, or at least London. *The Avengers* had a love affair with villains in wheelchairs. It certainly added colour to the character and increased the paradoxical eccentricity: on the one hand, they are presented as handicapped, yet on the other these villains have tremendous strength or power. [2]

As the plot thickens, Kane seems to be having more and more secretive meetings after hours. Mrs. Peel gets a lead from another store employee, but when she goes to meet him, he has also met his demise. In Kane's paranoid world, intruders are met with hostility and more than once meet their death. Any employee that questions the bizarre happenings in this place gets fired; any employee that discovers their devious plan is brutally murdered. Bizarre, seemingly inexplicable things are happening. Produce is disappearing nightly from the food market. Even honeyed bumblebees go missing.

A Professor Poppel, in one scene, is being threatened to work harder by Kane's henchmen. The very same nuclear physicist has been missing for months. And the same man has ordered various foods including the dead bees from the department store. We learn later that he is being forced to make a nuclear bomb against his will. It is interesting that he is eating something that, if alive, would sting him: bumblebees. In their current state they are, of course, harmless. It reminds me of how certain vaccines are made from the dead pathogen as a way to attenuate the virulent bug. The 'bug' here is Kane, a man who has had Steed punched and constantly 'stings' Professor Poppel with drug injections via various henchmen. It is a metaphorical way for the professor to control the virulence that has besieged him, to ingest it in an attenuated form.

Nuclear physicists being forced against their will to make a bomb for the country they reside in is not a new story. But for a department store? Only in *The Avengers*. As Steed points out, "What should Pinter's (department store) want with a bomb, anyway?" This episode comes not long after World War 2 and the concern over atomic bombings worried most countries. This was the Cold War era, after all. There is a parallel between the rising tension and fear, in the seemingly ordinary department store, and the apprehension viewers of the 1960s felt in their everyday lives. This was the era of duck and cover; in 1965, at any moment the bomb could drop. Kane's henchmen also reinforce references to World War 2 with 'D-Day' being 'the day'. But of what? We don't know at that moment.

After discovering the dead employee brutally murdered with a spear, Mrs. Peel gets down to business. Noticeable at this point is a change in her clothing from elegant skirts and blouses to her now infamous leather catsuit. The leather is Emma's way of saying she is in charge. Soon after, the Avengers discover the secret. When they insert ordinary-looking store receipts into the computer they learn that the receipts contain the code for the bomb. The startling discovery is that the bomb is indeed the building, when they see the layout of the marble design in the entryway that matches the very same code. "We found our bomb," Emma declares. "We're standing in it", Steed retorts. Kane soon confronts our heroes, with another eloquent delivery by Andre Morell:

"Inefficient, inefficient that's what you said. But what do you think now? My biggest takeover yet. Yes the store is the bomb: the entire fabric of it. I'm proud of my scheme. A takeover, Mrs. Peel. Tomorrow I am going to takeover the entire country; hold it for ransom with my bomb. Oh they'll believe me, after I've destroyed London. I told you, didn't I Steed? Horatio Kane is not finished yet. 'No grasp of modern techniques'. Let's see what they think after I turn their modern techniques against them: a demonstration of power. Tonight I and my special staff will be on our way to somewhere far away from here. Tomorrow the store will open as usual. And then sometime during the day, this store and fifty miles surrounding it will disappear completely from the map. That ought to convince them, don't you think? The bomb, this store, will explode with the first customer who buys a washing machine."

I see this episode more as an angry, impotent man's destructive fantasy of power and revenge on the city he felt had dismissed him as a "discontinued" line. What is unique here is that his building itself is the weapon of mass destruction. Kane at first seems more like the earlier 19th century English workman who would destroy labour-saving machinery, rather than create more. In his first speech, he let us know that he was a technophobe. Now we learn that he is the diabolical mastermind, re-creating the most sophisticated technological weapon of the time. [3]

In my chapter on *The Girl From Auntie*, I discuss the term 'phallic granny'. In this episode, we can coin the phrase 'phallic building'. The department store is 'aroused' (by a customer taking a lift to the basement). This triggers the phallic building to ejaculate its bomb, killing everyone. Quite a destructive fantasy of Kane's. What is also striking in this episode is Kane's delusional quality. It's as if in Kane's mind the building and he are fused as one, almost indistinguishable from one another. The building is thus almost the phallic extension of Kane, ready for its final destructive ejaculation all over the city of London. *The Avengers* has reached an unobtainable goal in this episode, of actually creating a building to appear sexy. [4]

Emma uses her feminine powers in her leather catsuit. As she is confronted with a loaded gun, she clicks her fingers and demands, "Give me the gun." She knows that the henchman will not shoot a woman. In addition, it is the same man who earlier hoped to be her lover, not to kill her. She uses this to her advantage by feinting, cleverly snapping her fingers to distract him from the karate kick that is about to come. The power struggle that ensues is one of the longest and most suspenseful in the series. What is ironic here is how Steed uses a low-tech device, a toy pellet gun, to undermine the most high-tech device of its kind. Kane's own downfall, however, is his manic grandiosity. Showing off his plan provides the Avengers with the time to stop it. Kane is determined not to lose; he pushes the button for the bomb. His empty wheelchair is seen falling down the stairs. And then, the ultimate climax, when we see Steed frantically looking for something in the hardware department to stop the lift before it detonates the bomb. The lift stops just inches above the detonator. This is the final blow for Kane, when the Avengers metaphorically castrate his phallic building by preventing its final bomb ejaculation. It is as if Kane himself dies at this moment. He has lost control.

In this post-war era, only a few developed countries possessed the power of the atom bomb. However, what makes this episode delightful is that the writer shows that even an 'ordinary' old department store owner can have one too. In fact, Kane is like his own little country, all contained inside a department store. He has the power to hold Britain to ransom with an atom bomb, like those countries behind the Iron Curtain in 1965. In the microcosm of this impending atom bomb department store, the Avengers become like the Allies in World War 2. After all, in *Death at Bargain Prices* they did save post-war Britain from the horrors of further bombings of London. No doubt this relieved the 1965 viewer who lived in fear of another attack, but this time by an all-destructive atom bomb.

During World War 2, Adolf Hitler had the most evil and bizarre plan: a quest for a master race. He planned to accomplish this by taking over the world and began by exterminating millions of Jews. He was the first diabolical mastermind of modern times. Post-war Britain needed to fantasise an 'avenge', and protect themselves after Hitler destroyed much of their beloved country. And could it happen again?

Week after week, *The Avengers* reassured the post-war audience that any diabolical mastermind could be avenged. Steed and Mrs. Peel showed them how to have nerves of steel in the face of danger. Indeed, in the following season "Mrs. Peel, you're needed" struck a chord with its audience. No wonder, then as now, her sage advice as she is leaving the show stays with us. "Always keep your bowler on in times of stress and watch out for diabolical masterminds."

© Margaret J Gordon

1. Interestingly, Mrs. Peel tells Steed that he too will be at home in the department of discontinued lines.
2. This might also be applied to one of the heroes of Season 6, Mother.
3. Is it significant that the washing machine, *the* modern symbol of labour-saving machinery, will be the catalyst?
4. A masculine, sexually destructive power, perhaps.

TOO MANY CHRISTMAS TREES

Filmed: 18th February – 1st March 1965

Exterior Locations:
Deserted country lanes
Storey's house: façade

Sets:
'Dream' sets
Steed's apartment
Storey's house: entrance hall, landing, mastermind's study, drawing room, Old Curiosity Shop guest bedroom, Hall of Great Expectations, Mirror Room, secret room

TOO MANY CHRISTMAS TREES

Main Character List:
John Steed
Emma Peel
Jenkins: Storey's butler
Martin Trasker: amateur psychic
Jeremy Wade: book dealer
Brandon Storey: publisher, mastermind
Felix Teasel: Security Intelligence – psychiatric division
Janice Crane: psychic

Too Many Christmas Trees clearly and splendidly demonstrates why it has such a prestigious reputation, one which places it among the best episodes in the series. We are immediately seduced by the *finesse* and quality of its recreation of the harsh yet magical world of the great English novelist Charles Dickens. The combination of sets, replica objects and fashions discovered in Storey's residence offers up a veritable gallery of scholarly images or portraits, yet also represents something exhilaratingly alive. Add in the costumes of famous characters, and the number of clever, veiled references for viewers is multiplied. One recognises the guillotine from *A Tale of Two Cities*, Little Nell from *The Old Curiosity Shop*, Miss Havisham's mansion covered in cobwebs with the Grand Hall of *Great Expectations*, and Charles Dickens' fascination with mirrors. The decades pass and yet Dickens remains a beacon of British culture, finding a natural and successful medium in the modern fields of television and film.

The new *Doctor Who*, besides offering us the rare privilege of meeting the author in person [1], has dedicated two episodes to his work, the horror-based *The Unquiet Dead* (2005) and the marvellous *A Christmas Carol* (2010), two fantastic explorations of Dickens' world, well after *Too Many Christmas Trees*. In 2011 the BBC created a sensation with its ambitiously aesthetic version of *Great Expectations*, with Gillian Anderson in the lead role. [2]. One could also mention the invigorating re-reading of Conan Doyle created by Steven Moffat's *Sherlock* (also the scriptwriter of a formidable *Jekyll*) or the clever recreation of Jane Austen in *Lost in Austen* (ITV, 2008). Certainly, in contrast to the never-ending drily academic approach in France, the British have the talent to draw on their literary heritage through innovative and dynamic television. *Too Many Christmas Trees* is a remarkable forerunner and trailblazer in this exhilarating movement. It is also a sparkling example of the intertextual presence of British culture in this fourth season. This makes its way not only into the subjects discussed and the characters encountered, but also through the sayings and quotations found in the dialogue, an element rarely found in the subsequent seasons. Season 5 would also offer us an episode based on manipulated dreams, *Death's Door*, but this time the artistic influence would be Alfred Hitchcock's *Spellbound* (1945). If *Too Many Christmas Trees* is not necessarily part of the tradition developed in this season of exploring hierarchical British society, it remains nevertheless one of the most intrinsically 'English' *Avengers* stories.

This dark and scary Christmas tale (first shown on 25th December 1965) is striking in its ability to combine or bring together all the strengths of the series, in an episode which provides us with harmonious perfection. Working for the first time here on the show, the talent and craft of veteran director Roy Ward Baker allows him to work wonders, creating with consummate skill a strange and disturbing atmosphere. This is particularly evident in the remarkable *oneiric* (dream) scenes which are childish in tone, offering a subtle mix of wonder and terror. His vision can also be seen in the striking discovery of a corpse, quirky camera angles, close-ups of particularly expressive faces and the masterful mirror scene. In this episode we find several of the best *Hammer* ideas from its artistic pinnacle. *Too Many Christmas Trees* marks the fecund arrival of one of the most talented British television directors to the *Avengers* team, leading to his creative achievements on a diverse range of episodes: *The Town of No Return*, *The Girl From Auntie*, *Split!* etc. This was a welcome 'signing' for a series which had lost Peter Hammond, its best director from the Cathy Gale era.

In addition to the sound and music, the photography is to be admired throughout the episode, Gerry Turpin establishing a particularly sumptuous black and white. Laurie Johnson offers us a full score, including the disturbing drums and strange chimes. The sets are impressive both in terms of quality and creativity, be it in the recreation of a dreamlike Dickensian Christmas or the world of nightmares. The choice of set designer Robert Jones for this unique episode was an excellent one. Harry Pottle, in charge, excels in 1960s design but also in practicality, ensuring that all his various creations are perfectly functional, even though we find them here in a completely, profoundly different context.

The cornerstone of this 'hour' is Tony Williamson's cleverly complex script which merges seamlessly with Roy Ward Baker's direction. Williamson, who delivers a number of the best Tara King episodes (*Wish You Were Here*, *Killer*, and *Stay Tuned*) understands the particular nature of this episode, drawing on fantasy rather than science fiction. In this sense *Too Many Christmas Trees* contrasts with other *Avengers* adventures (except *Warlock* and, in part, *Death's Door*). Fantasy is above all else about creating an atmosphere, while science fiction is a dynamic accumulation of facts or data. [3]

The plot understandably plays the atmosphere 'card'; in the world of Dickens you never totally leave the dream world behind. For his/her part, the viewer remains unsure about the events until the very end, but this – after all – is the very essence of dreams. Our only regret is the slightly hasty conclusion, with a return to the clichés of 'spy mania' (something written into the DNA of *The Avengers* and other British adventure series of the Sixties). At the heart of it we have the hackneyed cliché of the revelation of the identity of the leader of the baddies, hiding behind a mask. This is all the more damaging as it is wholly predictable. Retaining an element of the mystery would have undoubtedly added the perfect finishing touches to the story, but this would have required moving away from the *Avengers* formula, approaching the shores of *The Twilight Zone*.

The casting of talented and experienced actors provides a key element in the success of the project. Robert James (Jenkins) oozes delightful deceit, a butler who has no doubt been trained at The Butlers & Gentleman's Gentlemen Association [4]. His wonderful expressiveness reflects someone who is one of the regular guest actors in the series, appearing no less than five times in the show. In addition, Jeanette Sterke (Janice Crane) offers a dark and cold beauty, both cerebral and mysterious. The one-off appearance of this talented performer (who came from the Royal Academy of Dramatic Art) illustrates the lamentable lack of female antagonists in the series. Alex Scott (Trasker) effectively plays the role of the gang leader, although it is the performance of Edwin Richfield (Teazel) which we remember more, in the role of an intriguing and disturbing psychoanalyst; a red herring but also a perfect example of the mastery of this amazing actor, familiar to *Avengers* fans having appeared six times, spread over the entire series, and equally admired in *The Saint*. Veteran Mervyn Johns (Storey) dazzles, showing the mastery of a star of British cinema (most notably in *Dead of Night*, 1945, a memorable horror film). [5]

Our Avengers play their part in this important masterpiece. Long after his appearance in a minor secondary role in *A Christmas Carol* (1951), Patrick Macnee subtly plays an unusual, less confident and energetic Steed, even if in the end he turns out to have been pulling the strings. His scenes with his co-lead positively sparkle, especially as Mrs. Peel definitively finds her 'tempo', still with a malicious streak but now with more complicity and femininity than Cathy Gale (who benefits from a veiled reference here to Honor Blackman's role in *Goldfinger*). As so often in *The Avengers*, the humour is both compelling and in plentiful supply, finely interwoven in the story rather than invasively added on.

We note that Emma accepts with a smile the fact that she has been more or less manipulated, a rare magnanimity from a character that almost always reacts in the opposite way. *Too Many Christmas Trees* represents a milestone in so far as it is the first time that we are shown that our Avengers might make a couple. We gain this impression from the subtle suggestions or touches spaced apart over a number of scenes; from Mrs. Peel's 'epistolary jealousy' – when Steed is opening his Christmas cards – to the famous mistletoe tag scene. Here Diana Rigg demonstrates her dazzling beauty and talent; long before her Robin Hood (*A Sense of History*) and Cowboy Doctor (*Silent Dust*), she already excels at providing an aura of femininity in male costumes. Perhaps due to a love of great writers, she seems particularly pleased and satisfied to find herself immersed in the world of Dickens.

Superb both in terms of narrative and visual display, *Too Many Christmas Trees* is the first genuine masterpiece of this fourth season. It is also the moment where Mrs. Peel finally establishes her full identity, after the completion of a number of successful episodes in which she appeared to be still 'finding herself'.

© Bernard Ginez (© translated by Rodney Marshall)

1. Charles Dickens was played by Simon Callow.
2. She also played Lady Dedlock in the critically-acclaimed 2005 BBC serialisation of *Bleak House*.

3. It is worth noting that Williamson's original script was changed substantially, leaving us to wonder how hands-on Brian Clemens was in the process of producing the final shooting script.
4. In *What The Butler Saw*.
5. Bernard Ginez's reference here is an intriguing one. In *Dead of Night*, Johns played an architect who arrives at a country house for a party only to reveal to everyone that he has seen them all before, in a dream. The experimental film is structured through a number of 'sequences', one directed by Avenger Charles Crichton, and includes Christmas party and Haunted Mirror sections. Could this film have been a major influence on the episode and does this explain the casting of the actor? There is certainly a subversive, surreal horror at play in *Too Many Christmas Trees* which playfully connects with the sparkling wit, charm and mistletoe and Johns' presence adds another intertextual layer to this rich *Avengers* hour.

FAITES DE BEAUX REVES

Too Many Christmas Trees s'affirme clairement à la hauteur de la prestigieuse réputation le situant parmi les meilleurs opus de la série. On est ainsi d'emblée séduit par la finesse et la qualité de son évocation de l'univers à la fois dur et enchanté de cet immense écrivain anglais qu'est Charles Dickens. L'ensemble des multiples décors, répliques et vêtures découverts dans la résidence, en constitue une galerie de portraits érudite, mais aussi vivante et enthousiaste. Outre les costumes de célèbres personnages, les clins d'œil astucieux se multiplient. On reconnaît ainsi la Guillotine du *Conte de Deux Cités*, le Little Nell du *Magasin d'Antiquités,* le manoir tapissé de toiles d'araignées de Miss Havisham, avec le Grand Hall des *Grandes Espérances*, voire la fascination de Charles Dickens pour les miroirs. Les décennies s'écoulent et ce dernier demeure bien un phare de la culture britannique, trouvant une extension naturelle et réussie dans le domaine audiovisuel.

Le nouveau *Docteur Who*, outre le rare privilège de rencontrer l'auteur en personne, a ainsi dédié pas moins de deux épisodes à son œuvre, l'horrifique *The Unquiet Dead* et le merveilleux *A Christmas Carol* (autres variations fantastiques autour du monde de l'auteur, bien après *Too Many Christmas Trees)*. En 2011, la BBC fait sensation avec sa version ambitieusement esthétique des *Grandes Espérances*, avec Gillian Anderson dans le rôle principal. On pourrait également citer la revigorante relecture de Conan Doyle induite par le *Sherlock* de Steven Moffat (également scénariste d'un formidable *Jekyll*), ou l'astucieuse mise en scène de Jane Austen dans *Lost in Austen* (ITV, 2008). Décidément, bien loin du sempiternel académisme hexagonal, les Britanniques ont le talent d'allier leur patrimoine littéraire à une écriture télévisuelle innovante et dynamique. *Too Many Christmas Trees* représente un remarquable ancêtre et chef de file pour cette mouvance des plus enthousiasmantes.

De fait l'opus illustre avec un éclat particulier la présence de la culture britannique au sein de cette saison quatre. Celle-ci se traduira par les sujets évoqués et les personnages rencontrés, mais aussi par les proverbes et citations présents dans les dialogues, un élément bien moins présent lors des périodes ultérieures. De manière caractéristiques, la saison 5 proposera également un épisode basé sur les manipulations oniriques, avec *Death's Door*, mais la référence sera cette fois bien davantage le *Spellbound* d'Alfred Hitchcock. Si *Too Many Christmas Trees* ne se situe pas dans la tradition incisive envers la société britannique traditionnelle développée par la saison, il n'en demeure pas moins l'un des récits les plus intrinsèquement anglais des Avengers.

Ce sombre et angoissant conte de Noël (diffusé le 25 décembre 1965) marque les esprits par une impressionnante conjonction de l'ensemble des talents de la série, dans un tout parfaitement harmonieux. Œuvrant pour la première fois ici sur la série, le talent et le métier du réalisateur vétéran Roy Ward Baker, font merveille, avec un art consommé dans l'instauration d'une atmosphère étrange et angoissante. Cela ressort particulièrement dans les remarquables scènes oniriques à la tonalité enfantine, au dégradé subtil entre merveilleux et épouvante. Mais cette vision se retrouve avec les frappantes découvertes d'un cadavre, les angles biscornus, les gros plans sur des visages particulièrement expressifs ou encore la magistrale scène des miroirs. On retrouve à cette occasion plusieurs des meilleures idées de la Hammer au sommet de son art. *Too Many Christmas Trees* marque ainsi l'arrivée féconde d'un des metteurs en scènes les plus doués de la télévision britannique au sein de l'équipe des Avengers, annonçant plusieurs réussites de natures très diverses (*The Town of No Return, The Girl From Auntie,*

Split !, etc.). Un renfort bienvenu pour une série devant désormais se passer, avec Peter Hammond, du meilleur réalisateur des années Cathy Gale.

De même que l'accompagnement sonore et musical, la photographie se montre également admirable tout au long de l'épisode, Gerry Turpin instaurant un noir et blanc particulièrement somptueux. Laurie Johnson nous offre une grande partition, notamment ces tambours stressants et ces carillons étranges. Les décors impressionnent par leur qualité et leur créativité, que cela soit dans la reconstitution du Noël rêvé par Dickens ou du monde du cauchemar. Le choix pour cet unique opus du décorateur Robert Jones apparaît judicieux. Harry Pottle, responsable en titre, excelle dans le design Sixties mais aussi l'art de vivre pratique, mettant un point d'honneur à ce que ses diverses créations soient parfaitement fonctionnelles, or on se situe ici dans une sensation profondément différente.

Clef de voûte de cette convergence, le scénario savamment complexe de Tony Williamson fusionne pleinement avec la réalisation de Roy Ward Baker. Tony Williamson, à qui l'on devra nombre des meilleurs épisodes Tara King (*Wish You Were Here, Killer, Stay Tuned,* etc.) comprend admirablement la nature très particulière de l'opus, relevant davantage du Fantastique que de la Science-fiction. En ce sens *Too Many Christmas Trees* se situe à l'opposé d'autres aventures des Avengers (hormis *Warlock* et, partiellement, *Death's Door*). Or le Fantastique est avant tout une atmosphère, tandis que la Science-fiction est une accumulation dynamique de données.

L'intrigue joue donc judicieusement la carte de l'ambiance (avec l'environnement Dickens, on ne quitte jamais réellement le monde onirique). De son côté, le spectateur reste jusqu'à la fin dans l'incompréhension des évènements, mais telle est l'essence des rêves. On regrettera uniquement une conclusion légèrement précipitée, avec un certain retour aux poncifs de l'espionnite (certes inscrite dans l'ADN de *Chapeau Melon* et des séries d'aventures anglaises des Sixties). On trouve à la clef un poncif aussi rebattu que la révélation de l'identité du leader des méchants, dissimulée sous le masque. C'est d'autant plus dommageable que cette information s'avère à ce moment largement prévisible. Conserver une part de mystère et d'interrogation aurait sans doute parachevé le récit, mais il aurait fallu pour cela s'éloigner de la formule des Avengers, jusqu'à aborder les rivages de la *Twilight Zone*.

La distribution, talentueuse et expérimentée, apporte un élément clef au succès de l'entreprise. Robert James (Jenkins) suinte jouissivement la fourberie, en majordome sans doute déjà issu de *The Butler's and Gentleman's Gentlemen Association*. Cette merveilleuse expressivité explique que l'acteur soit l'un des grands habitués de la série, avec pas moins de cinq participations à son actif. Par ailleurs, Jeanette Sterke (Janice Crane) apparaît comme une beauté ténébreuse et froide, à la fois cérébrale et mystérieuse. Le non retour de cette talentueuse comédienne issue de la *Royal Academy of Dramatic Art* illustre le dommageable manque d'antagonistes féminins au sein de la série. Alex Scott (Trasker) campe efficacement le chef de bande décidé, mais l'on retiendra surtout la composition d'Edwin Richfield en psychanalyste intrigant et inquiétant; une habile diversion mais aussi un parfait exemple de la maestria de cet acteur épatant et familier des amateurs de la série (six participations, étalées sur l'ensemble de la série), admiré également chez Simon Templar. Le vétéran Mervyn Johns (Storey) brille de la maestria d'une figure du cinéma britannique (notamment dans *Au cœur de la nuit*, 1945, mémorable film d'horreur).

Nos Avengers ne demeurent certes pas en reste au sein de cet important chef d'œuvre. Bien après le *Christmas Carol* de 1951 où il apparaissait en second rôle passablement efflanqué, Patrick Macnee incarne avec beaucoup de crédibilité un Steed moins triomphant et irradiant d'énergie qu'à l'ordinaire (mais tirant évidemment le ficelles en ultime ressort). Ses scènes avec sa partenaire se révèlent cependant brillantes, d'autant que Mrs Peel trouve ici définitivement son tempo, toujours malicieux mais plus complice et féminin que ne le fut celui de Cathy Gale (celle-ci bénéficiant ici d'un joli clin d'œil autour de la participation d'Honor Blackman à *Goldfinger*). Comme si souvent chez les Avengers, l'humour se montre aussi irrésistible qu'abondant, finement entremêlé au récit et jamais invasif.

On remarque qu'Emma prend avec le sourire d'avoir été peu ou prou manipulée (un travers byzantin dont Steed ne se départira jamais vraiment), une magnanimité qui ne caractérisa jamais notre ethnologue préférée dans des circonstances similaires (bien au rebours !). *Too Many Christmas Trees* marque un jalon puisque c'est la toute première fois que l'on entrevoit la possibilité que nos Avengers puissent former un couple, par des touches subtiles espacées de scène en scène, de la jalousie épistolaire de Mrs Peel jusqu'au fameux final du gui. Diana Rigg se montre éblouissante de beauté et de talent, bien avant le Robin des Bois de *A Sense of History* ou le Cowboy de *Silent Dust*, elle excelle déjà à donner une aura toute de féminité à des vêtures masculines. Peut être est-ce dû à l'amour des grands auteurs, mais on la sent particulièrement ravie et épanouie de se retrouver immergée dans l'univers de Dickens.

Narrativement et visuellement superbe, *Too Many Christmas Trees* s'impose comme le premier authentique chef-d'œuvre de cette quatrième saison. Il s'avère également le moment où Mrs Peel achève de se dessiner, après la réalisation de plusieurs épisodes déjà réussis où elle apparaissait encore en recherche.

© Bernard Ginez

THE CYBERNAUTS

Filmed: 2nd – 14th March 1965

Exterior Locations:
Suburban road
Driveway

Sets:
Hammond's study
Office corridor
Lambert's office
Karate School
Reception of Harachi Corporation; Tusamo's office
Emma Peel's apartment
Showroom, Jephcott Products
Steed's apartment
United Automation: ante room, entrance hall, lift, library, air-conditioning shaft, corridor, maintenance unit, assembly unit

THE CYBERNAUTS

Main Character List:
Samuel Hammond: Electrical Industries
John Steed
Emma Peel
Bob Lambert: Industrial Developments
Sensai: Karate instructor
'Oyuka': female Karate expert
Tusamo: Harachi Corporation representative
Miss Green: Jephcott employee
Jephcott: electrical products manufacturer, 'Oyama'
Gilbert: civil servant
Benson: works for Dr. Armstrong
Dr. Armstrong: United Automation, ex-ministry scientist
'Roger': cybernaut
Maintenance cybernaut

Ask any fan of cult TV to name an *Avengers* episode and chances are *The Cybernauts* is the one they'll probably think of first. This instant classic was the sixth episode to be filmed on monochrome with delectable Diana Rigg during March 1965. Hard to imagine now, but at the time the script came in for a certain amount of criticism by Anthony John, the ABC executive. "The best thing I can say about this one is that it seems all right" was the only faint praise he could muster.

I beg to differ however. This first rate script was penned by newcomer Philip Levene, who was invited to write *Avengers* scripts by Brian Clemens after he'd heard one of his plays on radio's *Just After Midnight* during his car journey home.

A good many thrillers over the years have belonged to the 'less is more' school of thinking. *The Cybernauts* is no exception, and cleverly teases the viewer with the occasional hint as to its mystery, without revealing too much too soon. In fact, a Cybernaut doesn't make its initial appearance until 33 minutes into the 50 minute episode. Up until then the viewer has only been privy to the odd red herring and the occasional crushed pen. [1]

The 'pen' in question, in its pristine pre-crushed condition, is used to make the establishing shot of the episode, before the carnage of whipping sounds and splintering doors is heard. The ensuing scene is cleverly observed through the eyes of the intruder, ensuring the viewer is subjected to the full horror of the carnage without too much being revealed. We see the intended victim backing away in terror; we hear again that peculiar whip-like sound, we see the victim fall to the ground, and finally the pen being crushed. It is a cleverly filmed and rather unsettling beginning. Immediately the viewer knows this is no ordinary run-of-the-mill murder story. What he maybe doesn't know, on the first viewing, is that all the clues are there to be found in the opening scene, but clues that are impossible to fathom for a further 30 minutes.

Several red herrings are dangled before the viewer en route to the first Cybernaut. The first of these is discussed by John Steed and Emma Peel in the office of Lambert, the third industrialist to fall victim to the mysterious assassin. What could have killed a man, left him with a broken neck, and yet no trace of bruising? The answer: Karate, meaning 'empty hand'. A subject Emma knows rather a lot about. Could the answer belong at the local karate school? Emma pays them a visit and informs Sensai ('the knowledgeable one') of her interest in karate. "Interest is for the onlooker. Karate is a science, an art, a discipline," he informs her, suggesting that fencing may be more suitable, little realising that Emma is already an expert in both. Acala ('the immovable one') enters the room and Emma, having been invited to challenge her by Sensai, easily wins the fight. "You attacked her as a woman, but she has the skill of a man. A bad mistake," comments Sensai, an observation that offers a perfect description of Emma Peel. Indeed this is a mistake a good many will make over the course of the next two years.

After being shown this particular side to Emma Peel, the viewer is immediately privy to a scene that captures John Steed perfectly. He sits very elegantly in the office at Harachi, resplendent in his Saville Row suit, bowler hat in his lap and furled umbrella in one hand. To all intents and purposes the typical English gentleman. A little eccentric perhaps, but respectable and thoroughly harmless. Or so it would seem. While Tusamo, played by Bert Kwouk, has his back turned to Steed, this 'thoroughly harmless' Englishman presses a switch on the stem of his brolly to reveal a hidden camera, which is then used to photograph the list of names Steed needs on Tusamo's desk. This wonderful cover that Steed employs so ruthlessly certainly gives him the advantage his adversaries didn't see coming.

Who would suspect that this very picture of British respectability could pose a threat? Tusamo can count himself lucky that he wasn't considered a threat by Steed. The acquisition of the list of names was all that Steed required, and this he obtained with the minimum of fuss. Indeed Tusamo was none the wiser even after Steed had left. Those that have posed a threat to Steed however were dealt with rather differently. Countless villains have been rendered unconscious by the steel rim of Steed's bowler hat, or tripped over by his brolly, and on at least one occasion knocked out by gas released from the stem of his umbrella. The bowler hat and the brolly conjure up an image of a respectable businessman about town during the 1960s; however, in the hands of a ruthless agent, they become tools used to lure his adversaries into a false sense of security.

A nice feature of *The Avengers* was those scenes that featured the two leads discussing the case in hand. *The Avengers* was far too extraordinary a show to simply have Steed and Emma standing in a room and talking. This they of course did at times, but there was always some quirk or other added to the scene. Whether it was Emma fencing while she speaks with Steed, Steed producing tea-making facilities in a railway carriage, or here in this episode where Steed discusses the case with Emma, who continues to clean her flat with a feather duster, even pausing briefly at one point to dust off Steed! Another red herring, Oyama ('the tall mountain'), is discussed during this amusingly domestic scene. Similarly, Steed receives a visit from Gilbert, who while filling in Steed with details about Armstrong, displays a somewhat perfectionist side to his nature by straightening Steed's pictures and ornaments. This was a clever device employed for many characters in *The Avengers*, and successfully raised them above the mundane and into characters that were quite memorable. The character under discussion in this scene, Armstrong, proved to be a very memorable one in *The Avengers'* catalogue, and with him the trail of red herrings abruptly ends.

A good many villains in this type of genre are motivated by greed and profit. Villains in *The Avengers* however, while often motivated by these same aims, usually have some other unusual trait to elevate them above the run-of-the-mill villain and into someone rather more extraordinary. And so it is with Armstrong. In the short amusing scene with Steed and Gilbert, we are given Armstrong's history. We learn that Armstrong is not one to tow the line and follow orders. Disobeying orders from the top, and in his eagerness to test out his latest invention, he destroys the building he is working in and has been confined to a wheelchair ever since. We learn that he was ousted from his job and has hidden himself behind a veil of gadgets at United Automation, the company he now owns. Before we've even met Armstrong, we know he is going to be an interesting and slightly disturbing character.

The Avengers has always been a visually stimulating series. Unusual sets. Unusual camera angles that are almost Hitchcockian in style. The United Automation set is a strange combination of eye-catching elegance and disturbing shadows. As Steed, posing as a journalist, enters the elevator that takes him from the foyer to Armstrong's office, a sense of foreboding creeps into play alongside Laurie Johnson's brilliantly creepy score.

As Steed 'interviews' Armstrong, we learn that Armstrong has little regard for man. "We humans are fallible, temperamental, and unreliable. The machine is obedient, more competent." He has in fact surrounded himself with an automated workforce, and is perfecting a machine that will think for itself. In time, he informs Steed, machine could supplant the human brain entirely. "And will it?" Emma asks Steed. "Not if I have anything to do with it" is his response. A response that perfectly sums up Steed's attitude to life, whereby man lives and survives by his very wit and wily endeavours.

It is during this interview that Armstrong is revealed as the mastermind behind the Cybernauts, and at the interview's conclusion, Steed is given a pen, cleverly planting the seed of an impending deadly encounter the viewer now has to wait for. That moment duly arrives after Steed stealthily re-enters Armstrong's office later that evening. It is this very scene that provides the viewer with their first glimpse of a Cybernaut, 33 minutes into the episode. After being rendered unconscious by a Cybernaut, Steed awakens facing the barrel of a gun. It is here, faced with such impossible odds, that Steed has to use his wit and wily endeavours to outwit his adversary and his array of gadgets. Armstrong informs Steed of a new Cybernaut he has created, with an electronic brain, incapable of making a wrong decision. Steed knows he must act quickly as Emma, who is now in the elevator looking for Steed, is sent by Armstrong to the factory warehouse to face this new Cybernaut. Steed engages Armstrong in a conversation about his vision for a Cybernetic police state. As with all diabolical masterminds, Armstrong is only too willing to talk about his scheme. His adversary successfully distracted, Steed slams his fist down on all the controls activating every mechanical device, and throwing the office into the darkness that offers Steed his escape.

The final action-packed showdown in the warehouse is brilliantly staged and is one of the most memorable scenes in *The Avengers'* history. "There's no escape!" cries Armstrong, as he wheels himself into the warehouse to witness Steed and Emma facing two Cybernauts. It is a triumph of free-thinking humanity over machinery [2] when Steed has a flash of inspiration and places the pen in the new Cybernaut's lapel, thus creating a battle between the Cybernauts. The mastermind perishes at the hands of his own creation, but as is so often the case in *The Avengers*, every plot development has an extraordinary quirk which places the scene firmly in *Avengerland*. The final shot of Emma pushing over the now deactivated Cybernaut with her forefinger is one such quirk, and also the most amusing incident in the whole episode. This clever little touch was even resurrected two years later in *Return of The Cybernauts*, where Steed insists "It's my turn" before felling the Cybernaut with his own forefinger.

In an episode that is almost entirely studio-bound, the final exterior shot, one of only two exterior shots in the episode, sees Steed in his Bentley filling in a crossword with a pencil. Emma drives into shot and offers Steed the 'pen' when his pencil breaks. "I don't hold with those new fangled things" is both his response, and a reflection of his whole attitude throughout the series. He acknowledges progress and the modern era, even doffing his bowler hat at Emma's disappearing Lotus, the ultimate modern woman in her ultra-modern car, but Steed will always be a gentleman of Edwardian sensibilities, and one who prefers to live by his wit and wily endeavours.

© Richard Cogzell

1. This is surely the defining irony of *The Cybernauts*: that such a subtly-constructed episode is mainly remembered for the sight of the brutal robots, despite the fact that they remain off-screen for so long.
2. A recurring theme in this season and beyond. Steed prefers human imperfection to 'perfect' automation.

THE GRAVEDIGGERS

Filmed: 15th March – 14th April 1965

Exterior Locations:
Graveyard
Miniature train line

Sets:
Controller's office
Hospital: corridor, operating theatre, matron's office
Steed's apartment
Winslip's country house: station concourse area, main hall, carriage
Florist
Funeral parlour
Undertakers

THE GRAVEDIGGERS

Main Character List:
Palmer: early warning station
Baron: henchman
Dr. Johnson: chief surgeon, chairman of hospital
John Steed
Emma Peel
Dr. Hubert Marlow: ex-ministry radar expert
Sexton: at Pringby churchyard
Nurse Spray: at Railwaymen's hospital
Sister Thirlwell: at Railwaymen's hospital
Sager: henchman
Frederick: Sir Winslip's butler
Sir Horace Winslip: philanthropist
Miller: assists Dr. Johnson

The Gravediggers, sandwiched between the immensely popular episode *The Cybernauts* and the immensely unpopular episode *Room Without A View*, is the 7th of the 26 episodes produced for Season 4. It is arguably one of the weaker Season 4 episodes yet it is very watchable. It is after all a Season 4 episode, which is a little like being a top-flight football team. Even if you're in the relegation zone you're still better than 99% of the football teams in the country. *The Gravediggers* is the only Peel era *Avengers* episode written by Malcolm Hulke, and the only *Avengers* episode ever directed by Quentin Lawrence. Not that the script and the direction of it are completely poor, but it is not hard to understand why both the writer and the director were 'one and done' after this one.

Let's start with what is good about *The Gravediggers*. The teaser is very good. The scene is classic *Avengerland*: a picturesque graveyard, an old fashioned funeral party, wonderful funereal music, and ending with a classic avengerish touch, the antenna mysteriously rising out of the grave. It is a very vivid scene, visually and aurally. The music, also used in funeral scenes in other *Avengers* episodes, is unforgettable: haunting but somehow comic. (It is actually difficult for some die-hard *Avengers* fans to attend real-life funerals without hearing this music playing in their heads.) The scene sets up the storyline very well.

Also, the locations in this episode are very avengerish. Other than the early scene at the radar defence location and a brief scene in Steed's apartment, this episode is entirely set in various classic *Avengerland* locations: a hospital with no visible patients, a creepy mortuary that doesn't seem to have a proprietor on the premises, and the quirky house and grounds of Sir Horace.

Steed's first visit to Sir Horace is one of the episode's highpoints. It is played strictly for laughs and the deadpan efficiency with which

Frederick (Sir Horace's assistant) performs his absurd duties almost allows him to steal the scene from Steed. Steed, always comfortable no matter what the situation, doesn't bat an eye at any of the loony shenanigans that go on there. He graciously pays his pence to get in and good-humouredly lunches with the cartoonish Sir Horace on the fake train.

Later, he seems to be having the time of his life riding on Sir Horace's miniature train. One would never guess that the fate of Britain's missile defence system was at stake as a smiling Steed rides along, pretending to shoot birds with his umbrella. He leaves without learning very much but it is nevertheless an enjoyable excursion for Steed and the viewer.

The scene in which Steed rescues the damsel in distress is wonderful – funny and tense at the same time. It is a very clever homage to the silent film era with the telescope view beginning, the old-time piano music, and the speeded-up camera, which makes Steed look like an Olympic sprinter as he runs through the woods to catch up to the train. The fight on the moving train is, as are all movie fights on moving trains, very exciting.

What are the negatives with *The Gravediggers*? To start with, the supporting characters (with the exception of Frederick) are very weak. The Canadian actor Paul Massie as Dr. Johnson and Caroline Blakiston as Miss Thurwell are very generic villains. Blakiston has a much better role in the Season 5 episode, *The Positive Negative Man*, in which she plays Cynthia Wentworth-Howe, the confidential secretary whose ultimate ambition is to "achieve the special category of button-lip." Dr. Johnson and Miss Thurwell are serviceable villains, just not very interesting in the avengerish way that we have come to expect in Season 4.

Sir Horace, as played by Ronald Fraser, is simply bad. The writer was probably aiming for a typically English eccentric character here but instead ended up with a cartoon character. There's a big difference between the two. The viewer can sympathise and somewhat relate to the former but only laugh at the latter. Sir Horace is either a complete dolt or certifiably insane. His hair style held the record for the most bizarre ever until Donald Trump came along. Hair styles aside, this character is perhaps a missed opportunity by the writer and director of this episode to add some gravitas to it. If Sir Horace were more of a relatable human being and less of a buffoon the viewer could have empathised with his love for the bygone days of the railroad. Something *has* been lost in our society by the triumph of the automobile over the railroad and a chance to engage the viewer on this subject was lost here. [1]

The basic premise for the story, agents of a foreign power infiltrating Britain seeking to jam its missile defence system, is a fairly reasonable one but the gigantic holes in the plot logic are a little hard to take. There is no such thing as a Peel era episode plot without holes but *The Gravediggers*' logic flaws, unlike the flaws in most other Peel era episodes, are so glaring that they actually do detract from the quality of the episode. As a courtesy to the reader only one example will be offered. Any *Avengers* fan who has had the misfortune of watching an episode with someone who doesn't 'get' *The Avengers* has had to suffer through comments like "That doesn't make sense! How come the bad guys didn't …blah… blah… blah?" We all know how tedious these issues can be so only one will be mentioned, that of the antenna. The antenna was supposedly built to respond to sunlight, rise up out of the buried coffin, and transmit solar power back to the jamming device in the coffin. Since the antenna was inside the coffin six feet underground, how could sunlight get to it to activate it? Also, how could the raised antenna go unnoticed by anyone who happens to walk by? These obvious questions (and there are many many more in *The Gravediggers*) make it that much more difficult for the viewer to regard this episode as anything but a frothy one.

Another problem with *The Gravediggers* is how underutilised Mrs. Peel is. When a writer has at his disposal the most fascinating female character in television history he should make the most of it. Unfortunately though, Mrs. Peel's beauty, wit, and intelligence aren't very much on display in this episode. She does help Steed connect the dots plot-wise but she is relegated for the most part to unglamorous duties such as checking personnel files and impersonating nurses. Also, she suffers the ignominy of being captured and has to be rescued by her partner.

Malcolm Hulke, who wrote *The Gravediggers*, is more prominent as a writer for the *Doctor Who* series. He just did not seem to know how to showcase the Mrs. Peel character. [2] The same thing can be said of the Steed/Peel chemistry. There just isn't very much interaction between Steed and Mrs. Peel in this episode. That is a huge negative because, after all, that chemistry is what makes *The Avengers* truly great.

The direction by Quentin Lawrence is uneven at best. The fight on the moving train is very well filmed and edited but Steed's fight with the two villains at the hospital is very awkward and unrealistic, as weak as some of those murky and confusing fights in the Cathy Gale era. Also, the scene where Mrs. Peel ties up the villainous nurse Miss Thurwell and takes her place in the operating room is very confusing. First of all a huge casting mistake was made concerning Miss Thurwell. The actress is blonde, blue eyed, and shorter than Mrs. Peel. Even with the surgical mask on it is blatantly obvious that Mrs. Peel is not Miss Thurwell. Why didn't they cast a taller, brown eyed, brown haired actress for the role? Not that everything in *The Avengers* needs to make sense but this seems to be just plain shoddy craftsmanship on the part of the director and producer. And secondly, when Mrs. Peel enters the operating room the villains' eyes narrow and the viewer thinks "these guys are obviously on to Mrs. Peel" but they go ahead and proceed with the operation anyway. When the operation is complete the camera shows more close-ups of the villains' eyes looking very suspiciously at Mrs. Peel, but apparently they (despite the suspicious looks) still don't realise the deception. It is only when Miss Thurwell (who Mrs. Peel did not do a very good job of tying up) comes in and unmasks her that it dawns on them. The viewer ends up scratching his or her head over all this, wondering why the camera kept showing those suspicious looks if the villains apparently weren't suspicious after all. Those shots are probably just an attempt to increase the tension in the scene but they fail. Again, this is very shoddy craftsmanship, particularly for a Season 4 episode.

The Gravediggers episode has its supporters and it also has its critics. In its favour it does have a sense of fun going for it. The elements that make it a lot of fun, such as the teaser scene, the rolling scenery, the miniature train, the damsel in distress rescue, are enjoyable simply from a visual and aural standpoint. If the viewer is also looking for a reasonably well-crafted story, some subtle wit, some Steed/Peel magic, or a bit of human substance, he or she will be disappointed by *The Gravediggers*. It makes some *Avengers* fans' 'Best Ten' lists and others' 'Worst Ten' lists. It is a kind of litmus test for the type of fan one is. If one prefers more froth than substance one likes it, if one prefers more substance than froth, one doesn't.

© Dan O'Shea

1. It is interesting to note the fine balance which exists between 'eccentric' and 'cartoon'. Sir Horace and Colonel Rawlings (Bill Fraser) in *Small Game for Big Hunters* are, on the surface, similar characters and yet Rawlings – despite his racism – manages to be a far more interesting, well-rounded character that holds back – just – from being ridiculously over-the-top; I agree with Dan that in *The Gravediggers* both actor and character fail to do so.
2. Malcolm Hulke wrote a substantial number of Cathy Gale episodes and there is a Cathy Gale style to Emma Peel's role here as Steed sends her undercover. In Hulke's defence, this device is a formula used by plenty of other writers in Season 4 including Brian Clemens and Roger Marshall. The tied-up formula happens at least eight times in the season, including some of the 'classic' episodes such as *The Town of No Return* and *The Hour That Never Was*, continuing throughout the filmed era. At least it rarely involves chloroform, overused in the Tara King season.

ROOM WITHOUT A VIEW

Filmed: 15th – 29th April 1965

Exterior Locations:
Deserted country lanes
Grounds of Wadkins' house

Sets:
Wadkins' country house
Chessman Hotel: reception, lobby, guestroom 621, laundry room, owner's King suite
Nee San prison, 'Manchuria'

ROOM WITHOUT A VIEW

Main Character List:
Anna Wadkin: John Wadkin's wife
Grace: Anna's guest
John Wadkin: physicist, expert in cryogenics
John Steed
Emma Peel
Vernals: 'eager beaver' at the Ministry
Dr. George Cullen: ex-colleague of Wadkin
Leonard Martin Pasold: McBain's Chemicals
Mr. Carter: Chessman Hotel manager
Prison guard
Max Chessman: hotel chain owner
Pushkin: Russian Ministry of Interior

Room Without A View begins with close-ups of a series of fat, grinning, porcelain figures which become more and more bizarre, the final ones surrounded by baby gargoyles. The music matches the Oriental theme, the wind-chimes adding to the general atmosphere of an exotic 'otherness'. The swaying curtains become theatrical as they are gripped by a hand which then shakes as it rips a photo, before attempting to strangle the real-life woman whose still-life image we have just seen torn up. Once again, an *Avengers* teaser has offered us an unsettling mix of the 'real' and the surreal.

The post-teaser scene simultaneously reinforces and undermines social stereotypes. Vernals – from the Ministry – is the civil servant geek, an "eager beaver, everything in triplicate", governed by the theoretical rulebook of "standard procedure" yet totally useless when the threat becomes physically real. He patronisingly assumes that a woman will be lost in the male-dominated worlds of science and psychology. Rather than being bamboozled by the technical jargon, Mrs. Peel simply demystifies the language. 'Cryogenics' is translated as "the science of cooling things"; specialist, esoteric expressions such as "intensified re-orientation and auto-suggestion" become simplified to "brainwashed". Vernals criticises Steed for his (perceived) lack of textbook knowledge about the Nee San prison, only to be shocked – as we perhaps are – by Steed's in-depth analysis:

"Rice husks, gruel, shavings of bad pork and water. *Brackish* water tasting of dust. Some friendly sort of place, Nee San. You have nothing to do all day but lie in a cell listening to the world go by...marching feet, fog-horns on the ships going up river, and the chiming of the clock. And there's no sense of time because whatever the hour in Nee San, the clock always strikes three."

Steed is not just a suave salesman of adventures; he is also a great raconteur, able to paint a picture with words, offering us a pre-echo of the Nee San set we will see much later. His description has Mrs. Peel, Vernals and us spellbound. Steed is always capable of surprise. Racial stereotypes are playfully dealt with, Chinese Anna Wadkin telling Steed that "inscrutability" is meant to be her quality, not his.

Emma Peel's humane qualities are revealed as Vernals and Dr. Cullen dismiss John Wadkin as a "cabbage" and "a fish in a tank" respectively, while she perseveres, attempting to communicate with this wrecked man.

Vernals is a ridiculous figure, as his over-the-top spying techniques at the Chessman Hotel remind us. Steed's facial expression, as they silently communicate in the lobby, acknowledges this. The Chessman offers us sets within the set, chessboards springing up everywhere: reception, lobby, lift, and corridor. Even the exterior doors of the lift are decorated in chess graphics and the bedside lampshade bases are knights. When hotel manager Carter proudly explains the playful set-up, he could almost be talking about *The Avengers* itself:

"For your amusement...you may pit your wits against the grand master. The games are changed every day."

However, the chessboards – like the show's formula – provide a sense of continuity. The mystery of how Cullen and seven other physicists have "disappeared into thin air" is, like a game of chess, a puzzle which Steed is left to solve. As Steed searches Cullen's vacated room, he even pauses to move a chess piece, playfully reinforcing the chess game leitmotif in *Room Without A View*:

Steed: Fascinating game, chess. Pitting of wits, strategy, point, counter-point. Not unlike war.

As Steed and Vernals reflect on their failure to prevent another leading scientist from vanishing, we get a typically witty Steedism:

Vernals: Um...who's going to tell the Minister?
Steed: I will. Probably have to hand in my umbrella.

The humour in this leisurely-paced episode continues as Mrs. Peel attempts to refuse to go undercover again: "I've had my fill of 'fascinating new experiences'." The comment reflects Steed's often underhand use of Emma Peel in dangerous undercover roles, as well as offering us a self-referential touch. If Rigg plays a role each week, so too does Emma. Steed's take up of a role himself, that of Monsieur Gourmet, will allow light-hearted humour to interplay with a dramatic undercurrent in the second half of this episode.

The disturbing drama re-establishes itself as Pasold investigates Cullen's room. The moment he pulls back the curtains to reveal a metal board, rather than the spectacular cityscape view, we have been set a puzzle. How is Room 621 transformed from luxurious en-suite accommodation to claustrophobic gas chamber? From the hotel bedroom trap we are taken straight in to another one, the Nee San prison. The sounds which greet Cullen/us echo Steed's earlier description of Nee San, yet the presence of Cullen and the chess piece he is gripping warn us not to be taken in by this set-within-the-set. Wadkin's voice through the vent asks us to question where we are and even whether we really are still in 1965. The prison cell, with its basic walls and straw-strewn floor is simple yet atmospheric. One can easily imagine losing track of time here, of slowly losing one's mind even.

When we finally encounter the mastermind, Max Chessman, his round face bears a dramatic, striking resemblance to the grinning porcelain figures of the teaser. His masochistic secondhand savouring of the gourmet food is oddly humorous and warns us to expect a future scene in which he will encounter Monsieur Gourmet himself. Like a chess grand master, we should be anticipating the future moves. When Mrs. Peel, now reluctantly installed as receptionist, discovers that Steed will be "gourmandising" with Chessman while she works, she warns him with a hint of bitterness: "Well, don't come to me for the bicarbonate of soda."

Max Chessman is a diabolical mastermind with a plan to take his hotel empire further than Napoleon, east of the Black Sea. However, he is also a physical oddity:

"Look at me, one of nature's jokes, a fat man with thin blood. I have to keep the temperature at a steady eighty degrees."

This connects Max Chessman to other physically-challenged masterminds, such as Horatio Kane and Dr. Armstrong. Are their physical deformities meant to match or mirror their moral ones?

Steed's ridiculously remarkable vineyard knowledge in *Dial A Deadly Number* is matched here as he offers his expert opinion of the proffered cigar: "Cuban, sun-dried, hand-rolled, rolled against the thigh of *une jeune fille*." His description is humorous, but is also a cunningly playful one, as he is stalling while Chessman impatiently awaits the answer to an earlier question about Wadkin. The crispness of the verbal exchanges as Chessman tests Steed's cuisine knowledge is matched by the suspicious Carter grilling Mrs. Peel, the scenes mirroring each other:

Carter: For a receptionist you undertake a great many tasks, Mrs. Peel.
Emma: As a receptionist, Mr. Carter, I expect to.

Her discovery of Pasold's corpse in a laundry basket – the lid popping up conveniently to allow us/her to see inside – offers us a surreal coffin and enables the viewer to place the three sets/puzzle pieces together: hotel, laundry and prison are all housed under the same roof, intertwined enterprises/narratives. There is also a cyclical feeling developing, as Mrs. Peel is trapped – like Pasold before her – in Room 621. Her experience offers us an uncomfortable sense of *déjà vu*. This time, though, the scene takes us further, as a guard in gas mask emerges from the built-in wardrobe. However, if we appear to be making progress then the arrival of Steed in 621 moments later sets us back: the view is back and there is no hint of either gas or foul play. We may be a step ahead of Steed but we too are caught in a puzzle maze.

As *Room Without A View* reaches its climax, there is still time for leisured humour as Russian minister Pushkin complains about the nineteen seconds it took for the lift to arrive: "This would not be tolerated at home." Just as the Chessman is in the traditional service industry for its 'normal' guests, a more clandestine one is offered, as Chessman explains:

"A unique service. Information, at leisure, without risk...ready for questioning under ideal conditions."

Chessman's master plan is that of a businessman. He wants to create a global gourmet empire, an upmarket chain in which Chessman becomes a worldwide brand. This makes him very different from most other *Avengers* diabolical masterminds. His physical weakness also makes him strangely vulnerable, pathetically pleading as Steed lowers the room temperature. Once again, Steed finds time to move a chess piece as he waits for Chessman to reveal the whereabouts of Mrs. Peel. This seems appropriate as Steed's unravelling of the strange case is like that of a chess grand master.

With only five minutes remaining, Chessman finally explains the mystery behind Room 621: there is a fake version on the seventh floor. Steed's arrival in the room adds a third circle to the cycle, yet the atmosphere this time reassures us that he will not be trapped. As Steed discovers the hidden door in the back of the wardrobe, he still has time to replace the coat hanger, a typical Steed gesture which offers further evidence that all will be well now, while reinforcing our image of him as being almost meticulously camp. It intertextually connects to his careful removal of Emma Peel's ornaments in their fencing duel in *The Town of No Return*.

Everything appears to be false in *Room Without A View*: the hotel manager, the seventh floor room, the Far East prison and its 'everyday' noises. Even some of the guards and laundry men are no more Chinese than Steed is. It is appropriate, then, that both Steed and Mrs. Peel are also fakes – galloping gourmet and roving receptionist – actors playing roles on the hotel set. The fight finale is played out in front of the tape recorder, Steed employing a mop against the guards' bayonets. The tape reverses just as the villains' fortunes do – matching a similar scene in *The Master Minds* – and the scene revels in its quirky artificiality, as does the tag scene in which a speeded-up Steed takes Mrs. Peel off in a runaway rickshaw, along a familiar stretch of deserted country road, towards that bright horizon.

Despite the very strong supporting cast – which includes Peter Jeffrey, Philip Latham and Peter Arne – this is one of those rare unloved Season 4 episodes. Roger Marshall's script is well structured, the initial idea is a clever one, yet, despite the presence of wit and humour, the episode never quite develops the charm or the disconcerting avengerish atmosphere which we discover in other studio-bound episodes such as *Death at Bargain Prices*, *Dial A Deadly Number*, or *The Cybernauts*. It is, perhaps, the combination of a slow pace, the lack of any experimental/quirky camera shots, and truly outstanding, memorable scenes that holds *Room Without A View* back from being a 'classic' episode. In addition, one could reasonably argue that Diana Rigg is underused, a crime in itself. Nevertheless, for Steed/Macnee there is great fun to be had as Monsieur Gourmet and the episode deserves a more positive press than it has received.

© Rodney Marshall

A SURFEIT OF H$_2$O

Filmed: 30th April – 11th May 1965

Exterior Locations:
Fields

Sets:
Barker brothers' cottage
Jonah's ark barn
Grannie Gregson's Glorious Grogs wine factory: reception, laboratory, store
Storm drains

A SURFEIT OF H$_2$O

Main Character List:
Ted Barker: poacher in Little Storpington
John Steed
Emma Peel
Eli Barker: Ted's brother
Jonah Barnard: local barn owner, ark builder
Martin Smythe: assistant at Grannie Gregson's wine factory
Dr. Sturm: in charge of Grannie Gregson's wine factory
Joyce Jason: receptionist/sales at Grannie Gregson's wine factory
Sir Arnold Kelly: meteorologist
Frederick: henchman from Grannie Gregson's

In a season in which *The Avengers* consistently demonstrates its ability to offer an almost bewildering variety of themes and stylistic approaches, in which each episode is lovingly created as an individual 'film', *A Surfeit of H$_2$O* arguably represents the most individualistic of the lot. It is the only script contributed by Colin Finbow and the fact that Steed and Emma Peel leave their usual cars at home, driving around together in the roofless, jeep-like Mini Moke, highlights the one-off nature of this memorably bizarre episode. [1]

The teaser sees a country man setting wire traps in a field against the backdrop of rumbling thunder, representing both pathetic fallacy and a physical result of the experiments undertaken at the neighbouring wine factory. A sudden rainstorm erupts and the man drowns, lying there with his mouth opening and closing like a fish. It is an unsettling sight. In the post-teaser scene all that is left of him is a puddle in the shape of a man. This surreal image will be repeated later in the episode, and adds a hauntingly odd touch, almost like a liquid scene-of-crime tape. These initial scenes warn us to expect a visually startling episode.

Steed is in playful mode throughout *A Surfeit of H$_2$O*. He describes the drowned man, Ted Barker, in alliteratively poetic terminology, leaving it to Emma Peel to translate into layman's terms:

Steed: Snare setter, pheasant fancier, partridge pincher...
Emma: You mean the local poacher.

While both the Avengers acknowledge the inexplicable occurrence of a man drowning in a field – "impossible" (Emma); "strange" (Steed) – locals such as Eli Barker and Jonah Barnard consider the weather to be an Old Testament-style portent, a "sign". Their names tell us that they are strange, biblical figures, Eli talking to Mrs. Peel in his leaking cottage about demons and Jonah preaching about a coming flood in his barn where he is constructing an oak-framed Noah's Ark. If both figures are gently mocked by Steed and the script, Barnard's evidence of strange changes is not simply based on religious superstition; it is also founded on 'surreal reality': marshland butterflies and birds appearing in this historically dry area of the country; the scientific disturbance of the natural world:

"The balance of nature is disturbed; doom is in the air…the same cloud in the same position in the sky every day."

The episode is remarkable for its striking images. Steed's face is strangely distorted as he stares into the glass bottle of the preserved giant cucumber; Eli's face disconcertingly odd as he lies dead in the wine factory's water supply, eyes and mouth wide open. Humans – like Mother Nature – are suffering from the unnatural experimentation at Granny Gregson's.

The humour in *A Surfeit of H$_2$0* is as bizarre as the plot. Steed, under cover as a philandering wine merchant, goes wonderfully over-the-top in his sensual eulogy about wine when offered a lifeless catalogue:

"*Catalogue!* 'Honeyed blackberry wine'. That means nothing to me, Miss Jason. Where is the tang of blue blackberries gathered in the early morning dew by barefoot peasant girls? The rich nectar taste of honey syrup…The sun glinting on amber liquid…The nostrils assaulted by the heady aromatics of a perfect bouquet…Rolling smooth syrup-sweet liquid around the mouth, alerting the taste buds, savouring the sheer sensuality of a unique experience."

The shocked reaction of the receptionist is almost that of a blushing virgin, and the strangely humorous scene is made odder still by the portrait of Granny Gregson holding an enormous (phallic?) cucumber. Steed does a double take as he looks at the painting, encouraging us to do the same thing. There is plenty of cute/corny humour in the script, Mrs. Peel announcing that her knowledge of meteorological science is "bright in patches"; Steed's tasting of 'old bark wine' leading to his assessment that they "must have put the dog in it too".

When the aptly-named Dr. Sturm introduces Steed to one of his state-of-the-art pulping presses – describing it as "a gentle giant" – we are pre-warned that the machine will serve a far more ominous function later on. Indeed, as *A Surfeit of H$_2$0* reaches its dramatic climax, the darker drama bubbles to the surface like fermenting alcohol.

The introduction of Sir Arnold Kelly, a renowned meteorological expert, provides us with a typical *Avengers* victim: short-sighted, affably eccentric, and lost in his own world.

Martin: He's not wearing a mackintosh.
Sturm: Pity. Looks like rain.

As Sir Arnold drowns in another torrential downpour – taking us back to the teaser – the disturbing images are heightened by the sight of Sturm watching impassively from the laboratory window. It is a disconcertingly chilling sight. The shape of the surreal puddle is commented on by Steed who states that "I had an aunty who used to make biscuits like this." The bizarre connection Steed makes is as surreal as the image itself.

The climax of the plot dramatically switches between Emma Peel being tortured in the pulping press and Steed and Jonah journeying through the wine factory's drains.

Sturm: Another half an inch before breathing becomes difficult...a fraction more pressure and your ribs will bend, another fraction and your ribs will crack.

Emma Peel's pained facial expressions are genuinely disturbing, the potentially clichéd scene played effectively straight as Sturm promises to "squeeze the information" out of her. The idea that his ability to control rain "to order" represents the "biggest military weapon since the nuclear bomb" does not seem particularly far-fetched and, suddenly, Jonah's warnings about the dangers of scientific experimentation no longer appear ridiculously alarmist:

"Man has destroyed mountains with his science...Making rain! It's flying in the face of nature!"

As in *Man-Eater of Surrey Green* and *Silent Dust*, the potential ecological dangers created by scientists are made to appear very 'real', in the sense of possible. (This should not be taken as evidence that I believe in alien life form). Rachel Carson's eco-warnings in her 1960s bestseller *Silent Spring* would no doubt have been echoing in the minds of well-read contemporary viewers. Steed's arrival – just in the nick of time – allows humour to disrupt the drama:

Steed: What are you, the sparkle in the seaweed soda?
Emma: No, I'm the kick in the nettle noggin.

Despite Steed's reassurance that he understands how to operate Sturm's machine, we are left unsure whether Steed has cleverly outwitted the pulp press or simply guessed correctly as he releases

Mrs. Peel from the mechanical jaws. As his bowler is crushed, Emma Peel playfully reassures him that "it was over very quickly. I don't think it suffered." Once again, the humour here is surreal, playing on the idea of the faithful bowler almost being a canine companion.

The final fight scene which takes place in driving rain is as bizarre as the scenes which precede it, as two worlds/times collide: Jonah offering his Old Testament refrain of "Hallelujah! The flood is here!" while Sturm is appropriately dealt with, drowning in his own ultra-modern rain machine. The machine offers four choices – drizzle, shower, storm, tempest – and, like the drama itself, has been pushed into the highest 'gear' for this dramatic finale. The rain machine idea was reworked in the disastrous 1998 Hollywood movie; far better to simply show cinema-goers this delightfully different hour.

The tag scene of *A Surfeit of H$_2$O* does not require a themed-vehicle such as a hearse, rickshaw, milk float, or magic carpet. It already has one in the shape of the Mini Moke, a one-off, quirky mode of transport which zooms off towards that 'bright horizon', a symbol of this oddly-entertaining, unique episode.

© Rodney Marshall

1. It remains a mystery to me why, having produced such an atmospherically quirky *Avengers* script, Colin Finbow was never involved in the series again. For me, this episode represents a 'classic' Season 4.

TWO'S A CROWD

Filmed: 12th – 28th May 1965

Exterior Locations:
Embassy grounds/lake
Country road

Sets:
Steed's apartment
Aeromodel shop
Russian Embassy: outer office, reception hall, Psev's office
City bar
Fashion show

TWO'S A CROWD

Main Character List:
Ambassador Brodny
John Steed
Emma Peel
Major Carson: from the Department
Sergei Ivenko: minor official at the Russian Embassy
Alicia Elena: Russian Embassy, finance and administration
Boris Shvedloff: Russian Embassy, sabotage and elimination expert
Pudeshkin: Russian Embassy, cipher expert
Josef Vogel: Russian Embassy, planning and operations expert
Gordon Webster: model/actor, Steed lookalike (played by Steed)

In the dangerous arena of international espionage, death can come suddenly and unexpectedly. It strikes from unexpected directions, too – from the air, perhaps. From the shadows. From depths of dark water. Sometimes from a friend who is not what they seemed to be...

Twenty years after the end of the Second World War, the sunny clear skies over London are peaceful, the sound of an aeroplane engine no longer a signifier of danger from the skies – free from barrage balloons and other defences, the dockland vista is open and vulnerable...as a small aeroplane banks and descends, the droning of its engine growing louder, more insistent. The Houses of Parliament bask in the sun beside the lazy River Thames, but we become aware that the plane has a bomb or missile slung underneath. This sinister object must surely be intended for a target below, in London.

A well-dressed man – the ambassador, no less, for a major power which seems to be Russia – helps himself to another drink from a punch-bowl on the balcony of his embassy. Too late he becomes aware of the rapidly approaching engine noise...The plane releases its payload...and in a sudden realisation of scale, the small 'bomb' package plops into Ambassador Brodny's punch-bowl, comically wetting his face. From threat to humour, in the shrinking of scale from a large payload 'bomb' to a harmless little plastic toy; the first 'switch', of many to come. However, there is a real threat to Brodny, because the message means that the enigmatic masterspy Colonel Psev is coming to town (a telephone dial later on indicates the Russian Embassy is at Leadenhall in London). Specifically, Psev wishes to base himself in Brodny's embassy for the duration of a defence conference, along with his entourage, four dangerous and powerful agents whose orders must be obeyed to the letter.

Mrs. Emma Peel, dressed in a very striking white plastic tabard over a dark-sleeved jersey, gets no answer from pressing John Steed's doorbell. She enters his apartment and finds him unconscious, just as Steed's confederate, Major Carson, attacks. It has been a ruse to test 'security', Steed betting upon Emma's abilities to overcome the Major. Another twist, Steed was not in any immediate danger, nor actually unconscious. This play-acting, hiding the truth, however briefly, from Emma, could be seen as untrusting. She will get her own back on Steed...She gets her own back on the Major now by treading on his fingers to immobilise him. He is unable to return Emma's offer of a cordial handshake and honour is satisfied.

Steed makes it clear that Psev is one of the most important enemy agents: "There are spies and spies, but he's the king of them all". Steed remains casual, lounging about his apartment in a black roll-neck sweater (his clothes will vary wildly as the plot demands, later on. The other large drain on the wardrobe budget will be Psev's secretary, though with Emma sidelined for the early part of this episode an 'eye candy' quotient was possibly in play in the production team's thinking). Carson is wedded to his raincoat which, as Steed emphasises, the Major can't remove, even though we only ever see him in Steed's apartment!

There is a rival-cum-scapegoat of sorts for Brodny, his subordinate Sergei Ivenko who helps Brodny to do the bidding of the four VIPs who serve Colonel Psev. He is played by John Bluthal, a stalwart of British comedy over six decades, and his interactions with Brodny (Warren Mitchell) are a joy to behold. Emma Peel poses as an assistant in a model shop, aero-modelling being one of Colonel Psev's known hobbies. Ivenko visits, and is identified to Emma by Steed (lurking conspicuously behind a shelf). Emma wears some delightful spectacles as part of her disguise. She doesn't get much to do in this episode, and although what she does is marvellous, it is mainly near the end.

After tense exchanges at the Embassy – wherein Brodny is left in no doubt that if Psev does not get the defence conference information he came for, Brodny will be accompanying Psev's entourage home in ignominy – we switch to more humour. Ivenko accompanies Brodny to the Dandy Collection fashion show; Psev is also a dedicated follower of fashion, and keen to keep up with the newest trends. More opportunities for humour ensue: a male model, dressed in a James Bond style dinner jacket ensemble has his outfit touted as having "hidden extras", being resistant to flame and champagne; "the driest Martini just rolls off it...anyone for cocktails?"

Similarly, the next male model (who is dressed in the loud shirts and sunglasses of a beachfront Lothario) sports "lipstick proof" fashions. He is Gordon Webster, actor and wastrel, and we're instantly drawn to him as soon as we see his very familiar face beneath that "hat with a dash of panache".

Although Brodny repeatedly dozes off through boredom (my own reaction to fashion), he perks up considerably when Gordon Webster takes the stage, complete with "slacks built for action", a Leslie Phillips-style 'cad' moustache and that outrageously garish line in lipstick-proof shirts (not to mention pinching the bottoms of his female colleagues on the catwalk) – for Webster, crucially, is a man who looks virtually identical to Steed.

Brodny is on the forward foot again. Proving he is no buffoon, he takes the precaution of telephoning Steed's number. Brodny doesn't speak – yet Steed is there (or seems to be). Webster has left the stage only briefly during this call; surely there is not enough time for him to take a re-routed call if he is really Steed? We the audience are now led to believe that Webster and Steed are two different men. Brodny smiles smugly, as the camera lingers on his triumphant features partially hidden by 'fashionable' ferns in the foreground. Like Steed, he knows the game is afoot, and he can now be a big game hunter deep in the jungle of espionage; just as a deerstalker-topped "all huntin', all shootin', all fishin'" outfit modelled by Webster takes the stage (with more ludicrous posing by Macnee, who proves himself – once again – to be a comedy god).

Psev's assistants make their first mistake by calling off the man watching Steed's apartment. This will make coming and going a lot easier for Steed, and maybe for someone else…from now on, they will rely on sound. Later on, they will order Brodny not to be an eye-witness to Webster killing Steed…as they say in America, succinctly, "you do the math".

Brodny remains largely a bumbling comic character, but he has a few loveable traits, most notably a kind of devotion to remaining in England (and an ever-present fear of being returned home to Russia). He emulates Steed, even admires him, and speaks of their personal acquaintanceship proudly; although this, like everything, is trumped by Brodny's number one priority: his overwhelming regard for his own safety. Brodny is therefore not a reliable figure to either 'side' in the Cold War conflict; he professes not to be a "cloak and dagger" man, and even the simple mission of replacing an umbrella in Steed's apartment fills him with trepidation.

Brodny arriving at Steed's apartment with bowler and brolly is not suspicious; Brodny clearly views Steed as the height of English sartorial elegance and tries to copy his immaculate tailoring (with variable results, missing Steed's waistcoat and having a rumpled protruding tie). Whatever viewers may think of Brodny, it is impossible to fault his choice of role model!

Ivenko breaks the wing of one of Psev's half-completed aeroplane models whilst rushing to comply with an order to light Webster's cigar; whilst this gives Emma an excuse to visit the embassy (with a replacement), and see Webster for plot reasons, it is a horrible shock for Ivenko and twists the story away from humour (the louche Webster stringing along the Russians) and on to angry threats against the hapless Ivenko, made behind his back, showing the deadliness of Psev's quartet.

"People may look alike, but they don't behave alike," Steed reassures Emma – cue an immediate cut to a pinstripe-suited Brodny putting the finishing touches to a near-identical pattern suit on Webster. Nicely done. We're reminded that Brodny isn't actually evil or vicious; just a man under intense pressure from capricious bosses.

Macnee excels as Webster; he moves, talks and reacts very differently to Steed. Webster is a louche opportunist, charming in the sense of a 'rotter' always on the lookout for the main chance; his hairstyle is similar to Steed's but sloppily coiffed, hair oil applied in copious quantities and a wayward curl drooping down his left temple; he seems slightly dissipated, and drags on cigars and sups alcohol with alacrity. At the Embassy reception, he happily takes care of Emma's glass of champagne and so has two on the go at once (a metaphor?). Emma uses some kind of swizzle stick, presumably to reduce carbonation in her champagne – perhaps anticipating action; she wouldn't want to burp during a fight!

Alcohol performs several functions here. Brodny's panicky quest to secure the rare *La Crème de Violettes* liqueur, required by Colonel

Psev, ends when Steed offers a bottle to "cement relations". In return Brodny accidentally confirms Psev is indeed in town; eager to prove he is loyal, Brodny gulps down his loathed vodka – two glasses of it, for good measure; eschewing the London gin which Steed knows Brodny prefers. Steed sips a brandy, fully aware of the situation. Just as he was well-prepared in advance, obtaining the liqueur for Brodny, who knows how long he has been planning to infiltrate Psev's organisation, discover Psev's identity, and neutralise him? Similarly, Psev's mission is to infiltrate the Polaris submarine base-supply planning meeting, critical to Britain's nuclear safety. The man shown on television to be heading the security detail is…John Steed. We get some unintentional amusement as the Embassy's television turns on instantly (after Brodny has been grinning at it for a while, then gets ordered to switch it on!). Unlike every 1960s television it does not have to 'warm up', and the picture is high-definition film.

The actor Gordon Webster's past has been researched – quickly – by Psev's cronies. Webster was a fighter pilot, but was cashiered – meaning he was drummed out of the service in disgrace. His inveterate habits of gambling, drinking, and womanising means he is – unlike Steed – corruptible. Amusingly, when being groomed to perform as Steed, Webster is given a gigantic buttonhole carnation, resembling a frothing bouquet of foliage with stems wrapped in silver paper. It's not clear whether a preoccupied Emma notices this gigantic clue, but Brodny does, and predictably panics. Webster claims to quite like it – but Brodny tells the agents that they might as well put a stick of celery in the fake Steed's lapel! BBC costume designers for future telefantasy characters please take note. To unobtrusively rearrange the flower, Alicia Elena stands Webster closely under an unruly pot plant, so that Macnee's head is stuck in as much foliage as his poor carnation.

"A hostage in the hand is worth two in the tomb", quips Vogel. Oh dear. No wonder he credits the saying to Psev! Emma is held hostage, tied next to the fireplace in Psev's ante-room, and will be out of the action nearly as soon as she came into it – the episode's only real weakness. This room doubles as a control centre for the various mini-machines of death, the model planes and submarine.

At the point of presenting Sergei Ivenko with his ticket home (essentially a death warrant, since Ivenko has been earmarked for elimination), Brodny seems to take a malicious delight in the act. Either he is unaware of the seriousness of what awaits Ivenko, or Brodny is simply relieved that another 'incompetent' has been identified in Brodny's place. It's an ugly face of cowardice, but it is hard to condemn Brodny's relief, mainly thanks to Warren Mitchell's enjoyably nervous-looking performance throughout the earlier scenes. Or perhaps Sergei Brodny is merely glad to see the back of another Sergei; less confusion at the Embassy.

Ivenko is able to sneak through the Embassy at night in search of his file with its elimination order, and there is some gorgeous lighting with oppressive shadows in one of which Psev may lurk…we will see someone following as smart suited legs and fashionably sharp shoes – perhaps Psev's, or more likely Vogel's – move into the light, the mysterious figure clearly having overheard Ivenko's plea for asylum. Ivenko passes from the wide firelit hall under a halo of unfocussed lit chandelier, into darkness and long shadows. This reflects his passage of realisation – from free(ish) man, to a victim of accidents and others' incompetence, and sheer malevolence; an innocent man earmarked for destruction. This is our biggest indication of the viciousness of Psev.

It also marks another twist or change in perception – things just got very serious again. Fun is in another room. The writer teases our tastebuds with frequent change, but always driving the characters forward. The 'For Elimination' stamp is freeze-framed and zoomed, confirming Ivenko's immediate fears in a neat directorial flourish; the music, tense extended strings, emphasises the horror of a dead man walking. Death – even in a high-stakes espionage game – isn't always sudden or unexpected. It can be protracted, capricious and cruel.

Ivenko's only option is to seek asylum in the West. His fatal mistake is to ring Steed from within his own embassy. Although he plans to meet Steed in the grounds – "by the lake at the back" – Steed has to somehow get from his own apartment to the Embassy (where is Webster supposed to be now – do the Russians let him keep nipping out?). Ivenko is killed remotely, which at least explains why Webster/Steed isn't spotted in the grounds; Vogel has binocular-eyes only for Ivenko, presumably in order to range the submarine's weapon. The entire sequence is done in dumb-show mime, with Steed gesturing to Ivenko from the Tyke's Water Bridge, right up to the point he rolls over Ivenko's corpse. Music does the speaking. It's all very nicely done – quite eerie.

Steed finds Emma. As usual, he comes in through the window (in the Cathy Gale years, Steed is asked if he always enters by window; his answer is along the lines of "whenever possible"). He can't resist commenting on her condition: "All ready for broiling?" She is trussed like a chicken. Then we twist back again from the hints of cosy Steed/Emma familiarity – "Webster. Gordon Webster." The Psev agents are in control. Steed teases Emma – the miniature tie pin camera that he is given to break the defence conference security is a present from Emma (or replica of same). "Christmas, or birthday – or some...special occasion?" and he knuckles her chin playfully. Emma stares back impassively. They know the circumstances of the gift, just how 'special' the occasion was; we don't. This is how you should do the 'will they, won't they?' between the leads, subsequent TV show producers take note! [1]

There's a clever shot of the broken glass in the fireplace, after 'Webster' has thrown it there in a Cossack gesture after downing his drink, on his way to kill Steed and Carson. It's lovely because, although Emma doesn't realise it yet, it's suddenly clear to a viewer that this was no 'accident'; Webster really is Steed, and has left Emma a means of untying her bonds, the glass.

Eventually, of course, we realise (if we had not guessed already) that PSEV is in fact "four heads are better than one" – the four agents of the entourage make up PSEV itself, a group entity. Hence all the hobbies, the immense consumption of cigars, the requirement for pills, liqueurs, suits...'Webster', still not revealing himself to Emma, has effectively beaten PSEV – his developed microfilm reads 'Two's A Crowd'. This does not go down well with the humourless Soviets.

Mrs. Peel's expected fight never comes...the closest is when Emma prepares to put a bullet in Webster/Steed's head. She does get to overpower her guard once she has broken through her bonds; with her left hand, she 'nerve pinches' him into unconsciousness whilst advancing on Psev's group, the guard's gun in her right hand. This represented a big switch too, but a predictable one – from the tense (and intense) infiltration of the conference, all done on audio with swelling music and a tension-breaking harsh shrilling of the phone for the final result – towards which Vogel leaps most athletically and amusingly. Interestingly, *The New Avengers* 'doubles' episode called *Faces* involved telephones to inform the heroes of the fate of their partners: life or death. In this case, Emma may already think Steed is dead. The machines are a vital bridge between human lives in both cases, as Emma/Purdey await news of their friends and the fate of the duplicates.

There is one final switch before the tag scene tease of an equestrian Emma pretending to Steed to be someone else. It turns out the entire defence conference was bait in a trap to unmask and neutralise Psev, cooked up by Steed and a colleague. That he didn't trust Emma with this information chagrins her, although he does explain that he needed to be sure his Webster persona could fool anyone and Emma would be the most reliable test of it. Nevertheless, we can forgive Emma for taunting Steed at the end, before they ride off in harmony and Macnee gets to show off his lifelong equestrian skills once more.

There is a slight jolt for modern viewers who are aware of the later seasons of the show. Steed says, "Come now, Mrs. Peel. If I had a twin, I'm sure Mother would have mentioned it!" At the time, we must presume he means his own mother (which makes more sense anyway, since she would know if she had given birth to twins); we don't find out if Steed's parents are alive or dead. But the line leaps out once we are aware of Patrick Newell's character code-named Mother, Steed's boss in the final season.

Appropriately for an episode about doubles and being in two places at the same time, PSEV will have a tiny echo in a future episode. In *Small Game for Big Hunters* one of Steed's files (upset during the raid on his paperwork) is marked 'Pzev'. An inconsequential, playful in-joke, but we may wonder if Shvedloff has been replaced and the four-headed masterspy has been recommissioned. Stranger things have happened – if you're ever in Steed's department records room, just take a look at the Boris Kartovsky file (*A Touch of Brimstone/Split!*)...

The doubles idea has been done elsewhere (and in several *Avengers/New Avengers* episodes) but the cleverness here is in working out how Steed manages to juggle two identities at once, to at least two sets of colleagues. This episode rewards rewatching to try to spot all the tricks used to maintain the illusion by Steed and his colleagues. Colleagues both seen (Carson) and unseen (Plessey, referenced in the final scenes as a faker with Steed of the audio tapes used to enable Steed to answer the phone and appear on Psev's "bug" channel).

Whilst enjoying the exploits of Steed and his partner, connoisseurs of the espionage genre are usually aware of other literary and screen agents aplenty. So when spy film tropes crop up in *The Avengers*, there is a conspiracy between the makers of the series and the audience who participate in the fun of spotting their references. The fashion show 'James Bond', the scale models (as seen in many a spy film pretending to be full-sized military hardware), cunningly-disguised miniature cameras posing as items of jewellery, bugged umbrellas...

All these nods and winks provide levity, as does the relationship of Steed and Brodny, and that of Brodny and Webster; there is a froth of fun which can be tinged with dark humour too. The submarine model rising from Tyke's Water Lake and despatching the unfortunate Ivenko is amusing at first, but a tougher undercurrent is revealed when Steed – seconds too late for their rendezvous – turns over his body to reveal his dripping face and dead staring eyes.

At the climax, Steed's attempts to reach his contact by radio interfere with the radio-controlled flying model bomber built by 'Psev', sending it haywire. Even as we smile at the rickety model, and the exasperation of its 'cipher expert' pilot twiddling uselessly at the remote-controls, it is sent crashing, along with its explosive payload, into Psev's control room. Presumably the resultant explosion injures or kills the four enemy agents; they are "hoist by their own petard". Deadly danger and humour meet in this final confluence, joined by a hefty dose of poetic justice: a heady mix that remains, for many viewers, an essential element of *The Avengers*. These ingredients of hazard and humour are employed very deftly in this monochrome era of the show. They parallel the images we see: the physical light and shade in the carefully lit and framed shots, and the costume and set designs. It is all part of a constructed whole where nothing, however odd it may appear, is accidental.

With levity and wit, darkness and death, suspense and mystery, bright sunshine relaxation and dark night time plotting, country and town, and hints of a more intimate relationship between Steed and Emma, this is an episode that constantly twists and turns. It develops the characters and plot in consistent and satisfying ways, and rewards the viewers. It is a worthy member of the best season of *The Avengers*, and therefore an adventure befitting Steed and Emma; the kind of story that *The Avengers* is all about. The semi-comedic acting (especially of John Bluthal and Warren Mitchell, alone or together) is subtly done, and a real high point of the series. It is a story ripe for reappraisal.

© Frank Shailes

1. Frank refers to the SEDDI members: those who believe 'Steed and Emma Definitely Did It'. This enigma was encouraged by Brian Clemens himself, as I suggested in my introduction. The debate still continues. Some episodes (monochrome and colour) clearly hint at the possibility, or

probability as in the tag scene in *Epic*; others suggest otherwise. This uncertainty adds yet another subtle level of humour (and mystery) to their on-screen rapport and chemistry.

MAN-EATER OF SURREY GREEN

Filmed: 31st May – 11th June 1965

Exterior Locations:
Botanical gardens
Sir Lyle Peterson's House: façade, grounds
Moat Farm outbuildings
Deserted country lanes

Sets:
Steed's apartment
Sir Lyle Peterson's house: plant room, study
Surrey Green Arms pub

MAN-EATER OF SURREY GREEN

Main Character List:
Laura Burford: botanist
Alan Carter: botanist
John Steed
Emma Peel
Lennox: Sir Lyle's butler, henchman
Sir Lyle Peterson: horticulturist
Wing Commander Davies: War Department
Dr. Sheldon: expert botanist
Publican of Surrey Green Arms
Joe Mercer: farm supplier
Professor Taylor: germination expert working for Sir Lyle
Professor Knight: botanical expert working for Sir Lyle
Dr. Connolly: irrigation expert working for Sir Lyle

Man-Eater of Surrey Green isn't any more fantastical than the cult science fiction novel *The Day of the Triffids*. The key difference is that Wyndham's novel is able to terrify readers because the images are co-created by our vivid imaginations; we paint the pictures, as it were. With television and cinema we are forced to rely on the images provided for us by the director and camera crew. These nearly always fall short of those projected by our over-active minds. It is, after all, one of the great advantages of books. Thankfully, this only becomes a problem in the final few minutes of this *Avengers* episode, thanks mainly to the brilliant direction.

The teaser for *Man-Eater of Surrey Green* sees amorous botanists Alan Carter and Laura Burford at work in a ministry greenhouse before plant-loving Burford encounters a strange hypnotic sound which sends her trampling through precious plants and bushes as if she is sleepwalking, before getting into a waiting, chauffeur-driven car. Carter is oblivious to the strange events, his hearing aid encasing (and protecting) him in his own private world of research. Once again *The Avengers* offers us an image of benevolent scientists as being cut-off from reality. The sight of zombified figures – effectively portrayed in *The Master Minds* – will be repeated or re-used throughout this story. However, it is, arguably, the strange sound which creates the unsettling atmosphere, here, rather than the sight of the 'walking dead'.

The post-teaser scene sees Steed playing his formulaic role of suave salesman of adventures, offering a rose to the suspicious Mrs. Peel:

"What nasty situation have you got in store for me this time, hm? You have your own built-in early warning system, you know. A certain look in the eye."

Emma Peel is not simply demonstrating her ability to read Steed's cunning, underhand nature. She is voicing our own ability to recognise the series' formulaic approach as Steed takes her/us off for another extraordinary adventure. For us, the 'early warning system' is the music and opening credits as we (voluntarily) head off for our weekly fix of fantasy.

The experimental direction of Sidney Hayers is one of the highlights of *Man-Eater of Surrey Green*. The quirkiness of the camera work is first in evidence as Steed visits Sir Lyle Peterson's country home. As he stands in the entrance porch, we get a close-up of Steed examining a strange plant, the image framed by its strange 'tentacles'. This odd sight – which offers us a playful piece of delayed decoding – is immediately swapped for another, as Lennox, the powerfully-built young butler, answers the door. Lacking the world-weary charm of most *Avengers* butlers, he is menacingly resplendent in boots and an old-fashioned, buttoned-up tunic; more guard dog than manservant. He offers Steed a frosty welcome, warning us to expect something unpleasant inside.

It is the glass-ceilinged plant room – which we will return to for the final scenes – that adds the avengerish, surreal atmosphere to the mansion. Naked female mannequins stand guard, with climbing plants their only attire. Steed doffs his bowler to them, warning one of them that "come autumn, I hope to see more of you." The comment, on every level, is wonderfully strange. The set is effectively bizarre, as the figures create a brooding presence, almost as if they are watching him/us. As a recurring leitmotif in *The Avengers*, they always seem to unsettle us. Equally effective is Steed's spying on the botanists through the glass doors, as the camera constantly switches between Steed's view and close-ups of his spying eye.

Steed's interview with Sir Lyle offers us more early hints of the plot's main strand. In passing Steed his brandy, Lyle draws connections between human/plant life:

"Man differs little from plant life. Liquid nutriment is vitally essential."

More female waxwork dummies – with real hair – decorate his office, Lyle drawing a polarity between the "passive, inanimate" figures and the living plants which "feel, perhaps even think." The disturbing sight of Lyle feeding his 'pet' Venus fly-traps offers another miniature fore-echo of what is to come. Steed cannot bear to look at these hungry, "gourmet" creatures, closing his eyes before changing the conversation.

Hayers' interesting direction comes in to play again as Steed leaves. We catch Lennox's menacing face in Steed's rearview mirror, having just 'planted' something deadly on the driver's seat. These little touches from the camera transform the episode, adding an extra creative and playful layer, sculpting a genuine work of art.

There are a number of science fiction and ecology episodes in Season 4, including some which combine the two, such as *A Surfeit of H$_2$O*. Serious questions about the potentially destructive results of scientific research are raised, even if they are quickly dropped again or forgotten amidst the action-adventure. *Man-Eater of Surrey Green* takes the science fiction/ecology theme to its extreme as the Avengers move on to the episode's most atmospheric location, the abandoned Moat Farm.

The scenes set at Moat Farm cleverly contrast with each other. The initial one sees Steed and Mrs. Peel drive along a deserted country lane, arriving at a collection of charmingly dilapidated outbuildings: weather-boarded wooden barns, brick outhouses and rusting corrugated sheds, surrounded by nettle-strewn, neglected grass. The haunting music teases us, as does the tile dropped by a startled dove. However, there is nothing sinister lurking in the interiors. It is the mound outside which we are asked to focus upon. As Steed is forced to swap umbrella for agricultural fork, the scene moves from realism to surrealism with the uncovering of a skeleton in a space helmet.

The macabre discovery moves seamlessly into the following scene at the same location. The previous rural silence has been shattered. The farm is now a hive of activity, the courtyard populated by military personnel and vehicles, winching equipment and metal detectors, scientists with testing tables. On a superficial level, it instantly transforms the previously brooding atmosphere to one of action. Wing Commander Davies' space ship explanation is at once pure fantasy yet also chillingly surreal:

"Poor chap died...up there...alone...five thousand miles up in the cosmos...since, the ship and the body have been circling in orbit."

The arrival of the wonderfully enthusiastic and eccentric Dr. Sheldon enables the team to verify Mrs. Peel's theory that the creature which the space ship collided with was vegetable, rather than animal or mineral. Steed's praise is offered in a patronisingly teasing manner, reminding us that he is not always the egalitarian, feminist sharer of adventures: "Very observant of you, my dear." The interplay in these twinned scenes between realism/surrealism is fascinating, the rural, isolated setting at odds with the unearthly, bizarre discoveries:

Sheldon: Imagine a plant that could think...*think*!

It is the surrealism which often lacks a dramatic undercurrent in *Man-Eater of Surrey Green*. Conversely, the 'realistic' deaths of a labourer and Alan Carter are atmospherically, chillingly filmed. As the butler shoots the zombified agricultural worker with his double-barrelled shotgun, the television screen is covered with smoke, obliterating any sight of the killer. The visual effect is horribly real. In the following scene on Lyle's estate, Laura Burford watches impassively as her fiancé is electrified by the perimeter fence, his hands remaining glued to the barbed wire.

Emma Peel's dry humour lightens the mood in an episode with plenty of charm and wit. As Dr. Sheldon collects her deadly herbicide, Mrs. Peel warns Steed:

"She'd better be quick or we'll all be on the menu."

The scene closes with Steed emphasising the importance of wearing a hearing-aid; however, she now plays the nonchalant role. After all, "the plant's only *man*-eating!"

It is in the final ten minutes that *Man-Eater of Surrey Green* suffers, visually. Up until now, the writer and director have kept the giant plant under wraps, quite literally. As Steed, Emma and the elderly Dr. Sheldon enter Sir Lyle's surreal plant room, the sense of the creature covering the whole building, blocking windows and pressing down on the glass roof is effective, adding an uncomfortably claustrophobic feeling. However, the sight of its fat 'tentacles' dragging bodies away to be devoured does not work, neither on a dramatic nor a self-referentially artificial level. The images become ridiculous and it is left to Steed and Emma to provide the surreal spectacle.

Their fight with each other works on a number of levels. It upsets our sense of the correct order of things, forcing us to take sides. On an artistic level it is effectively shot, with their figures often foregrounded with vegetation which frames the images. On a comic level, the pauses to either pick up or tip over the herbicide container add a subtly silly element.

As the herbicide takes hold, the avengerish atmosphere is maintained by the strange sight of the mannequins crashing to the ground, rather than the sound of the man-eater screaming as it shakes furiously in its death-throes.

The episode loses its hold or grip on us when we are forced to see the plant close-up. The old adage of 'less is more' should have been adhered to here; perhaps even 'none is more'. In every other respect, *Man-Eater of Surrey Green* is an enjoyable, visually-striking episode, topped off with the sight of Steed and Emma relaxing on the hay bales of a tractor trailer, as the vehicle recedes along a deserted country lane towards that 'bright horizon'.

© Rodney Marshall

SILENT DUST

Filmed: 14th June – 2nd July 1965

Exterior Locations:
Arable fields
River estuary
Woodland
Country lanes
Manderley dead zone
Barn
Clare's studio garden
Stirrup Cup Inn yard
Spinney
Tumbledown farm outbuildings
Stables
Open countryside

Sets:
Rolls Royce interior
Barn
Fertiliser laboratory
Clare's studio
Stirrup Cup Inn
Omrod's sporting room
Tumbledown farm outbuildings

SILENT DUST

Main Character List:
John Steed
Emma Peel
Quince: birdwatcher
Minister: hockey selector
Mellors: Omrod's gamekeeper
Peter Omrod: country squire, mastermind
Phil Juggins: henchman working for Omrod
Sir Manfred Fellows: ministry scientist
Clare Prendergast: daughter of Silent Dust inventor
Croft: rose grower
Beryl Snow: local landowner
Ponsford: publican of the Stirrup Cup Inn

The opening scene begins with an idyllic, peaceful English countryside which abounds with life and joy. A succession of pirouetting animals – wrens, chaffinches, ducks and crows – symbolises an Earthly paradise, but the sense of a rural arcadia is short-lived as a horrible scarecrow seems to strike down all these inoffensive creatures merely by its strange stare. The teaser remains faithful to the season as a whole in offering viewers a charming backdrop undercut by a sudden, violent event. Unfortunately, the stuffed birds (which follow the bucolic music and cosy nests) are poorly done and undermine possible references to Hitchcock's famous film. The special effects are not strengths of the episode, as exemplified later on when Mrs. Peel is almost struck by a fake bat. It is one of the rare weaknesses in this gripping, fascinating and topical adventure which is underrated by many British and French fans.

The original title was *Strictly for the Worms*. It is fortunate that *Silent Dust*, with its far more unsettling connotations, was retained. The title was surely inspired by *Silent Spring* which had been published in September 1962. This bestseller is often considered to have initiated the environmental movement in the West. In the book, the marine biologist Rachel Carson described the deadly consequences of pesticides (notably DDT) on the environment, more specifically birdlife; this phenomenon is directly alluded to in the episode's teaser. Carson even pointed the finger of accusation at the chemical industry. *Silent Dust* arguably belongs to a sub-genre of ecological episodes including *A Surfeit of H_2O* and *Man-Eater of Surrey Green*. A group of villains has managed to get its hands on a powerful pesticide called 'Silent Dust' which is capable of destroying nature and wildlife within a selected area. These landowners intend destroying the county of Dorset in order to blackmail the government to the tune of £40 million. Prendergast, a civil servant, invented the pesticide but was subsequently discredited and thrown out. His invention has been recuperated by Omrod, an agricultural advisor, who is the brain behind the fiendish plot (the term diabolical mastermind is perhaps an exaggeration in his case). Omrod has managed to gain the trust of Clara Prendergast, the daughter of the dead chemist, and has attracted the interest of three accomplices to his deathly project. He is ready to destroy the entire country, like many other warped minds of the season and series. Prendergast, like Dr. Armstrong (*The Cybernauts*) and Marlow (*The Gravediggers*), has been disgraced and disowned by his government superiors.

The artistic success of an episode, particularly in the sumptuous fourth season, often resides not only in the originality of the plot, but also in the humorous exchanges between Mrs. Peel and Steed. The post-teaser scene sees the Avengers appear in a boat and is one of the best moments of the episode. Steed and Mrs. Peel are boating on a lake and the logical, traditional roles have been reversed: Steed is relaxing underneath an umbrella while Mrs. Peel handles the pole; the brief exchange between our heroes is superb:

Steed: Tired?
Emma: Exhausted!
Steed: No stamina.
Emma: No comment!

As is the case on a number of occasions during this season, Mrs. Peel is the brain and the brawn, while Steed uses his charm, his Epicurean knowledge and his contacts in high places. He takes out a bottle of rosé which he has been keeping at river temperature, confirming his wine knowledge which we have already seen in *A Surfeit of H$_2$O* and the legendary sequence in *Dial A Deadly Number* (another episode written by Roger Marshall). Soon afterwards, while Mrs. Peel investigates, as so often, under cover (the British Trust for Ornithology), Steed has a meeting with a minister which allows viewers to become aware of the danger menacing the country. The professional relations between Steed and Mrs. Peel are typical of the season here: Mrs. Peel investigates on her own in the village while Steed returns to London (to encounter the minister) before travelling to Manderley, a place abandoned ten years ago. He gets to know two pretty women in an attempt to investigate further, Clara Prendergast and Miss Snow; his two meetings with Miss Snow are closely scrutinised by Emma Peel, who throws him some wonderfully disapproving, irresistible stares full of suspicion and jealousy. Emma's comical expression is superb while Steed, bristling with intentions – "I'll see what I can pick up here" – tries a sleight of hand approach on Miss Snow. Besides, even for the landlord, there are no two ways about it: Mrs. Peel and Steed represent a couple!

Another highlight of this season is the omnipresent cultural references, which are unfortunately erased in the French translations. This intertextual richness is a quality specific to this monochrome season. It tends to disappear in the following seasons as the series became 'international'. *Silent Dust* contains a number of references to English literature which disappear in the French version. In the initial post-teaser scene, for example, Steed evokes the disappearance of a species of bird, the martlet, by quoting a Shakespeare verse: "The temple-haunting martlet." Mrs. Peel replies: "*Macbeth*, Act 1, Scene 6. Banquo." In the French version, Steed evokes the martlets but instead of citing *Macbeth* he asks Mrs. Peel if she knows the bird and she gives him a description. Perhaps the translators took viewers for idiots! Later, Croft and Mrs. Peel recite verse from the poets Francis Thompson and Robert

Herrick, which are replaced by French poets in *Chapeau Melon et Bottes de Cuir*. Mellors, the gamekeeper, has the same name as the lover of Lady Chatterley, from DH Lawrence's infamous erotic novel. Lawrence's Mellors is also a gamekeeper and when Emma says that she has encountered Mellors, Steed replies: "Not THE gamekeeper?" There is also Clare Prendergast's use of "To err is human, to forgive divine", a citation from Alexander Pope's famous *An Essay on Criticism*. These cultural references, which are very difficult to rework in foreign language versions, add a touch of Britishness and provide a unique aspect to the fourth season. [1]

Silent Dust has the advantage of being filmed almost entirely on location and it celebrates the English countryside. [2] The magnificent outside footage, with the added charm of a pleasing musical score (in particular during the hunting sequences), offer an undeniably rich extra layer to this episode and reflect the advantages of moving on to film for the series. There is a subtle mixture, of music already heard in the season – when Steed is snooping around – and new elements, when Emma is searching for him. The pub, as is often the case, is the place which allows the Avengers to encounter the enemy (as in *The Town of No Return*); it is there that Mrs. Peel encounters Croft, the lover of roses, and where Steed has a chummy conversation with Miss Snow.

There are no 'secondary roles', in the sense that every character is convincing and striking. The bunch of *Avengers* baddies is a varied one. Omrod (William Franklyn) is a money-grabbing landowner and is prepared to do anything to achieve his aims; Mellors (Conrad Phillips), the gamekeeper, is a thick brute with an appropriate name; and Miss Snow (Joanna Wake) uses her charm wisely on Steed ("He is just the sort of risk I fancy"). My favourite character is Juggins (Jack Watson), the killer of wild boar and a cynic ("The winner gets the ears"). He reveals an unhealthy attraction for 'Snowdrop' and tries to win her over with his homemade scrumpy. The viewer knows that it was he who killed Quince once we have seen the familiar forearm tattooed with a rose when Juggins eats some crisps at Omrod's house. The more minor characters are equally interesting and captivating: Quince, translated as Antoine in French ("Where have all the martlets gone?"), Sir Manfred Fellows (and his excellent retort: "We had a winner last year. Smelt like old socks!") and Clare Prendergast, played by the pretty Scottish actress Isobel Black. Only Croft, the rose-grower, leaves me indifferent and it is quite surprising that it is he who is chosen to eliminate Steed, because Juggins, the thug, would have been far better equipped. Obviously this does allow a lightly humorous confrontation, with no violence whatsoever. Each episode has its eccentric character; here, it is the hay-fever suffering minister, who is more concerned with his hockey team than the menacing situation faced by Her Majesty's country.

The plot, still plausible nowadays, is relatively simple: it's enough to listen to the explanation Steed receives from the minister opposite the dead Manderley tree ("It is lifeless, just like dust.") Ecology and money are the two great themes of this adventure. The four stooges are prepared to destroy Dorset in return for £10 million each. Their motives and manners are totally different from each other but their aim is the same. Omrod has a purely financial motive, while Croft wants revenge on a country which has failed to acknowledge his various new rose creations, and Miss Snow owns land which is now barren. The ecology theme shows once again that the series was ahead of its time. The danger of pesticides is perfectly demonstrated by the discovery of the dead zone of Manderley where just a single tree is left standing. We should note the unbelievable scene where Steed recovers dust in an envelope and then grabs hold of an apple which he tastes, all achieved solely with his right hand! Despite the seriousness and dramatic aspects, there is still plenty of room left for humour and light entertainment, as much in the witty repartee as the dramatic situations. This balance between the serious and the playful is also proof of the season's artistic achievement, particularly when that balance or tension is found within a single scene. The whipping sequence here is far less controversial than the equivalent one in *A Touch of Brimstone*, possibly helped by the more 'decent' attire worn by Mrs. Peel. Nevertheless, we should also bear in mind that the music employed by Laurie Johnson is more pleasantly cheerful here than unsettlingly frightening. Look at Emma and Juggins' faces as the whip traps her foot and one notes a certain amusement, as if they are about to burst into laughter. Two scenes which appear to be similar have been treated in very different ways. It is a shame that we notice Diana Rigg's stunt double during the somersault and the extended whipping scene. This is the second and final fault in the episode, after the stuffed birds at the foot of the scarecrow in the teaser.

There are two other moments of note in the episode. One of the strangest scenes in the series is Steed's hallucination in which he is a wounded sheriff (not a drop of blood; the series' unwritten rules insist on this!) Mrs. Peel, wearing a doctor's moustache, extracts a disproportionately large bullet! One has changed genre or shifted register, and find ourselves in a Western with a spittoon. Everything is exaggerated, just like the enormous bullet for a superficial wound. This dream does not have any direct repercussions in terms of plot but is part of the series' code: a mixture of realism and surrealism, which one finds in even greater measure in *Too Many Christmas Trees*. On Mrs. Peel's arrival at the ruin, one is struck by the horrible headscarf she is wearing, but it thankfully serves a practical purpose as a splint for Steed. The long hunting sequence is very well filmed and the prey soon becomes Mrs. Peel, much to Juggins' pleasure and taste. Despite the supposed dangers, the finale is accompanied by light-hearted music and scenes, such as the one in which Mrs. Peel throws off her gloves and boots. In seizing hold of a placard ("Down with violence") in the manner of a polo match, Steed eliminates the final opponent in comic strip fashion. As usual, the series combines some shocking images or scenes – Prendergast's ashes in an urn on the mantelpiece; Quince dead in the midst of the apples – and daringly light-hearted moments which deal with serious subjects and dramatic consequences.

Silent Dust has a leisurely pace but the humour, suspense and several 'classic' scenes allow it to obtain 'four bowlers' in my classification. The episode can be watched and re-watched with pleasure. A simple and topical plot, a constantly present, avengerish humour, an erotic touch and the attractive English countryside allow us to pass an agreeable moment, something which is nearly always the case with *The Avengers*.

© Denis Chauvet (© translated by Rodney Marshall)

1. In addition, Quince is an indirect reference to Peter Quince, one of the 'rude mechanicals' (labourers) in Shakespeare's *A Midsummer Night's Dream*. Manderley refers to the atmospheric estate in Daphne du Maurier's gothic romance *Rebecca*.
2. There is a certain paradox or irony that having written a number of studio-bound episodes such as *Dial A Deadly Number* and *Room Without A View*, Marshall is responsible for the two Season 4 episodes which are almost exclusively location-based.

LA POUSSIERE QUI TUE

Tout commence dans l'ouverture par une idyllique et paisible campagne anglaise qui regorge de vies et de gaité. Une succession d'animaux virevoltants - des roitelets, des pinsons, des canards et des corbeaux - symbolise le paradis terrestre, mais la plénitude est de courte durée car un horrible épouvantail semble terrasser toutes ces créatures inoffensives de son étrange regard. La scène d'introduction est fidèle à la série en présentant aux téléspectateurs une séquence charmante troublée par un évènement violent et soudain. Malheureusement, les oiseaux empaillés, qui succèdent à la musique idyllique et aux nids douillets, ne sont pas du meilleur goût et ils gâchent la possible référence au célèbre film d'Hitchcock. Les effets spéciaux ne sont pas par conséquent un atout de l'épisode, comme plus tard, lorsque Mrs Peel est presque heurtée par une fausse chauve-souris. C'est un des rares défauts de cette aventure passionnante et d'actualité qui est à tort déconsidérée par beaucoup de fans britanniques et français.

Le dernier épisode de l'année 1965 pour les Londoniens – il fut diffusé à la St Sylvestre à Londres et au Nouvel An dans les Midlands– fut initialement appelé *Strictly for the Worms*. Il est heureux que *Silent Dust*, à la connotation plus inquiétante, ait été retenu. Le titre est sûrement inspiré par l'ouvrage *Silent Spring* paru en septembre 1962. Ce best seller est souvent considéré comme l'initiateur du mouvement écologiste en Occident. La biologiste américaine Rachel Carson y décrit les conséquences mortelles des pesticides (notamment le DDT) sur l'environnement et plus particulièrement les oiseaux, un phénomène auquel fait directement allusion la séquence d'ouverture de l'épisode. La responsabilité de l'industrie chimique était également pointée du doigt. *Silent Dust* est une sorte d'épisode écologique un peu dans la lignée de *A Surfeit of H2O* et *Man-Eater of Surrey Green*. Un groupe de malveillants a réussi à mettre la main sur un puissant pesticide appelé Silent Dust, capable de détruire la nature et la faune dans un périmètre sélectionné. Ces propriétaires terriens ont l'intention de détruire le comté du Dorset pour extorquer quarante millions de livres au gouvernement. Prendergast, un fonctionnaire du ministère, a inventé ce pesticide, mais il fut déconsidéré et renvoyé comme un malpropre. Son invention fut récupérée par un conseiller agricole, le dénommé Omrod, le véritable cerveau du complot (le terme *diabolical mastermind* est peut-être exagéré pour lui). Omrod est parvenu à amadouer Clara Prendergast, la fille du chimiste décédé, et à intéresser trois autres complices à son funeste projet. Il est prêt à détruire tout le pays, comme beaucoup d'esprits tordus de la série. En tout cas, Prendergast, tels le docteur Armstrong (*The Cybernauts*) et Marlow (*The Gravediggers*) a été disgracié et déshonoré par ses supérieurs gouvernementaux.

La réussite d'un épisode, particulièrement lors de la somptueuse quatrième saison, réside souvent non seulement dans l'originalité de l'intrigue, mais également dans les scénettes humoristiques entre Mrs Peel et Steed. La séquence suivant l'introduction typique *Avengersland,* qui marque l'apparition des Avengers dans un bateau, est pour cette raison un des meilleurs passages de l'épisode. Steed et Mrs Peel sont dans un bateau plat et les rôles sont inversés à la logique : Steed se repose sous une ombrelle tandis que Mrs Peel manie la perche et le bref échange entre nos héros est superbe. Steed: « Tired? », Mrs Peel: «Exhausted! », Steed: «No stamina», Mrs Peel: «No comment! ». Comme de nombreuses fois au cours de cette saison, Mrs Peel est la tête et les jambes, alors que Steed use de son charme, de connaissances épicuriennes et de ses relations haut placées. Ainsi, il sort une bouteille de rosé qu'il gardait à la température de la rivière et confirme ses connaissances en la matière que nous avions déjà constatées dans *A Surfeit of H2O* et la séquence d'anthologie de *Dial a Deadly Number* (un autre épisode écrit par Roger Marshall). Peu après, tandis que Mrs Peel enquête, comme souvent, sous une couverture (la British Trust for Ornithology), Steed rencontre un ministre et permet aux téléspectateurs d'être au courant du danger qui menace le pays. Les relations entre Steed et Mrs Peel sont conformes à l'ordinaire. Mrs Peel enquête seule dans le village tandis que Steed doit rentrer à Londres pour rencontrer le ministre et se rendre à Manderley, un village abandonné depuis déjà dix ans. Il fait la connaissance de deux jolies femmes pour faire avancer l'enquête, Clara Prendergast et Miss Snow, et ses deux rencontres avec Miss Snow sont étroitement surveillées par Emma Peel, qui lui lance de superbes regards désapprobateurs irrésistibles remplis de méfiance et de jalousie. La mimique d'Emma est superbe lorsque Steed, plein d'intentions (« I'll see what I can pick up here »), essuie un revers auprès de Miss Snow. D'ailleurs, même pour l'hôtelier, il n'y a pas de mystère : Mrs Peel et Steed forment un couple !

Un autre atout de cette saison est la référence culturelle britannique omniprésente, qui est malheureusement gommée dans les traductions françaises. Cet aspect culturel est une spécificité de la saison monochrome. Elle aura tendance à disparaître dans les saisons suivantes lorsque la série deviendra internationale. *Silent Dust* a de nombreuses références à la littérature anglaise qui ont disparu dans la version française ! Dans la première scène, par exemple, Steed évoque la disparition d'une race d'oiseaux, les martinets, en récitant un vers de Shakespeare : 'The temple-haunting martlet.' Mrs Peel répond: 'Macbeth, Act 1, scene 6, Banquo'. Dans la version française, Steed évoque les martinets mais au lieu de citer le vers de Macbeth, il demande à Mrs Peel si elle connaît cet oiseau et cette dernière lui donne la description. Peut-être que les traducteurs ont pris les téléspectateurs français pour des idiots ! Plus tard, Croft et Mrs Peel récitent des vers des poètes Francis Thompson et Robert Herrick, qui seront remplacés par des poètes français dans *Chapeau melon et bottes de cuir*. Mellors, le garde-chasse, a le même nom que l'amant de Lady Chatterley, célèbre roman érotique de DH Lawrence. Le Mellors de cette œuvre littéraire est également garde-chasse, d'où la réplique de Steed à Emma qui dit avoir rencontré Mellors : «not THE gamekeeper ?». Sans oublier la citation *The err is human, to forgive divine*, formulée par Clare, qui est un extrait du fameux *An Essay on Criticism*, d'Alexander Pope. Ces références culturelles, très difficiles à retranscrire dans les versions étrangères, donnent une touche de Britishness et un aspect unique à la quatrième saison.

Silent Dust a l'avantage d'être tourné pratiquement entièrement en extérieur et sent bon la campagne anglaise. Les magnifiques séquences en extérieur, agrémentées d'une musique plaisante (en particulier pendant la chasse à courre), sont indéniablement un plus pour cet épisode et cela valorise le passage de la série sur film. Il y a un subtil mélange de musique déjà entendue - lorsque Steed fouine autour de la remise- et d'airs nouveaux, quand Emma est à la recherche de Steed. Le pub est comme souvent le lieu qui permet aux Avengers de rencontrer l'opposition (c'est également le cas dans *The Town of No Return*) ; Mrs Peel y rencontre Croft, l'amoureux des roses, et Steed a une discussion campagnarde avec Miss Snow.

Il n'y a pas de second rôle en évidence, car ils sont tous convaincants et marquants. La brochette d'opposants aux Avengers est variée. Omrod (William Franklyn) est un propriétaire terrien cupide et prêt à tout pour arriver à ses fins, Mellors (Conrad Phillips), le garde-chasse, est une brute épaisse au nom révélateur et Miss Snow (Joanna Wake) use de son charme sur Steed à bon escient (« He is just the sort of risk I fancy »). Mon personnage préféré est Juggins (Jack Watson), le tueur de porcs rustre et cynique (« The winner gets the ears »). Il éprouve un peu d'affection malsaine pour 'snow drop' et il essaye de la convertir à sa gnole faite maison, et le téléspectateur constate qu'il a tué Quince lorsqu'il laisse apparaître son avant-bras tatoué d'une rose en prenant des chips chez Omrod. Les personnages plus mineurs sont également intéressants et attachants : Quince, traduit par Antoine en français («Where have all the martlets gone ?»), Sir Manfred Fellows (et son excellente réplique : « We had a winner last year. Smelt like old socks! ») et Clare Prendergast, interprétée par la jolie actrice écossaise Isobel Black. Seul Croft, le rosiériste, m'est indifférent et il est assez surprenant que cela soit justement lui qui ait été choisi pour éliminer Steed, car Juggins, la brute, aurait été plus approprié. Evidement, cela permet de voir une confrontation de comédie légère, sans aucune violence. Chaque épisode a son excentrique ; ici, c'est le ministre qui souffre d'un rhume des foins et qui est plus préoccupé par son équipe de hockey que par la situation menaçante pour le pays de Sa Majesté.

L'intrigue, toujours plausible de nos jours, est relativement simple : il suffit d'écouter le commentaire que fait Steed au ministre face à l'arbre desséché de Manderley («It is lifeless, just like dust »). L'écologie et l'argent sont par conséquent les deux grands thèmes de cette aventure. Les quatre comparses sont prêts à détruire le Dorset pour dix millions de livres chacun. Leur mobile et leur comportement sont totalement différents mais leur but est le même. Omrod a un motif purement financier, tandis que Croft veut se venger du pays qui n'a pas reconnu ses créations de plusieurs sortes de roses et Miss Snow possède des terres devenues infertiles. L'écologie montre encore une fois que la série était en avance sur son temps. La dangerosité des pesticides est parfaitement rendue par la découverte du village moribond de Manderley où seul un arbre mort est encore debout. A noter la scène incroyable lorsque Steed récupère de la poussière dans une enveloppe puis se saisit d'une pomme qu'il déguste ; le tout avec la main droite ! Ce sujet particulièrement sérieux et dramatique laisse néanmoins une grande place à l'humour et la légèreté aussi bien dans les réparties que dans les situations ; cet équilibre entre le sérieux et la folâtrerie est aussi un gage de réussite, surtout lorsqu'on le retrouve à l'intérieur d'une même scène. Ainsi, la séquence du fouet fit beaucoup moins de scandale que celle similaire de *A Touch of Brimstone*. On peut supposer que la tenue plus décente de Mrs Peel y est pour quelque chose. Néanmoins, on remarque également que la musique utilisée par Laurie Johnson pour ce passage est plus enjouée qu'effrayante. Regardez les visages d'Emma et de Juggins lorsque le fouet attrape le pied et on discerne un certain amusement, comme s'ils allaient éclater de rire. Cela explique que deux scènes apparemment similaires aient eu un traitement aussi différent. On peut regretter la présence visible de la doublure de Diana Rigg lors de la cabriole et des plans éloignés de la scène du fouet. C'est le second, et dernier, défaut de l'épisode après l'entassement des oiseaux empaillés au pied de l'épouvantail du début.

Deux autres passages sont particuliers à cette histoire. L'une des scènes les plus étranges de la série est le délire de Steed en shérif blessé (pas une goutte de sang, critère de la série oblige !). Mrs Peel en doc moustachue extrait une balle disproportionnée ! On change de registre et on passe soudainement dans le western avec le crachoir. Tout est exagéré comme cette grosse balle pour une blessure superficielle. Ce rêve n'a pas de répercussion directe sur l'intrigue mais il fait partie des codes de la série, un mélange de réalisme et de surréalisme, qu'on retrouve avec une place plus essentielle dans *Too Many Christmas Trees*. A l'arrivée de Mrs Peel dans la ruine, on est frappé par l'horrible fichu qu'elle a sur la tête, mais il aura heureusement son utilité en servant d'attelle à Steed. La longue chasse à courre est très bien filmée et la proie devient rapidement Mrs Peel, ce qui est au goût de Juggins. Malgré la supposé dangerosité de l'opposition, le final est accompagné d'une musique plaisante et de scènes légères comme la façon avec laquelle Mrs Peel se débarrasse de ses gants et de ses bottes. En se saisissant d'une pancarte « Down with violence » dans un simulacre de match de polo, Steed élimine le dernier opposant d'une manière surtout vue dans les bandes dessinées. Comme à l'accoutumée, la série sait allier scènes chocs – l'urne des cendres de Prendergast sur la cheminée, Quince mort au milieu de pommes - et passages légers pour un sujet grave et lourd de conséquences.

Silent Dust a un rythme parfois lent mais l'humour, l'intrigue et quelques scènes d'anthologie lui permettent d'obtenir quatre melons à mon classement. L'épisode se laisse voir et revoir facilement. Une intrigue simple et d'actualité, un humour *avengeresque* à tout instant, une pointe d'érotisme (la beauté de Diana Rigg parée dans un drap est mise en évidence) et une campagne anglaise accueillante font passer un agréable moment, ce qui est (presque) toujours le cas avec les *Avengers*.

© Denis Chauvet

THE HOUR THAT NEVER WAS

Filmed: 5th – 20th July 1965

Exterior Locations:
Fields
Country lanes
Bridge
Airbase: wire-fence, runway, hangar, control tower, airstrip, dustbin area, officers' mess façade

Sets:
Airbase: officers' mess, baker's shop, officer quarters, control tower, fall-out shelter, main entrance barrier, dentist's room, corridor

THE HOUR THAT NEVER WAS

Main Character List:
Rosey: airbase guard dog
John Steed
Emma Peel
Milkman
Benedict Napoleon Hickey: airbase tramp
Geoffrey Risdale: RAF officer
Wiggins: RAF officer
'Porky': RAF officer
Phillip Leas: camp dentist, mastermind

"This script was so visual…it was a cinch: the nodding dog in the back of the car, the petrol pump overflowing, the rattling chains, the milkman and milk float. I couldn't really believe my luck because it was an exceptionally good script; in fact it became the best script that I ever got hold of." (Gerry O'Hara, DVD commentary, Optimum /Canal)

High praise indeed for Roger Marshall's sublime *The Hour That Never Was* from its acclaimed director Gerry O'Hara. *The Hour That Never Was* represents *The Avengers* as a film series at its new, location filming best – for the four previous years it had been restricted to the cramp, claustrophobic confines of Teddington television studios. Now it had broken free and 35mm film gave it so many new possibilities but perhaps the most enticing of all was to bring the outside world of quaint middle England into the television sets and homes of the viewing public, particularly those in overseas markets such as Australia and the USA.

The tranquillity of a wonderful summer day in England, beautiful lilies on a lake, cows slowly chewing the cud, majestic shire horses, a quiet country lane with a vintage Bentley tootling along are all suddenly shattered by a crazed dog chasing nothing in particular. That the dog is actually very small and can cause such a beast of a car to crash adds greatly to the teaser in this episode. [1] A cracked dashboard clock showing 11am and superimposed episode title give tantalising clues as to where the next 50 minutes are actually going to take us.

Laurie Johnson's whimsical score is the perfect accompaniment to the opening scenes of Steed and Emma walking through the pleasant countryside. The dialogue is sharp and witty as Steed regales Emma with his wartime adventures of being based at their destination, RAF Station 472 Hamelin. With the base due to close the following day, Steed has been invited to one last party and send off for all leaving airmen so it is not a total surprise that it is looking somewhat worse for wear.

The mood suddenly changes when Steed and Emma hear loud piano playing from the officers' mess, only to discover that it is empty and the piano is mysterious playing by itself. Emma questions Steed as to whether he might have been mistaken as to day of the party but he reassures her, and himself, that he is right and the mood lifts again as he suggests his former colleagues are out and about on the old training plane. A cut to the dead goldfish and the mess clock stuck at 11am tell us they have overlooked something.

A delightful visual gag starts the next set of scenes as Steed acknowledges his bowler is similar in design to the base's Gunnery Dome. Steed and Emma then discover the overflowing petrol pump as they continue to wander around the deserted RAF station – for over a minute, there is no dialogue, the only sound being a sparse piece of music, all of which enhances the eerie feeling and there is a similarity here to Patrick McGoohan's masterpiece, *The Prisoner*, in particular the episode *Arrival*. (*The Hour That Never Was* predates *Arrival* by over a year).

The short scene of Steed and Emma discovering a 'Sergeant Henderson Special' cake is used to continue the sense that Steed is so caught up in looking forward to the party that he is missing some glaringly obvious peculiarities. It's left to Emma to question events but she is cut short by the sound of a milk float. For over a minute that is the only sound heard as Steed and Emma investigate the base further as they try to locate where the sound is coming from. It is hard to imagine a modern day television series having such long periods of time with such minimal audio; this illustrates perfectly that *The Avengers* production team knew that the two leads could hold the audience's attention even in absolute silence. [2]

Gerry O'Hara's framing of leaning tower of milk crates is a visual delight, beautifully pulling back to allow Steed and Emma to enter the frame and show them in scale next to the tower and the enormity of the base. A brief visit to Squadron Leader Geoffrey Ridsdale's apartment brings more questions than answers although they do discover he is being posted on to Singapore.

Steed and Emma's visit to the control tower not only reinforces the enormous scale of the base but also the peculiarity of the events and gives them (and us) a grandstand view of the shooting of a milkman. It should be noted that the milkman represents the first person seen outside of Steed and Emma and we are a third of the way into the episode.

The fighter aircraft gives Steed more nooks and crannies to investigate while Emma's discovery of an unconscious rabbit near the undercarriage has an unsettling feeling that whatever is wrong extends beyond humans.

O'Hara's framing is again sublime, as first Steed and then Emma are seen as tiny in comparison to the cavernous hanger they enter. These shots are pure *film noir* and look closely at how the director places ambiguous objects in the foreground corners that greatly enhance just a few seconds of on-screen time. The echoing dialogue is another example of the production team daring to do things differently from many of its contemporaries.

As Steed and Emma split up to try and find the body of the now missing milkman, O'Hara provides us with lots of unusual hand-held camera angles and the base itself is a huge supporting star of the story. The tension builds superbly as it feels like we are experiencing an earth tremor: the clattering milk crates, piercing high-pitched noise and clanging, hanging chains are excruciating for Steed and Emma and you wonder when it might stop.

Steed is clearly getting frustrated with the situation and in a rare show of losing his temper smashes a glass as he cannot find any answers. It is 25 minutes into the episode before we are introduced to the first non-Avenger character with dialogue, the wonderfully charming tramp Benedict Napoleon Hickey. The child-like Hickey thinks with his stomach, likes a good drink and is a serial RAF dustbin raider. While Steed struggles to get any real answers from the gibbering Hickey, he tolerates the homeless down-and-out to the point of getting the idea to search the guard hut at the main gate. There is no sign of Mrs. Peel at the hut and an unseen villain drops the gate barrier onto Steed, knocking him unconscious.

Déjà-vu! Steed awakes in his crashed Bentley! Hasn't he/we been here before? But where is Mrs. Peel? He retraces his steps along the short cut to the base and once again it seems deserted. However, to his surprise, on entering the officers' mess he finds it is packed to the rafters and the party is in full swing. Ridsdale is a typical RAF flyer, a product of the private school/Oxbridge university system and is clearly fond of his old friend Steed. Part of the brilliance of Roger Marshall's script is that we still have no idea of what might have happened earlier at the base or who the villain of the piece is; the tension builds nicely as Steed discovers a murdered Hickey shortly after leaving the party for a breath of fresh air. [3]

The familiar sound of clinking milk bottles and an electric milk float captures Steed's attention and another unconscious body being couriered adds to the sense of mystery. O'Hara again gives us another wonderful shot as he frames the opening double doors on a hut through the back of the skeletal milk float, pulling back and round to reveal Steed hiding behind the vehicle.

There is a wonderfully witty line as Steed discovers the tied up Emma in a dentist's chair and there are some lovely details played out as the scene develops – just look at how the conversation flows as the dentist's chair moves from a reclined position to upright (eagle-eyed fans might even notice a tiny hair in the camera at the top of the screen!) and how at-ease Steed and Emma are when talking about things seriously.

The revealing of camp dentist, Philip Leas, as the villain behind the piece is somewhat underplayed compared to other episodes in the series and this is a nice touch. He is no devious mastermind with grand plans of world domination but more simply a man motivated by greed and money. The ensuing fight between Steed and Leas is full of fun, making use of the dentist's laughing gas and giving Leas a real sense of a deranged, drill-happy dentist.

The end tag is typical *Avengers* with Steed and Emma having a 'quiet' ride in the country (or runway) on the milk float but here I think the producers spoilt what would have been the perfect episode. The speeding up of the last ten seconds of action gives us a slapstick send off that is ultimately not needed and feels like a whimsical cop-out on the part of the producers. [4]

© Jaz Wiseman

1. There is a further irony that the diminutive dog, Rosey, is meant to be a RAF guard dog.
2. Possibly even *The Avengers* would not have been so daring in the subsequent colour seasons.
3. Holding back on the identity of the diabolical mastermind is, arguably, something *The Avengers* doesn't do often enough.

4. Roger Marshall has never (openly) objected to this but it feels to me almost like an attempt to undermine the perfection of what came before. Brian Clemens also speeded up the rickshaw in Marshall's *Room Without A View*. To me the effect is more Benny Hill than *Avengers*.

CASTLE DE'ATH

Filmed: 2nd – 20th August 1965

Exterior Locations:
Loch
Castle façade, battlements, grounds and courtyard
Moat

Sets:
Castle: entrance, banqueting hall, galleries, guest bedrooms, dungeons, submarine control room, cell

CASTLE DE'ATH

Main Character List:
McNab: Angus' right hand man
Ian De'Ath: 35th laird of the castle
Emma Peel
Angus De'Ath: Ian's cousin, mastermind
John Steed
Roberton: henchman
Submarine controller

Castle De'ath has a unique charm about it, helped by the wonderful location of Allington Castle in Kent. The plot about vanishing fish and a crisis in the British fishing industry is soon forgotten and the charm and fun of the episode lies in the red herrings – no pun intended – and the atmospheric setting. The fact that we never leave the location/set adds both to the magic and to the sense of claustrophobia.

Not a word is spoken in the teaser, which opens with the brooding loch landscape at dusk and the castle exterior. Against an aural backdrop of bagpipes, the hand-held camera takes us on a tour of the castle's interior, past suits of armour and eventually heading down into the dungeons where, finally, we encounter a human being, suffering on a medieval rack. At this point the bagpipes reach a crescendo. The areas which we have jerkily journeyed through will become familiar during the course of the episode, while the dungeons themselves will feature heavily. The title appears as we focus in on an Iron Maiden, racking up the dramatic tension in unison with Laurie Johnson's score.

The post-teaser scene sets up the polarity which will tease us throughout the episode: Ian De'Ath – the 35th Laird – is a traditional, fiercely-proud man, while his cousin, Angus, appears to be a modern playboy. It is Angus who has invited Mrs. Peel and 'Jock McSteed' to the castle, in an attempt to market Castle De'Ath as a tourist attraction. However, both Emma and we are led to believe that it is the Laird who wants the Avengers' visit literally terminated. The playfulness of the script encourages this belief but the signs that Angus is the diabolical mastermind are there from the start if we can read *Castle De'ath* against the grain. Angus' reckless firing of the crossbow in this scene warns us that he is a dangerous man yet we dismiss this as simply an example of his high spirits or extrovert character.

In *Dial A Deadly Number* Steed publically, playfully tests Mrs. Peel's cover story of coming from the West Indies. Here, Emma gets her own back as she interrogates him in front of the De'Aths:

Emma: You don't have a Scots accent.
Steed: I was carried south by marauding Sassenachs when I was a bairn.

Underneath the public conversations about castles and dungeons, Steed offers Mrs. Peel the private information that the dead frogman who the owners have been talking about "was four inches taller when he was dead than when he was alive." This immediately tells us that it is the same figure we saw being tortured on the rack in the teaser.

Much of the following storyline is wittily playful. Roberton spies on Steed who is testing the water in the moat: "Man, that's ridiculous. He's sailing a wee paper boat." Steed is happy to hide behind the jovial Jock McSteed, a historian tourist with the leisure time to fish and set paper boats on the water. Steed seems to actively enjoy – revel in – his undercover roles such as Gordon Webster, Monsieur Gourmet and Jock McSteed. Unlike Emma Peel's, his are often glamorous or artful, reminding us that *The Avengers* was capable of sexism. [1] As usual, he is happy for people to misread the 'signs', dismissing him as en eccentric fool. He stirs things up, openly mocking the stereotypical castle ghost legends:

"The first thing a ghost learns is to walk through walls. It's a fundamental part of any self-respecting spirit's basic training."

The tongue-in-cheek comment echoes his earlier observation that "no self-respecting castle would be without [dungeons]." The light-hearted feel of the episode is maintained by the memorable scene in which Emma plays a set of miniature bagpipes while Steed does some impromptu Scottish dancing. Meanwhile, our suspicion of Ian De'Ath is cranked up by his ominous comments:

Steed: How deep is your moat?
Ian: Deep enough for its purpose.

After Steed's four-poster bed is flattened by a deadly concrete ceiling which descends on his bowler, Ian comments that "perhaps we'll be more successful with another room." These seemingly dark observations are simply red herrings, preventing us from seeing the real mastermind who is under our very noses. Even the bed-crushing scene is turned into humorous material by McSteed:

"They've got a spot-on service here...tried to press my best shirt last night while I was still wearing it."

Scottish stereotypes abound in *Castle De'ath*, from the loch/castle setting, kilts and bagpipes to the porridge-eating scene in which Steed finds it impossible to eat his while the De'Ath cousins cover theirs with thick layers of salt. The look on Steed's face as the food is eaten adds humour while sending-up the traditional Scottish breakfast.

There is a cyclical nature to the episode, exemplified by Emma Peel's four visits to the dungeons. It is on her third trip down to the cobwebbed basement that she discovers the secret door to the submarine control room. The fact that this is hidden inside the Iron Maiden should have been obvious to us, given its prominence in the teaser. There is something symbolically fitting about Emma Peel using the Iron Maiden entrance to undermine the mastermind's plans.

After Ian De'Ath has politely asked Emma Peel to leave, apologising for his "apparent rudeness" – another clue that he is not the villain of the piece – we witness the fascinatingly shot scene in which the cousins confront each other, the darkly unreadable McNab standing between/behind them while their argument is played out. This becomes – in the atmospherically vast banqueting hall – an ideological debate as they argue their opposing sides of a "pompous" tradition versus "greedy" money-making polarity. It is appropriate that this medieval/modern argument takes place in an ancient castle, in the *olde worlde* setting of the hall, while down below Steed and Mrs. Peel are caught up in an attempt to wreck the modern technology of the submarine control room, (re-modelled from the set first seen in the bunkers of *The Town of No Return*.)

Despite Angus De'Ath's decidedly modern interests in technology and money, he is forced to fight McSteed in truly traditional Scottish fashion: with swords and shields in corridors, landing, and even on the banqueting table itself. It seems appropriate that his fatal demise is finally sealed in the medieval Iron Maiden, the portal between the ancient torture dungeons and the modern submarine pen. Emma Peel's change from a check, tartan-style outfit into her leather fighting gear is another visual reminder that *Castle De'ath* revolves around a traditional/modern binarism. This is lavishly illustrated in the tag scene as Steed and Emma veer off the main road in an amphibious car, driving/sailing across the loch against a timeless backdrop.

The lightweight storyline or plot of *Castle De'ath* doesn't bare close scrutiny, yet this hardly matters in an episode which is wonderfully playful. We do not even feel cheated by the red herrings. The Scottish location – filmed in Kent – the castle setting and bagpipe music conjure up a sense of adventure in which dungeon, rack, Iron Maiden, secret passageway and suits of armour help to create the noirish, atmospheric, brooding mood.

The episode lacks the cutting-edge surrealism and quirkiness of some of the season's 'classic' episodes, but in terms of charm there is nothing better in Season 4. That this charm is based around faked, clichéd Scottish Gothic story-telling – Black Jamie's "ghost walks, playing the lament of Glen De'Ath on the bagpipes" [2] – simply adds to the spectacle, rather than undermining it.

© Rodney Marshall

1. As he had done with Cathy Gale, Steed frequently treats Emma Peel as his 'hired help' and her undercover roles in Season 4 often reflect stereotypical female roles: primary school teacher, nurse etc.
2. Both the Kent location and Jock McSteed add further fake, clichéd elements to the mix.

THE THIRTEENTH HOLE

Filmed: 6th - 15th September 1965

Exterior Locations:
Craigleigh Golf Club: entrance, car park, buildings, fairways, greens, bunkers
Country lane

Sets:
Ted Murphy's flat
Craigleigh Golf Club: secretary's office/shop, bar/lounge, corridor, phone booth
Professor Minley's office at Greenwich Observatory
Concealed sand trap bunker control room

THE THIRTEENTH HOLE

Main Character List:
Frank Reid: golfer, technician
Jackson: caddy, henchman
Ted Murphy: agent
Emma Peel
John Steed
Dr. Peter Adams: scientist
Jerry Collins: club professional/acting secretary
Colonel Watson: senior golf member
Bertie Waversham: club captain
Professor Minley: Greenwich Observatory

Steed: Do you play [golf] at all?
Gambit: I agree with the Bishop of Lichfield. He said golf is a game of propelling a small ball into a hole, with the aid of instruments singularly ill-fitted for the purpose.

The above quotation is, quite obviously, not from *The Thirteenth Hole*, but *The New Avengers* episode *Angels of Death*. However, it encapsulates a common sentiment shared by many regarding the game of golf. Broadly speaking, people are either ardent fans of the game, or fail to find anything remotely interesting or appealing about what they consider to be a tedious pastime. The challenge for *The Avengers* in setting an entire episode on a golf course, and having the plot revolve around the game of golf, was to make it interesting for the scores of *Avengers* fans who would normally have been bored silly at the mere mention of the game.

The episode opens with Reed (Patrick Allen) playing a round of golf, accompanied by his caddy, Jackson (Victor Maddern). This opening scene adheres to the audience's perceptions and expectations of the game of golf as Reed ponders his next shot, then asks Jackson for the appropriate club. The stereotype of golf as a staid, sedate, unremarkable game is reinforced as Reed moves at a leisurely pace through what appears to be a perfectly ordinary golf course. But this is *Avengerland*, and nothing is ever quite what it seems. Soon, Jackson and Reed spot agent Ted Murphy poking around a sand trap. Reed asks Jackson for his "303" in much the same way as he has asked for all of his clubs. Jackson obliges by producing a rifle that definitely isn't part of any golfer's standard kit. Reed kills Murphy in cold blood, then swaps his rifle for a club as if nothing has happened. Not even three minutes into the episode, the show has already exploded the stereotype of the boring old golf game and given it a sinister, deadly edge. The non-golf fans in the audience are assured that the episode will be much more exciting than they might have at first thought. As a finishing touch, the camera then zooms in to show us that the murder has taken place at "the thirteenth hole", ratcheting up the tension by adding a dash of triskaidekaphobia. [1]

The next scene opens with Jackson turning over Murphy's flat, before being interrupted by Emma. In a break from the standard *Avengers* formula, we have one of the leads engaged in a fight immediately after we learn the episode's title. Normally, if there is an action scene early in the episode, it comes before the episode title, and involves characters other than Steed and Emma. The post-title scene, in which Steed and Emma are introduced to the case and examine the crime scene, or some other setting, is usually relatively calm, with Steed and Emma exchanging friendly, witty dialogue while puzzling over their latest assignment, giving the viewer a chance to relax after the shock of the teaser. Fights are saved for later in the episode, and are used to punctuate the plot with action, with the grandest sequences saved for the episode's climax. By putting even a short fight scene at the beginning of the episode, *The Thirteenth Hole* shakes up the *Avengers* formula. It does so again when Emma expresses her annoyance at Steed's failure to stop the escaping Jackson, making their initial encounter less-than-cordial where it would normally be friendly or playful.

Steed informs Emma that the flat belongs to the late Murphy, whose remit was to keep tabs on British scientists. Emma searches through Murphy's closet, finding his newly-purchased golf clubs, and suspiciously marked golf cards. As Steed laments the fact that Murphy "never had a chance to swing his steel-shafted, handle-to-head balanced niblick", Emma shoots him a look that is just two steps up from an annoyed eye-roll, a reaction which will typify her attitude toward golf throughout the episode, on which more later.

Arriving at the Craigleigh Golf Club, Steed and Emma are accosted by Collins (Francis Matthews), who informs them that it is a members-only weekend, clearly intending to send them away. This highlights a recurrent theme in the series, used most effectively in *The Town of No Return*, where Steed and Emma are cast as unwanted 'outsiders', excluded by the people they are investigating. Ironically, Collins, the man attempting to keep them out, shares similar goals with Steed and Emma – he, too, suspects something untoward is going on at the club, and is trying to work out what it is – yet his first onscreen act is to attempt to turn his would-be allies away. It is tempting to think that the irony is not unintentional.

The rest of the episode takes place either on the course, or in the clubhouse. Harkening back to her reaction to Steed's enthusiasm for Murphy's unused golf club, Emma spends the entirety of the episode seemingly attempting to have as little to do with the game as possible. She is portrayed as a competent golfer, initially joining Steed on the green and teeing off with ease. However, while the implication is that Emma understands the rules of the game, and is capable of playing a reasonable round, her time on the course is marked by a distinct lack of enthusiasm. This is unusual for her character, a woman normally typified by her interest in just about every subject known to man, and who often manages to connect the story of the week to one of her areas of expertise. But after her initial tee-off with Steed shortly after their arrival at the club, Emma forgoes golfing altogether, choosing to walk the course to conduct her investigations, rather than play it. She is equally unenthusiastic about the company in the clubhouse. She barely tolerates the advances of Captain Waversham (Donald Hewlett), at one point tuning him out entirely; when he asks if he is boring her, Emma responds with a distracted, "Hmm?" It is unusual for Emma to be unable to feign interest for the sake of the case, particularly when she risks antagonising the people she is investigating. She even seems to take a measure of perverse pleasure in acting as Steed's "fairy godmother"—predicated by a vaguely Shakespearian speech that perhaps harkens back to Diana Rigg's theatre background—by fixing Steed's game against Reed. She grinds Reed's ball into the green with no small measure of satisfaction, and is pleased with her work as she manipulates Steed's own ball by moving it up the course. No doubt some of her enjoyment stems from foiling Reed, but is she also happy to be destroying the purity of the game held sacrosanct by people like Waversham?

It is safe to assume, therefore, that Emma is not a fan of golf, immune to its supposed charms. She would probably be perfectly capable of entering the ranks of the enthusiasts, but she has no desire to do so. Whether this is simply a trait of the character, or meant to highlight Emma's role as that of a futuristic woman who is not part of 'the establishment' who often play the game, is up to the viewer.

Steed, in contrast, and in keeping with his persona as a traditionalist, is a golfer. The character is shown golfing as early as the Gale era, and goes on to hit a few balls in *The Murder Market*, *Take-Over* (although they are invisible ones), and *Angels of Death*, though *The Thirteenth Hole* is the only episode where he plays outside the confines of his home; he usually opts to hit balls into his upturned bowler. [2] On all occasions, Steed enjoys the game, but his enjoyment does not mean he is incapable of poking fun at it. This is most clearly evidenced during his game against Reed, in which Steed arrives decked out in an over-the-top golfer's outfit (eschewed, ironically, by all of the other members of the club), and proceeds to evaluate the course using a bizarre array of instruments that would put the most avid golf enthusiast to shame. In the process, Steed manages to be both a lover of the game, and to subvert and poke fun at it at the same time. This reflects his character as a whole, a man who, on the surface, appears to be a member of the establishment and all it entails, and yet frequently exhibits sides of his personality that clash violently with his persona of a well-bred, well-to-do man-about-town.

Perhaps if Steed did not work in his chosen profession, he would be more like a standard aristocrat, his game as sacrosanct to him as it is to the members of the club. However, unlike some golf 'nuts', Steed is acutely aware that it is only a game, and there are much, much more important things in life that need worrying about. As a result, he treats the game as it should be treated—as a source of fun, rather than a matter of 'life and death', much the way he treats the perks of his upper-class lifestyle. However, Steed is perfectly capable of acting as golf-mad as his persona would suggest. This affords Macnee the opportunity to turn in one of his brilliant, over-the-top performances as Steed plays the role of the boisterous, eccentric aristocrat with more money than sense, able to shoulder his way into where he is unwelcome, simply because his charm and bonhomie are so overwhelming; it seems churlish even for his enemies to turn him away with harsh words.

However, in classic *Avengers* tradition, the other golfers also do not conform to the golfer stereotype. While they appear to be standard-issue golf enthusiasts, harmless if a little dull, they are revealed to be something much more sinister. They are involved in a plot to sell Dr. Adams' secrets to the Russians, and are willing to kill to keep the set-up secret. Ironically, they are more guilty of disrespecting the game than either Steed or Emma is, as they are exploiting the course and the house rules (tee-off times, no late-night strolls to protect the green, sand traps) in order to achieve their own ends. In this way, they, like Steed and Emma, are not quite what they seem, with the possible exception of Waversham, who seems to be nothing more than a legitimate golf bore!

There are some small, subtle moments where real-life seeps into the episode. Macnee and Rigg ad-lib their game of pick-up sticks by reacting to the actual results of their play, creating a natural intimacy between them in the process. Rigg turns in a repeat performance with a game of tiddlywinks played using Steed's chainmail lined hat (note that after he puts it on, she retrieves her tiddlywinks, which are still sitting in the crown!) Macnee works off the cuff again during the final fight, in which he mistakenly attempts to pull his swordstick from the wrong club, a genuine blooper that was left in the episode. The television audience is also neatly mirrored by the Russian scientists watching events unfold on television via the satellite feed, although they happen to be rooting for the opposite side!

A final point of interest concerns Collins' death. Collins meets his end by being shot with a golf ball using a golf ball gun wielded by Jackson. When it is initially revealed, the gun looks ridiculous. It bears a striking resemblance to the gun that shoots around corners, which Steed planned to gift to his nephew in *The Gravediggers*, though its ammo was harmless ping pong balls. However, as the full implications of the weapon's potential sink in, it becomes something much more sinister. Golf balls are unforgiving, and taking one to the temple could easily kill. This is *Avengerland*, so we are spared gruesome deaths, the imprint of the ball's mark on the victim's head the only evidence of its force of impact. The audience is left to fill in the visceral details of a crushed skull, but the effect of the weapon is still conveyed. This illustrates that, while *The Thirteenth Hole* may not be the best episode that Season 4 has to offer, *The Avengers* could take something as innocuous as a golf ball, and the game of golf, and, by employing its usual subversiveness, put a sinister spin on it. In doing so, it took an episode that could have been dragged down by its subject matter, played with the preconceptions of that subject matter, and made an enjoyable hour of television. Not every series could manage such a feat.

© JZ Ferguson

1. A fear of the number 13.
2. He also gives his umbrella a golf swing in the modified opening titles of *The Forget-Me-Knot*.

SMALL GAME FOR BIG HUNTERS

Filmed: 16th September – 1st October 1965

Exterior Locations:
Shrubs, trees and lakeside
Country cottage façade, courtyard and grounds

Sets:
'Jungle' areas, fence boundary
Country cottage: hall, bedroom, living room
Tropical outfitter's shop
Colonel Rawlings' home: study, conservatory
Kalayan club house

SMALL GAME FOR BIG HUNTERS

Main Character List:
Jack Kendrick: farmhand
Emma Peel
John Steed
Dr. Gibson: medical doctor
Professor Swain: entomologist, formerly at the Kalayan University
Shop assistant: tropical outfitters
Razafi: Lieutenant of the Kalayan Intelligence Service
Simon Trent: adventurer
Colonel Rawlings: former senior military officer in Kalaya
Fleming: 'rubber expert'

A deadly voodoo-like curse called Shirenzai is spreading its evil spell across *Avengerland*...

Before we begin, the elephant in the room must be addressed (no, despite the African influence, there are no literal elephants in this episode - for that see the Cathy Gale era – here, the deadly enemy is at the other end of the size scale). We must address the question of race in *The Avengers*. Like uniformed policemen, mundane criminals such as drug dealers, and most of the working class, characters from ethnic minorities in Britain are largely absent from *The Avengers*, which was intended to have the surreal air of an almost deserted, idealised England of the early 20th century as embodied in Rupert Brooke's poem, *The Old Vicarage, Grantchester* (written in 1912, in Berlin). This poem describes a pastoral, already lost (and probably mythical) England and ends with the celebrated lines:

"Stands the Church clock at ten to three?
And is there honey still for tea?"

It has been cited by an *Avengers* writer/producer as encapsulating the never-never land which Steed and Emma keep safe from devious diabolical masterminds on a regular basis.

Rupert Brooke, famous as a war poet, died from sepsis from an infected mosquito bite far from home in 1915. A feeling of danger and distance and discomfort, and of hidden, unpredictable threats of death is something *The Avengers* captures and forcefully promotes - both in the sharp focus of its plots, and in its background 'atmosphere', working on multiple levels along with the humour and companionable warmth of our leading couple. It is notable that Brooke's poem includes such subversive imagery as English country towns and villages where the supposedly everyday folk possess "twisted lips and twisted hearts", inhabiting places "full of nameless crimes", whilst the poet himself is "sweating, sick, and hot." Danger, deceit, disease and crime are never far from the surface in the pretty and innocuous-seeming *Avengerland*. Let us prepare our tropical kit, and enter the far-from-urban jungle...the jungle of human pride, anger and revenge...a jungle of vengeance and Avengers...

One of the greatest joys of watching *The Avengers* for the first time is never knowing, from episode to episode, where one will 'end up' – where the action will take place. It is like taking a space-and-time-travelling trip in the TARDIS in *Doctor Who*: the destination is almost completely random. [1] You may have a location in Britain (and even that is not guaranteed, in *The New Avengers* and in the stories before Emma Peel joined Steed on his adventures), but it will be somewhere the public can not normally visit: a deserted WWII aerodrome, a private Scottish castle, after-hours in the backrooms of a massive department store, a sinister research establishment...

Long before urban explorers' websites came along, *Avengers* fans were detailing their visits to the odd and charming places our TV show had visited. But watching the show itself...it's immediate. We are planted in the midst of the action, bewildered and grasping for clues to places, people and motives. The same glorious confusion every week. No escape now – we find ourselves concentrating on another world. In *Small Game for Big Hunters* it is a pestilential, hot, and diseased place, indicative of threats to come. We are attacked by throbbing drums, the oppressive squall of insects and croaking swamp-frogs, lunged at by looming twisted tree trunks, and we find a harsh sun beating down on the reed beds of a mosquito-infested swamp as a lone, desperate man flees from – what? A feverish dream, or imprisonment, or a deadly pursuer?

Splashing waist-deep in a river of decaying vegetation, a small machete almost inadequate to hack his way through so painfully slowly, he makes landfall (shouts of triumph from unseen pursuers, ululating war cries; horrifically, a picked-clean skull watches on, embedded in the bifurcation of a branching tree – imagery referenced later in the James Bond movie *Live and Let Die*). Our persecuted hero staggers to a twisted wire fence, perhaps the last stage in a prisoner-of-war breakout. Climbing now, exhausted, agonisingly close to making it over the top, the poor, bedraggled escapee gasps and collapses. A deadly arrow – poisoned? – plunges into his back.

We never see the attacker. Murderous death comes from the jungle – the killer, expected by Kendrick (the victim), and feared by us (the viewers of this tragedy), remains unseen. Kendrick nearly escaped – onto the road outside the fence, with its trimmed verge and milestone: '23 miles to London'. Wait…what?? We know we're watching *The Avengers* now, not a prisoner-of-war film, and snuggle into our armchairs for intrigue and Steedian *bonhomie* aplenty. More strangeness awaits…we find out later that the man is not dead. It could be a very unusual *Avengers* episode indeed.

The intrepid machete-wielding explorer we saw in the earliest scenes, Kendrick, is merely an English field worker, a 'common farmhand'. An ordinary man, a working-class man, caught up in *The Avengers*' bizarre and deadly world. He saw too much of the villains' plan. Along with three other locals he was extracted to be a 'sample' or control for the experiment. There is no trace of a drug on the arrow (which has a nice dangly 'Shirenzai' attachment). His highly-exciting action scenes, and the fact he isn't actually killed, show humanity and empathy in Philip Levene's story-telling, no class snobbishness here. [2]

Humanity and empathy are the greatest calling-cards of *The Avengers*. For all its being steeped in death, its heroes ending the stories with humorous vehicular exits or with champagne toasts, the show has never been accused of callousness – and there is a reason for that. It is because the writers have always tipped a wink to the audience: life matters. We're having fun here, and we're escaping the Ten O'clock News; all the violence is pulp adventure and comic book. Steed and Mrs. Peel realise the value of life. That's why they're risking theirs, all the time.

Professor Swain is deeply unpleasant; in modern parlance, he has no 'people skills' whatsoever. He doesn't even have the dithery charm of other *Avengers* eccentrics (*The New Avengers*' Lopez in *Target!* would be his nearest equivalent and he's a delight by comparison). Emma Peel treats the victims of 'Shirenzai' with compassion, whilst Swain is only interested in how they confirm his own (apparently crackpot) theories. He messes about with a pendulum that seems to be a nail affected by a magnet (we never see how he works this trick). Ultimately, he himself is 'abducted', though Steed spends the rest of the day presumably downing brandy and Sundowners with the Colonel, and Emma doing goodness knows what (that 'lost evening and night' is never explained – perhaps she spent it trying to find the professor, though in all likelihood he's surely going to be in the house at the end of the garden where everybody else is).

Simon Trent (James Villers), the rifle-toting, supercilious colonialist is a great foil for Steed. Ostensibly a gentleman, he is an early riser, unable to resist taking a pot shot at anything that moves, cocking his rifle as a warning to Steed. He eventually admits it is empty, but we know his ammunition is not far away and he can't wait to bag "a big one". His contemptuous behaviour makes him highly amusing, and we anticipate a big fall for this sneering bully.

The other villains turn out to be either patsies or concealed heroes. Razafi appears to be a dangerous Kalayan hit man, daubed in facepaint resembling the Shirenzai curse symbol and with orders to harm Steed, but he is an ally, expositing to Steed important plot points regarding the villains' plan before being bumped off by the one female character (besides Emma). Lala promptly runs off into the 'jungle' allowing Steed to take advantage of his position as apparent murderer; holding the bloodied knife that killed Razafi whilst a suddenly affable Trent treats him as 'one of us' and explains the rest of the plot.

There are revengers – rather than avengers – here. Like the best villains, they totally believe they are in the right; in this case, the far right (politically speaking), because it all comes down to colonialism. *The Avengers*' plots often combined two or more seemingly unconnected locations or ideas to give some interesting dynamics. The location also has to be interesting or unusual, which it certainly is in *Small Game for Big Hunters*.

This time, writer Philip Levene addressed a more gritty and hard-hitting subject than the usual fare of the increasingly fantastic 1960s spy genre; later, some thriller series like *Man In A Suitcase* would address the dangers of British Empire colonial masters who could not 'let go' of newly-independent states. It seems out of place in a charming and larger-than-life show like the 1965/66 incarnation of *The Avengers*. But is it? The very fact that the show can take a sharp turn into contemporary concerns makes us sit up. The confrontation of British Empire and social responsibility is a fertile area for the 'conservative' Steed – whose humanitarianism triumphs, once again.

The physical danger is real. Despite the hints of a "voodoo" cult early on, and the apparently supernatural 'Shirenzai' curse, the more deadly danger of hard-faced, intelligent men with rifles makes Steed more than usually sombre, and when Steed looks worried, then we worry. We know he isn't being flippant.

We enjoy numerous humorous references to Trent's ever-closer bull-elephants, culminating in an unflinching reference to a ten-paces shot. By this stage, audience, writer and cast are complicit in laughing at 'fisherman's tales' of the ever more ridiculous hunters' escapades. For his shooting of a bull elephant Steed used F8 at 5/100ths of a second, and a small roll of film – i.e. a sedate camera safari, emphasising Steed's distaste for guns.

Steed and Emma are separated, not by far (geographically), though Steed is "down river" and unable to communicate with Emma, who has her hands full caring for the victims of the sleeping sickness. This is exacerbated by everyone's inability to secure the house (the door is repeatedly left open despite abductions, curse symbols, and strange footprints. Emma leaves a window open despite claiming later to have shut them all).

Dr. Gibson, who tended Kendrick, has by now also been infected with Shirenzai. Eventually both comatose victims are relayed to the 'jungle', apparently still alive. This enables Swain and Trent to ensure no-one can pre-empt their visit to Kalaya where they will cause chaos by releasing their tsetse flies, hospitalising most of the population and taking over. However, Steed spots the victims being brought in; he gets more suspicious. Emma goes to the heart of the action and takes over Lala's costume (towel-like wrap dress and flower in hair). Emma and Steed get to do Tarzan/Jane impressions, delightfully.

The bio-engineered threat of the tsetse flies is rendered impotent by English rain and low temperatures. Kalaya remains independent.

Emma and Steed get to paddle off, really "up river" this time, in a canoe in the tag scene; oh, but it's wonderful that they always end up together, every week. (Never mind 'in the end'. Peter Peel? Shouldn't he be stuck up the Amazon somewhere?) Emma Peel and Steed have their own river to paddle, and we love them for it.

As for the *Avengerland* setting...Once Upon a Time in the Far East? Or Africa? Or the Home Counties of England? The German title for this episode is *Afrikanischer Sommer*, whilst Professor Swain, the diabolical mastermind behind the tsetse fly operation, claims to have spent a large part of his career as an entomologist in the Far East and is thus qualified (he claims) to speak about the strange sleeping death which the curse represents. From whence does this knowledge originate? Asia or Africa? An example of the slightly confusing and disorienting story, which nevertheless works because of the difficulty the viewer has in getting a grip on its shifting elements. The apparent jungle setting is unusual for the film-era *Avengers*, which invariably have a British setting (unlike the globe-hopping studio adventures of the Cathy Gale years). [3]

This is rapidly revealed to be the Home Counties, and the incongruity of tropical curses and folklore, jungle drums, arcane symbols and displaced colonials at the bottom of the garden is only allowed a little time to settle in the imagination before a full-blown jungle reappears, this time in an oversized conservatory attached to a pleasant Hertfordshire retirement house. Within is the owner, Colonel Rawlings, whose mental state cannot grasp his displacement, and he is carefully cultivated (like the hothouse plants and insects of the jungle) to be stuck in the past on another continent. [4] Worlds within worlds – something *The Avengers* effortlessly manages every week.

I love Professor Swain's rendition of the Sheranzai curse warning "Aradi" (or "the sweet sound of hell, the inescapable sound that precedes the everlasting sleep") on his bamboo pipe. Mainly, because it doesn't appear in any of the sequences where 'Sherenzai' is inflicted, and is never referenced in Laurie Johnson's delightful incidental music. It is a huge clue that the man is a fraud, and I love it when the audience – us – are given massive clues; part of the fun of the show. This playfulness reminds us that the *Avengers* writers, actors and directors are sharing a game with us, not being 'superior' like some other shows. *The Avengers* is a very 1960s thing: a collective, communal experience as we are all having fun together – *Avengerland* lovers who have taken over the TV, if only for the weekly, magical hour.

© Frank Shailes

1. This, surely, is one of the principal delights of *The Avengers* in general, but this season in particular. Each week we head off into *Avengerland* for an adventure, 'destination unknown'. The dazzling variety of settings/locations reminds me of the childlike excitement of watching the fantasy adventures offered by the BBC's *Mr. Benn*. As Frank reminds us, not knowing where we are going is part of the fun, as we set off on a magical mystery tour.
2. Having said this, being a working-class character he has a non-speaking part! By contrast, the Kalayan Razafi is portrayed as a humane, articulate, refined man, his character contrasting with the stereotype costume he poses in. *Small Game for Big Hunters* can be considered to be both anti-colonialist and anti-racist.
3. The Emma Peel colour episode *The Superlative Seven* also takes us off to foreign soil, a fantasy island.
4. Is the Colonel simply a caricature, the British colonialist who cannot comprehend that the world has moved on and that the Empire is now a fantasy, like *Avengerland* itself? He is

not one of the villains, but can he be considered to be a victim? He tells Steed that he would like to return to Hertfordshire – where in a geographical sense he already is – but would he cope in the 'real' world? On reading my notes, Frank responded with the following comment: "The Colonel cuts a tragic figure at the point he wishes he were at home in Hertfordshire; the dramatic irony is that we know he is just yards away from his own country house, in which Trent no doubt enjoys breakfast every morning before swaggering about with his rifle. No damnable jungle heat for him! They're exploiting his money, of course. The swines!"

THE GIRL FROM AUNTIE

Filmed: 4th – 23rd October 1965

Exterior Locations:
Country house gateway and road
West London airport terminal
Emma Peel's apartment
London streets

Sets:
Corridor outside Emma Peel's apartment
Emma Peel's apartment
Taxi
Art Incorporated: reception, outer office, auction area, store room/cage
Theatrical agency
Advertising agency
Solicitors' office
Theatrical costumiers
Knitting circle
Office block
Ivanov's flat
Prison cell

THE GIRL FROM AUNTIE

Main Character List:
Emma Peel
'Old Lady'
John Steed
Taxi driver
Georgie Price-Jones: impersonating Emma Peel
Gregorie Auntie: art dealer, Art Incorporated
Receptionist: Art Incorporated
Aunt Hetty: a real auntie
Arkwright: knitting circle instructor
Ivanov: Russian spy
Russian auction bidder

In the Emma Peel era, we deal with all kinds of diabolical masterminds: metal men and buildings that are murderers come to mind. But what if the hit-man attacking could be your auntie, or even your grandmother? Welcome to *The Girl From Auntie*.

The name is clearly inspired by the 1960s spy show, *The Man From UNCLE*. The teaser shows a girl in a bikini leaving a fancy dress party and kissing a man with a pig face mask. Then our heroine appears, supposedly dressed as a bird. Suddenly, Emma Peel sees an old woman, who easily could be the age of her grandmother, take a traumatic fall off of a bicycle. The audience can see Emma's look of deep concern, as she is pulled to aid this motherly figure. But in a bizarre *Avengerish* twist, what happens next is completely shocking for both the viewer as well as for Emma Peel. She is violently attacked by this grandmother figure and is injected with a huge hypodermic needle, which makes Emma immediately pass out. The look on Emma's face during the struggle with 'granny' is that of betrayal, that this motherly figure would harm her, but also bewilderment as to her possible motivation. At this moment, the camera pans to the fallen basket with its contents sprawled over the ground: a knitting-needle and a ball of yarn. Then, the title appears.

This episode is not subtle. There are eleven people that drop dead from attacks with knitting-needles. In the first nine minutes of the episode, there are ten knitting-needle fatalities: seven of them dramatically fall out of closets and three are found dead in a car. The final victim is stabbed while in prison. During the episode, there are two other violent attacks, involving needles of some sort, where the people survive.

This episode is a contender for one of the more extreme parodies of all the Season 4 *Avengers* episodes. But I would argue that underneath this parody was a serious message. As the English poet and satirist Churchill said, "A joke's a very serious thing". If I were the father of psychoanalysis, Dr. Sigmund Freud, I would venture to say that the knitting-needle in this episode was a potent phallic symbol. Normally a phallic symbol associated with murder and violence is attributed to men. What makes *The Girl From Auntie* novel is that one is led to believe that the potent phallic symbol of the knitting-needle actually comes from a woman, and not just any woman: an elderly, frail grandmother figure. One would not expect her to be capable of violence, nor a knitting-needle a weapon. Maternal images of love and kindness, knitting warm fuzzy clothes for their kin come to mind. The knitting-needle is mother's tool to make these warm soft clothes that feel comforting and remind us of soothing motherly images.

The brilliance of this episode is in the use of the knitting-needle as a powerful phallic weapon. What could be a more powerful disguise for a hit-man? To a certain degree we all have an automatic assumption that a granny is as safe as her knitting tools. No wonder then that Mrs. Peel (as well as the other victims) lets her guard down around this motherly figure. Neither does the normally suspicious Steed seem to question the grandmotherly hit-man he meets leaving the multiple crime scenes he enters. In fact, he tips his hat to her.

The other hallmark of this episode is how effectively the audience is conned. Which 'Auntie' is the real killer? There may be more fakes in this episode than originals. There is even a fake Mrs. Peel. It creates a suspense that is meant to tease and confuse the viewer. The baddie in this episode turns out to be a powerful underground art thief who steals famous treasures. What makes him unique is that he not only steals works of art, such as the *Mona Lisa*, he will even steal the Eiffel Tower for the right price; and, of course, the most precious item for sale: Mrs. Peel. Like most con-artists, he replaces the original with a fake. But a fake Mrs. Peel? Absolutely. This is *The Avengers*.

Steed gets back from holiday only to find that Mrs. Peel has been replaced by a blonde impostor. Steed at this point pretends to be delivering a lobster to the fake Mrs. Peel, telling her that it is a gift from Steed, "a small fat man with a grey moustache." There are layers upon layers of deception in this episode. This is only the beginning. Steed leaves and then rings Mrs. Peel's flat with a delightful new accent. "Emma, it's ol' loverboy back from Karachi. Be with you in a couple of jiffs." The impostor quickly leaves. Steed has the taxi driver, who is now wearing Steed's diving mask, follow her. Throughout the episode, the taxicab driver is instructed by Steed to amuse himself with the numerous items of sporting gear Steed brings back from holiday: a nice *Avengerish* touch, to see him playing with oars, a diving mask, boxing gloves and a fishing hat in his taxi.

Meanwhile, at the office of Art Incorporated, the secretary tells her boss that lot 17 has been safely delivered. She smiles as she hears the order, "Everyone associated with the fake Mrs. Peel will be eliminated, beginning with the theatrical agents." Eventually, Steed confronts the impostor in a vacant office. She admits that she was hired to impersonate Mrs. Peel. Her name is Georgie Price-Jones. What happens next is quite unexpected. Georgie innocently sees a ball of yarn on the floor and pulls on it, only to find it attached to a dead body stabbed in the back with a knitting needle. A body dramatically falls out of a cupboard. [1] The next stop is a visit to two theatrical agents. Another ball of wool leads them to two more cupboard fatalities. Georgie is delighted she has been paid half her salary, as she finds her cheque skewered on the knitting needle in the victim's back, drawn against the account of a firm Barrett, Barrett and Wimpole. It is soon discovered that all of these three gentlemen are dead as well, found in a car outside the office. "Six bodies in an hour and twenty minutes! What do you call that?" Georgie's reply is delightfully self-referential: "It's a good first act."

Our journey, tracking the serial knitting-needle killer, continues at the theatrical costumiers' office: John, George, Paul and Fred, clearly a parody on *The Beatles*. The closet is opened once again, only to find all four costumiers fall out, stabbed with knitting needles. "Auntie, Auntie did it," are the final words of one victim before he dies. The character actress Sylvia Coleridge enters next, and steals the show. In walks Auntie, Auntie Hetty looking for her knitting pattern.

Our first introduction to her is when she discovers her knitting pattern strategically placed next to her four nephews. What is most striking is that she does not seem to notice that the four nephews she adores are dead. "They are my favourite nephews, and I like to think I am their favourite Auntie", she beams. Aunt Hetty is a true *Avengers* eccentric. She attributes their stillness to being asleep or playing a game. At one point she admits that they are "absolutely dead". There is a long pause followed by, "...to the world. Runs in the family you know: very heavy sleepers." Her only concern is knitting. From the audience's perspective, we wonder if this is our diabolical mastermind at work. During a pleasant chat, drinking tea with Steed, she offers to knit him a "poodle" sweater, or as she puts it, "I would love to do you in poodle wool, with a V neck double rib bottom and raglan sleeves". The phallic knitting-needle, in this example, appears to be Auntie's attempt to emasculate Steed. Once again, a tool associated with maternal comfort is being used as a metaphorical weapon. Here is an attempt to wound and humiliate Steed, through the 'kind' gesture of knitting him a sweater, albeit an effeminate one.

Steed's reaction is brilliant, as somewhere between horror and offence but in a beautifully British subdued way. What is disconcerting for the audience is the sight of a seemingly sincere, sweet old lady with a kind, gentle, grandmotherly voice smiling softly at us. Behind the exterior of maternal warmth, we wonder, could this same motherly figure be capable of murder, and of her own kin at that? [2] Ironically, Arkwright, the eccentric knitting instructor, tells us that knitting "binds the family together and brings peace to the home." What we actually see looks like anything but peace in the home. Is she the phallic granny trying to kill off her family? Or is the script writer conning us?

We are introduced to Mr. Arkwright, and his knitting circle. To make matters more confusing, Auntie is a member, as well as a dozen other grandmotherly figures that could fit the bill of the killer Auntie. We soon learn that the so called harmony of the knitting circle is being undermined by a burglar who is stealing Arkwright's knitting needles. Arkwright appears to almost be singing nursery rhymes, in the form of knitting instructions, to his students.

"Fingers nimble, fingers spright. Cast to the left. Cast to the right. First one pearl, then one plain. Then two pearl, and back again".

A true *Avengers* eccentric, Mr. Arkwright chats with Steed, but then gestures angrily with a knitting-needle when he learns his double 0 size needles have been stolen. Is he our killer? To investigate, Steed has the fake Mrs. Peel join the Arkwright knitting circle, only to find

Auntie Hetty pulling a gun on her. "I got it to deal with my nephew. This should keep him quiet. Don't you think?" The gun is a fake. Add that to the rest of the fakes in this episode: a toy gun made for Auntie's six year old nephew. We see her childlike nature suddenly appear as she pulls the trigger and squirts water from the gun. It eliminates this Auntie from our list of suspects.

The phallic granny hit-man is still on the loose. She is instructed to kill the fake Emma Peel, Georgie. The granny hit-man enters Mrs. Peel's apartment with her phallic knitting-needle only to be met by Georgie reading a step-by-step guide on how to defend oneself from an attacker from behind. With the usual *Avengers* sense of humour, Georgie follows the guide and throws her opponent to the ground, avoiding the deadly knitting-needle thrown at her. "She was old enough to be someone's grandmother", Georgie tells Steed. "Or Auntie", Steed muses.

So how does one find Mrs. Peel? Steed cons the con artist. He goes undercover as Wayne Pennyfeather ffinch. He obtains several works of art from museums that he strategically places in his apartment. The unobtainable is obtained, this time by Steed instead of Art Inc. The baddie has the granny hit-man check out Steed's art collection, and is duly impressed. To the audience's surprise, we learn the name of the head baddie: "Auntie. Gregorie Auntie".

Now that he has his attention, Steed, disguised as "ffinch, with two small f's", tells Auntie that he wants to buy Emma Peel. Auntie refuses. Emma Peel is not for sale. She has already been sold. Why is Emma Peel so valuable? For her secrets. "She carries most of the dispositions of western defence bases in her head. A splendid addition to any intelligence system in the world", according to Auntie. But Steed has a hunch that Ivanoff, a Russian diplomat seen leaving Art Inc., has bought Mrs. Peel.

Clearly Steed has only one option. Kill off the competitor, so to speak, which he does as usual with great skill and agility. Steed knocks out the Russian diplomat, Ivanoff, calls the police and has him escorted to jail. Meanwhile Auntie, who is worried that Ivanoff will talk, sends out the phallic granny to have him killed in prison by the usual method: the knitting-needle. Here is another fake. The granny hit-man enters the jail cell by informing the guards and Ivanoff that she is, who else? Ivanoff's mother.

Without a living buyer, there is a new auction for Mrs. Peel. Steed, disguised as ffinch, buys Mrs. Peel only to be uncovered as yet another fake. A fight ensues and Steed hits Auntie over the head with what we are told is the real *Mona Lisa*, completely destroying the painting. "Very enigmatic", Steed replies. Steed runs into Arkwright's knitting circle to find the phallic granny knitting away. A fight ensues and we soon learn that the granny hit-man is not really a woman at all. Steed peels off the hit-man's mask to find the phallic granny was, well, really a man after all. Suddenly, there is order to the universe. The audience no longer has to worry that hit-men can be motherly figures. The phallic knitting-needle can now be passed on to its rightful owner, a man. We are much more at ease with the phallic symbol belonging to a male owner. [3]

Steed finds Mrs. Peel in a cage behind the knitting store. But what happens next is also enigmatic. Mrs. Peel bends the steel bars of her cage, grabs the guard's head and strategically places it in between the bars. She then walks out of the cage. This episode is a stark change for Emma Peel. Her onscreen time is minimal, as are her clothes. In *The Girl From Auntie*, she at first glance comes across as a very weak Avenger. She may have been a *femme fatale* in Epic but she put on both a performance and fight that any female Avenger could be proud of. In *The Girl From Auntie* much of her entire performance consists of being stuck in a cage. She appears helpless and bored. This is the only Emma Peel episode where she seems completely unmotivated to escape. She seemingly just accepts her plight. Or does she? Is this yet another deception? We discover that she has created an escape hatch by dismantling part of her cage. Yet at the same time we wonder why she waited so long. Although we don't know the length of time she has spent in the cage, we are told that she was bought ten days earlier.

In addition, the sexually provocative outfit she wears is dramatically different from her others. It was one of the first episodes where leather was not used to provoke intense sexuality. We are told she is dressed as a bird for a costume party. But she more aptly looks like she was transformed into a playboy bunny. This makes Emma Peel appear as if she is naked. The frill that covers her seems to sexually objectify her even more. The leather that created the sexual dominatrix persona gives Emma Peel sexual power and lets you know she is completely in charge. In contrast, the exposed look of her costume makes Emma Peel appear to be feeble and ineffectual. Things are being done to her. She is being victimised and controlled and put into slavery. And the chosen outfit here certainly reflects that.

Or was Mrs. Peel in complete control for the entire length of her captivity? Hard to believe given the frightened look she gives the audience when she is told that she will be transported in two days to a more uncomfortable place. Perhaps she was just waiting to find out who her buyer was, before she made her escape. The script took a calculated risk to change Emma Peel's character from an Amazonian-like woman with superhuman abilities, to a seemingly playful playboy bunny. This new anti-feminine character of Emma Peel that is portrayed (until the surprise ending) is forever etched in stone into the minds of the viewers. Although she appears to have been able to escape all along, it is easy to forget this, unlike her costume. Mrs. Peel creates more questions than answers in this episode.

The way the episode gets away with her new image is with humour. We are repeatedly told that it is Emma Peel's top level secrets (her mind) that are being bought (not her body of course). On the other hand, Emma Peel's strength has been her 'man appeal' and of course how her name originated. One could argue that the knitting-needles were not the only dangerous weapon used in this episode. Emma Peel's raw sexuality is perhaps the second most powerful secret weapon of the episode. The sexual excitement she creates in her audience may perhaps be more powerful here than in any other episode. It would be the ultimate male fantasy to have 'man appeal' under his complete control, locked in a cage at his beck and call. Her sexuality is so provocative, and no doubt the male audience excitement so great, there is little option but to lock her up and contain this dangerous weapon. Her greatest power in this episode is her ability to seduce and mesmerise all the men around her into a fierce competition to win and own her.

The Avengers broke the glass ceiling with gender roles. Young women could be nuclear physicists, judo experts or both. Elderly women could (seemingly) be killer hit-men that carry phallic looking knitting-needle tools to murder. It appeared that elderly women no longer had to be sweet little old ladies in a knitting circle. And men? Well we learn two seasons later that men could be 'Mothers'.

There are plenty of references in this episode. One in particular merits special interest. The 'Bates and Marshall advertising agency' is a reference to Roger Marshall the writer and Richard Bates, the videotape era story editor. Bates and Marshall are killed, or more accurately found dead. On first glance, is this a not so funny inside-joke? [4] It is well known that Brian Clemens began to control the jobs of his talented staff during Season 4. Not long before this episode, Roger Marshall wrote the very witty *Dial A Deadly Number*. Yet *The Girl From Auntie* was heavily rewritten by Clemens. [5] There almost seems to be a parallel between the missing Mrs. Peel and the missing writer, Roger Marshall. Mrs. Peel becomes 'a bird in a cage' and her usual acting role virtually eliminated. Similarly, Roger Marshall suddenly vanishes from his behind-the-scenes role as well. With Clemens killing off the names of his head writer and ex-story editor, it makes one wonder if he was letting us know that he was taking over. Nearly fifty years later, I wonder, 'what if Roger Marshall's original script had been used?' The episode no doubt would be more subtle, witty and with a clever twist to the plot. Perhaps the audience would have enjoyed it more. Sadly we will never know; I think all of us fans are still longing to.

© Margaret J Gordon

1. The light-hearted music is at odds with the macabre vision.
2. I have always found this Auntie decidedly creepy, despite her being named after my wonderful great aunt.
3. The killer auntie/grandmother is a fake on a literal level as well; the part is clearly played by an elderly actress until that final 'uncovering' scene.
4. Brian Clemens tried a similar 'joke' with *The Hour That Never Was*, attempting to rename it *Roger and Out*.
5. In the absence of Roger Marshall's original script it is impossible now to work out what Brian Clemens changed. The episode is undoubtedly a Marshall/Clemens 'hybrid'.

QUICK-QUICK SLOW DEATH

Filmed: 25th October-12th November 1965

Exterior Locations:
Suburban streets
Country House grounds
Mackiedockie Street

Sets:
Willi Fehr's Cell
Fintry's Tattoo Parlour
Litchen & Co. (dress hire shop)
Piedi's & Co. (shoe shop)
Mulberry's Bank
Purbright & Co. (office shell)
Terpsichorean Training Techniques ballroom dancing school: foyer, ballroom, locker room

QUICK-QUICK SLOW DEATH

Main Character List:
Willi Fehr: enemy agent
John Steed
Emma Peel
Captain Noble: ministry interrogator
Fintry: tattooist
Huggins: dress hire shop assistant
Ivor Bracewell: assassin, senior male dance tutor
Syder: dress hire shop assistant
Arthur Piedi: shoe shop owner
Bernard: traditional cobbler
Bank Manager: Mulberry's Bank
Lucille Banks: principal of Terpsichorean Training Techniques
Nicki: dance instructor
'Arthur Peever': foreign agent
Chester Read: band leader, the 'commander'

Quick-Quick Slow Death is one of Season Four's lighter episodes, and it makes absolutely no attempt to hide that fact. Plenty of the scenes offer no more substance than the tulle that fills out the skirts of the ballroom dancers at the Terpsichorean Techniques' gala night. This is an episode that opens with the amusing image of an enemy agent pushing a pram, after all, though this scene also, strangely, breaks the *Avengers'* rule of empty streets with no passersby. The street traversed by Willi Fehr (Michael Peake) is chock full of commuters, passersby, traffic, and even workmen repairing a pavement, which is very rare for *Avengerland*. Quite why such a busy street was chosen, or why so much of it is shown in the scene, is unclear, though it is possible that the intention was to contrast the ordinariness of the setting with the unusual sight of a man pushing a pram, particularly since all the other prams in shot are being pushed by women.

In classic *Avengers* style, the pram – and the scene – is soon upturned to produce a dead body with a collection of bullet holes in his chest. In spite of this sudden, shocking and sinister twist, humour remains at the forefront of the episode, with scene after scene played for amusement, rather than dramatic effect. A clue to the identity of a murderer is tattooed on a garlic sausage (which Steed advises Emma to "destroy" by eating). Steed interviews a banker with a habit of moving unpredictably from wicket to wicket. Chester Read (Larry Cross) conducts a band consisting of cardboard cut-outs of himself. Captain Noble's (John Woodnutt) attempts at communication vary between hoarse utterances and whistling in Morse code. Steed manufactures a cover as a representative of 'Baggy Pants Limited' ("Where do you think they get those terrible clothes from?") Emma's stint as a dance instructress is marked by her rapidly-diminishing enthusiasm for the position as she faces the prospect of dancing with yet another flat-footed student – many of whom are much shorter than she is, undoubtedly cast for comic effect—while displaying suitably exasperated facial expressions. She pulls a whole new set of expressions during her visit to Piedi, the shoe designer and foot fetishist, who waxes lyrical about Emma's feet, and cringes in horror at the very idea of a dance school where people "[thrash] their poor arches to distraction." Steed gets in on the silliness by spinning an over-the-top back story, evoking a tragic, lonely life by laying on the pathos and making sad eyes at Lucille Banks (Eunice Gayson) as he regales her with tales of his crocodile-consumed girlfriend.

The episode climaxes with a fight/action sequence that is also played for laughs rather than drama, as Steed and Emma foil a plot to swap Steed for an enemy agent. Emma ensures that it is her partner, Ivor Bracewell (Maurice Kaufmann), who is replaced, forcing him behind a screen where the swap will take place by leaping at him chest-first and thrusting him bodily backwards. When he is coshed into unconsciousness, Emma takes up with his replacement without batting an eye, or missing a step. Further swaps occur behind the screen, including one ridiculous (and impossible) exchange, in which Steed and Emma manage to accidentally swap one another with enemy agents when the two dancing couples collide. When they realise their mistake, the fight that ensues is played for comic effect as Steed and Emma easily dispatch their opponents with techniques that owe more to dance moves than any fighting technique. Emma swings her 'partner' round and round, before Steed 'cuts in' and spins the man artfully above his head. If there were any doubts that 'fun' was the episode's main purpose, they've been easily dismissed by the end of the fight.

However, the lightness of touch is leavened with dark, dramatic overtones. The violence, whether onscreen or implied, is a step up from the series' usual treatment. The scene where Willi Fehr strangles Captain Noble nearly to death is startlingly visceral, right down to the choking sounds Noble makes as he struggles to breathe. Noble winds up shooting his would-be murderer in the side, leaving Fehr to stagger to the telephone and make a call, before dying himself. Fintry, the tattooist, is shot in the head. No blood is shown, but the gun is pointed directly at his temple when the trigger is pulled, which is unusual given the series' tendency to confine gunshots to the body, rather than the head. Piedi's assistant, Bernard, is suffocated in plaster, though the episode attempts to soften his death by having Emma 'excavate' him later on, using a small hammer to tap away at his 'cast'.

There is also a tragic element to the dance school's operation. Steed lays his sob story on thick, telling Lucille that he is alone and bereft, his mournful expression exaggerated for comic effect. However, this cannot conceal the fact that Lucille Banks and her accomplices are, in reality, preying upon exactly the sort of men Steed is posing as: lonely individuals seeking human companionship. It is insinuated that the real Arthur Peever was so starved of affection that he tattooed the name of his dance instructress on his forearm, where one would normally etch the name of a wife or girlfriend, because she was the only woman to whom he had any sort of close or intimate connection. Lucille's clients are not professional agents or cunning businessmen, but vulnerable people who reached out to her for help, and ended up dead for their troubles. Lucille herself confides to Steed that many of her students are in the same position as him, and claims that she hopes to help them, when in fact she is using their situation to her advantage. The episode skirts neatly over this fact in its bid to explain the dance school's scheme to the audience, but it lends the episode a definite sense of tragedy, a weightier dimension than the delivery would otherwise suggest.

Deserving of closer examination is Nicki. As played by Carole Gray, she is a somewhat unusual character for *Avengerland*. Despite working at the dance studio, she plays no part in the scheme; she is simply an overworked employee guilty of nothing more sinister than griping about her job. She does not wind up dead in the course of the episode. At worst, she is out of a job when Steed and Emma shut the dance school down. And she is not connected in any way, shape, or form to Steed's employers. These are the usual roles played by incidental characters in *Avengers* episodes, but she does not slot neatly into any of them. She is there, ostensibly, to feed Emma, and the audience, information and clues to assist in the unravelling of the plot of the week, but her character rises above the status of a mere plot propeller. Where she could have been a bland pretty face, Robert Banks Stewart imbued her with a biting, sarcastic wit, and the hair and costume department set her up with an elaborate hairdo and a nice line of frocks, as opposed to their usual strategy of toning down the looks of the other female characters so that they do not 'compete' with the *Avengers* girl. Nicki is even revealed as a canny entrepreneur, brokering an agreement with Piedi's assistant Bernard to sell dance shoes on the side in order to make a little extra money.

However, Nicki is most interesting because of the way she interacts with Emma. Where she could have been written as catty or threatened by the 'new girl', Nicki instead shows Emma the ropes and offers her hard-earned wisdom for surviving the trials of a dance instructress: "Put [your feet] above your head…[it] soothes them to such an extent that the agony is only excruciating." It is rare to have the opportunity to see Emma interact with another female character for any extended period of time, even rarer for her to do so for any reason other than to extract information. Many of those interactions are marked by antagonism, because the other female characters are often involved in the plot of the week, and regard Emma's presence and questions with suspicion. In contrast, Emma's dynamic with Nicki is one of friendly camaraderie, free from antagonism. That dynamic also highlights the admirable qualities of Emma's character. Emma is sophisticated, well-educated, independently wealthy, multi-talented, and took the reins of her father's company at the tender age of 21. [1] Nicki has, presumably, had none of Emma's advantages, but at no time does Emma treat her as any less than an equal, deserving of respect. This reflects Emma's characterisation as the 'modern woman'—she looks to and appreciates the quality of the person, rather than measuring them relative to her own position in society. Her dislike of her 'superior', Lucille Banks, in contrast, is thinly veiled at best. While Emma may not have to dance to pay the rent, as Nicki does, for the brief period that Emma is employed at the school, they are in the same boat, comrades-in-arms who commiserate about their aches and pains on their breaks, awaiting their next pupil with dread.

Emma is afforded plenty of opportunity to interact with Nicki due to the fact that she and Steed spend the majority of the episode apart. However, when they do reunite, however briefly, they are a delight, playful and completely at ease with one another, right from their very first scene where Emma catches one of the victims of Steed's beer can target practice with a cheerful "How's that?", and then happily agrees to launch his targets for him (even if she does accidentally send his "lunchtime refreshment" into orbit!) Their playfulness endures throughout the course of the episode, lending it a host of wonderful little touches that emphasise how *in simpatico* the two leads were, from their impromptu sashaying departure as they leave Captain Noble ("Carry on dancing!"), to Emma (miraculously) producing a needle and thread post-fight to fix Steed's damaged suit ("You'll lose your deposit"), culminating in the surreal, dreamlike tag, where Steed and Emma eschew their usual, unique form of transport in favour of dancing off, together, into the mist until they fade from view.

The episode also treats fans to a couple of (almost) in-jokes. Honor Blackman's then-husband, Maurice Kaufmann, appears as instructor Ivor Bracewell. Having wed Blackman shortly before she began her tenure as Cathy Gale, Kaufmann 'played' Steed in an unofficial capacity throughout Seasons Two and Three, reading Patrick Macnee's lines in order to help his wife learn her parts during the punishing recording schedule. Even if viewers were unaware of it at the time, there is humour to be gained from the sight of 'Mr. Gale' attempting to put the moves on Mrs. Peel—and ending up with his hand slammed in a door for his efforts. Perhaps harkening back to that same period of the show's history, shoe designer Piedi offers to create "Wellington boots, in the kinkiest black leather" for Emma, a line which is almost certainly a nod to Blackman and Macnee's *Kinky Boots* single.

Quick-Quick Slow Death is played largely for laughs, and it gets them. There is plenty of fun to be had, and the result is a light, amusing episode that gives viewers a break from some of the darker, more intense entries in the season's repertoire. However, it still manages to slip elements of tragedy and brutality into the mix, along with an innovative secondary character, all without sacrificing the episode's humorous bent, demonstrating that there was always more going on in the series than met the eye. Even when it was having fun.

© JZ Ferguson

1. This character detail – provided in the later episode *The House That Jack Built* – is referred to by a number of writers in *Bright Horizons*. I wonder, though, whether it can hold sway throughout the Peel era as a 'fact' outside that specific story. Cross-references do exist in *The Avengers* – such as Cathy Gale in *Too Many Christmas Trees* and between the cybernauts episodes – but these are exceptions rather than the rule.

THE DANGER MAKERS

Filmed: 15th November – 13th December 1965

Exterior Locations:
Country road
Military hospital
Drill parade
Air base
Country lanes
Manton Military Museum: façade, stairs

Sets:
Hospital: Long's office, bedroom
Colonel Groves' office
Grenade bay
Emma Peel's apartment
Manton Military Museum: gallery, Black Rose chamber, test room, cellar, corridor

THE DANGER MAKERS

Main Character List:
Emma Peel
John Steed
Harold Long: Psychological War Department, 'Apollo' mastermind
Stanhope: soldier
Major Robertson: army officer, 'Mercury'
Peters: army officer, 'Jupiter'
Colonel Adams: curator of Manton House Military Museum

The Danger Makers, the 20th of the 26 Season 4 episodes, was filmed in December 1965 and first broadcast in February 1966. Although at this point Great Britain had lost most of her empire and was no longer a major military power, these were heady times on the British pop culture scene. The world in the mid 1960s could not get enough British music, fashion, movies, and, in the case of *The Avengers*, television. This creative explosion in Britain came for the most part from the young. Britain's declining role on the world stage seemed to liberate the new British generation, to free them from their parents' traditions and values, and allowed them to more fully express themselves, often in irreverent and rebellious ways.

An exception to the youthful aspect of this creative cultural explosion in 1960s Britain was *The Avengers*, arguably the best and most influential television series of all time. The creators of the series were not particularly young, and Steed and Mrs. Peel are unquestionably adults, unapologetic members of the British 'Establishment'. Yet in Britain and around the world, when an *Avengers* episode was being broadcast, millions of long-haired, unkempt, rebellious, dope-smoking young folks tuned in and loved every minute. Why? The show, particularly in Season 4, was very, very hip – surrealistically creative stories filmed in fresh and original ways, with interesting and eccentric guest characters, and most importantly, with the two most fascinating main characters in television history.

The Danger Makers is in some ways a very typical Season 4 episode. It has the classic structure: our heroes investigate a series of mysterious deaths, discover a nefarious organisation guided by a diabolical mastermind, bring it to justice, and ride off into the bright horizon. Along the way there is plenty of witty banter, lots of action, and some pleasant scenes of the English countryside. And (not that this matters in any way) the story is, of course, full of holes too numerous to mention, as is every *Avengers* episode in the Peel era. However, there are also some aspects of this episode that are not typical of Season 4, and they contribute to making *The Danger Makers* special.

The basic plot is not typical because it is actually a plausible one, probably the most plausible plot in Season 4. The idea that an unscrupulous psychiatrist – psychiatry doesn't get a very good rap in *The Avengers*; see *The Master Minds* – could manipulate a group of combat veterans addicted to danger (a very real addiction) in to participating in criminal activities – because there is no possibility of danger in their current military duties – is not at all out of the question. [1]

Another atypical aspect of this episode is the lack of *Avengerland* sets. The military base is not deserted, there is traffic on the country lanes, and there are no scenes that take place in empty public spaces. All this helps to make *The Danger Makers* a more reality-based episode than most in Season 4.

The storyline is also untypical in that it could be viewed as a commentary on Britain's declining role on the world stage. This is unusually controversial. The series does take a few gentle jabs here and there at Britain's upper class, politicians and even its space program, but it normally takes a very affectionate and certainly uncontroversial tone towards its homeland. The basis for *The Danger Makers*' storyline is nominally the lack of risk and danger in modern warfare methods. Current wars have become "push button affairs" according to Major Robertson. However, modern warfare methods were not the real problem for these frustrated military men. The real problem was that Britain was now on the sidelines.

The Vietnam War that was raging at the time was certainly no push button affair. *The Danger Makers* seems to be indirectly alluding to this situation, and possibly in a regretful manner.

This brings us to a final atypical aspect of this episode, the character Major Robertson, played by Nigel Davenport. There are many memorable guest characters in Season 4, but for the most part they were memorable in a humorous way: Brodny, Sir Horace Winslip, and Roy Kinnear's tramp character in *The Hour That Never Was* come to mind. Major Robertson is something else entirely. He is, as Mrs. Peel describes him, a "paranoid, schizoid, psychopath". He murders two people and tries to murder Steed. And yet this deluded, demented man is in some ways a sympathetic character. He is, after all, a courageous and gallant soldier in an army that seems to have no need for his courage and gallantry. And he has been psychologically manipulated by the evil psychiatrist. Davenport portrays this tragic character superbly. His is the most nuanced performance given by any guest character in any episode in Season 4. Mrs. Peel is certainly right about the Major but the viewer can't help liking him a little. The scene in which he is tricked by Steed into relinquishing his gun is a great one. Steed understands this man and plays him perfectly when the Major comes to the basement to murder him. Steed's casual attitude towards his own demise, and his pointing out the lack of danger in shooting a handcuffed prisoner, was guaranteed to lead to the duel for the gun. Steed, of course, obtains the gun by cheating, and the Major's response is priceless. The look of outrage on his face says it all about this complex man - Murder is OK, but cheating is going too far! The viewer finds himself almost agreeing with him.

The script, written by Roger Marshall, is excellent. For *The Danger Makers* Marshall came up with, as has been already discussed, a plausible plot and a truly complex character in Major Robertson. Perhaps its greatest strength is the dialogue, some of the best in the entire series. The exchanges between the Major and Mrs. Peel when they discuss their thoughts about living in such a safety-conscious society are first rate. It's more like dialogue one would hear in the legitimate theatre than on a television show. Mrs. Peel is simply baiting the Major into disclosing information about the organisation but her words and his responses are at the same time so passionate and yet not entirely outlandish that the viewers can be excused if they start nodding their heads and saying, 'Yes - we agree!' The "show him your bumps" and chocolate box scenes are also first rate, adding some avengerish lightness to the story.

The direction by Charles Crichton is also excellent. He uses camera angles and crisp editing to very good effect to ratchet up the tension in the many dramatic scenes in *The Danger Makers*. The scene in which Mrs. Peel is undergoing her initiation into the organisation really should not be genuinely tense - the viewer knows perfectly well that the main character is not going to die here - but it is. The quick cutting back and forth between camera shots showing the trial from her point of view and then from the point of view of the spectators leads the viewer to clearly understand the difficulty in concentrating on two things at once and makes the viewers imagine how they would handle it if they were in Mrs. Peel's shoes. It becomes truly terrifying and the viewers join Steed in a collective sigh of relief when she finally completes it. The chicken-run in the teaser scene, the box of chocolates scene, the Major and Mrs. Peel's drive to Manton are all very well filmed and edited. It is remarkable what Crichton and many other *Avengers* directors did on the skimpy budgets they had to work with in Season 4.

The main characters, however, make or break any television series and the Emma Peel era *Avengers* episodes were truly blessed in this area. Mrs. Peel certainly has plenty of 'man appeal'. Diana Rigg was in her absolute physical prime in her Emma Peel days and the form-fitting outfits she wore displayed it for all to see. If one didn't like anything else about the series, Rigg's physical beauty alone could cause one to tune in. Mrs. Peel is obviously much more than that though. She somehow manages to be regal and warm at the same time, and by the way also has a genius level IQ, a great sense of humour, and can kick the stuffing out of just about every person on the planet. She is every man's desire and at the same time what every man hopes his daughters would turn out like. Women love watching this strong independent woman too. Her poise, intelligence, and beauty are never more evident than in her scenes with Major Robertson. It is not difficult to see how he is duped into thinking she shares his views. Mrs. Peel in some ways probably does share them, just not to the fanatical extent of the Major. In the most memorable scene in this episode, her initiation test, her physicality is fully on display. Her encyclopaedic mind becomes evident when she corrects Steed's probably facetious claim that Colonel Adams' ancestor was killed falling off his horse.

And Steed - what makes him so fascinating? Why did all those shaggy-haired pot smokers love him? Despite being the quintessential English gentleman, Steed is fun loving and irreverent and at the same time the master of every situation. The fact that Patrick Macnee's personal charm and good looks are such a perfect fit for the character is very understandable - Macnee basically creates this character himself. Steed's old school Britishness actually worked in his favour. Most of the outwardly rebellious British youth of the 1960s still had strong if hidden patriotic feelings for their country and its traditions, and the rest of the world also had a lot of (possibly misguided) affection for traditional Britain too. The worldwide popularity of *Downton Abbey* demonstrates that this is still true today.

The 'case' in *The Danger Makers* pretty much solves itself, so Steed's sleuthing skills aren't really tested, but his charm and sense of fun are well displayed in the box of chocolates scene, in his interactions with Colonel Adams, and in his using the code name 'Bacchus'. His understanding of the psyche of Major Robertson and the way he uses it to turn the tables on the Major is classic Steed. The coolness, the cleverness, the ruthlessness, are all qualities that define Steed and allow him to win in the end every time.

And, of course, there is that chemistry, the best since Tracey and Hepburn. The Steed/Peel relationship is so affectionate, elegant, and effortless that it was inevitable that the question of whether or not they were lovers would be raised. And raised it definitely was - raised and debated endlessly among fans of the series. The writers and producers of *The Avengers* played their cards brilliantly here, never making it conclusive either way and leaving contradictory clues strewn throughout the episodes.

Some of the earlier Season 4 episodes had echoes of the Steed/Gale conflict-ridden relationship, but that is long gone by the time *The Danger Makers* was produced. By that time this very modern woman and very seemingly old-fashioned man are completely comfortable with each other. Mrs. Peel is so sure of herself that she can accept Steed's courtly (some would say sexist) manner without getting defensive and Steed is also so sure of himself that he can accept Mrs. Peel's superiority in so many areas without getting defensive himself. The look on Mrs. Peel's face when she realizes that Steed was playing a joke on her with the box of chocolates is a good reflection of her bemused affection for Steed. Steed's demeanour when Mrs. Peel is risking her life in the initiation scene reflects very well his respect for Mrs. Peel and her abilities. He looks relieved when she completes it but doesn't really look overly-concerned while it is in progress. He seems to be very confident that she would succeed. Concerning the "are they lovers?" debate, the "show him your bumps" scene begins with a conversation between Steed, who is mixing drinks in Mrs. Peel's living room, and Emma while she is getting dressed in her bedroom. One could wonder why she was getting dressed – we know it isn't morning time. What had they been up to? Who knows? We are in *Avengerland* after all.

Where does *The Danger Makers* fit in the Season 4 hierarchy? Very high, probably just below the three truly iconic episodes, *The Hour That Never Was*, *The Town of No Return*, and *Too Many Christmas Trees*. This episode is not in that very top tier because it lacks the surrealist atmosphere that these three episodes have in abundance. *The Danger Makers*' well directed, subversively controversial story makes it a very good episode. What makes it a unique one is that it addresses in a thoughtful way (thanks to Nigel Davenport's portrayal of Major Robertson) a very universal dilemma: 'what should a nation do with its warrior caste during peacetime?'

© Dan O'Shea

1. The idea is effectively reworked in *The New Avengers* episode *Dirtier by the Dozen*.

A TOUCH OF BRIMSTONE

Filmed: 12th – 24th December 1965

Exterior Locations:
London theatre (stock footage)
Country road

Sets:
Courtyard
Theatre
Car
Darcy's study
Steed's apartment
Cartney's bedroom
London club
Hellfire Hall: courtyard, banqueting hall, catacombs, circle of justice
Coach and horses

A TOUCH OF BRIMSTONE

Main Character List:
Boris Kartovski: peacemaker
The Honourable John Cleverly Cartney: Hellfire Club member
Emma Peel
John Steed
Lord Darcy: Hellfire Club member
Horace: Darcy's butler, Hellfire Club member
Sara Bradley: lover of Cartney
Willy Frant/Lord Cartigan: Hellfire Club member
Tubby Bun/Lord Ragslan: Hellfire Club member
Roger Winthrop/Lord Lacon: Hellfire Club member

There are few episodes of *The Avengers* more famous than this, and there are few scenes more contentious than the Queen of Sin one. For this reason, this episode has long been considered a 'fan favourite' but has recently come under some reappraisal. This is strange because notoriety should not devalue an episode; prudishness over a costume and a few minutes of footage should not devalue the whole. There is much to be enjoyed here.

From the outset, James Hill makes this a *tour de force* of his directorial skill, as does Alan Hume of his cinematography. *A Touch of Brimstone* bursts onto our screens with a dramatically-lit shot of an armchair apparently moving of its own volition towards us. The agent of this, the as-yet unnamed Cartney, comes into shot, a devilish smirk on his face as he pedantically arranges chocolates on the arm of the chair to sample as he watches a mundane diplomatic announcement on the television. The reason for his mirth is quickly revealed as the Eastern Bloc politician is humiliated by a joke cigar and storms out. Cue opening titles.

When we return, Steed and Mrs. Peel are at the Opera and Steed explains they're there to see that a visiting sheik is not inconvenienced by another practical joke. Our heroes are in sparkling form and the scene shows the extraordinary chemistry between Rigg and Macnee. Unbeknown to them, Cartney is in the audience behind them, waiting malevolently. Comic relief is provided by the audience bobbing up and down like novice Catholics, unsure when the sheik's anthem finishes. All are astonished when the sheik's chair collapses beneath him and he storms out, an oil treaty now in jeopardy. Steed tells Mrs. Peel the chief suspect is our smirking villain, John Cleverly Cartney and she goes to visit him, purporting to be collecting for a charity.

Emma: I've come here to appeal to you, Mr. Cartney.

Cartney: You certainly do that!

Considerable restraint is shown in the production of this episode. Peter Wyngarde is cast as John Cleverly Cartney and he doesn't speak in that rich, theatrical voice until Mrs. Peel visits him some five minutes into the show. While Cartney writes her a cheque for 1,000 guineas – an inordinate sum, the implication being that Cartney is trying to buy Mrs. Peel's favours as well – she surreptitiously checks his diary. Cartney twice asks Mrs. Peel to dine with him; she declines, but takes his cheque. He tries one last attempt, suggesting a trip to the George V in Paris, but she declines that too. Her interview is interrupted by the arrival of a young foolish toff whom Cartney introduces as Lord Darcy, explaining they have dreary business about the estate to discuss.

Here Brian Clemens revels in stereotype, so marked a feature of his *Avengers* scripts. It is the foundation of *Avengerland*: Cartney is the handsome, fiendish lord manipulating events from behind the scenes; Lord Darcy plays the idiot aristocrat; Willy Frant, when he appears a moment later, is the sadistic country squire.

Darcy's manservant is vacuuming when Steed appears at the window and breaks in. Steed casually pours himself a drink and starts to rifle through the desk. Would any agent ever do that? Of course not, that's what makes this *The Avengers*. Finding little of interest, he turns to the wardrobe and discovers a Rococo costume and some rubber scissors. Horace, the manservant, discovers Steed at this point and Steed beats a hasty retreat.

Our heroes compare notes and realise the next target is the opening of the Hall of Friendship that afternoon. They rush off, belting through the countryside in Steed's Bentley with Emma watching the in-car television; again, only in *The Avengers*! Gadgets in the dashboard of both Steed's and Emma's cars are a frequent device, including radios, the television here, telephones, and an altimeter. They are subverting the genre wherein more prosaic devices such as Bond's radar screen behind the tachometer in his Aston Martin were already stretching credulity. Clemens writes a delicious piece of pompous drivel for the announcer on the television, which is an aside to the action. They both watch in horror when the ambassador is electrocuted by the charged ribbon. "Well, it's no joke anymore", Steed observes with the wry *sang froid* of the professional. (The scene is slightly marred by the backdrop remaining unchanged as the camera tracks in when he speaks. Backdrop projection and green-screen techniques of the time were fairly rudimentary, certainly by modern standards; many colour episodes of the time receive a green cast from the projected action, and they are often too pale, which is noticeable in the black and white episodes.)

A dejected Darcy returns home having wandered disconsolately in the rain, appalled at the dignitary's death. Horace removes his wet coat and prepares some cocoa while Darcy rings Cartney, who refuses to discuss the matter. Here the crew really work together with great lighting and cinematography and Hill's extraordinary direction, turning what could have been a mundane scene of Cartney languidly resting with Sara on a divan into a pivotal scene. Starting with a wide top-down shot, directly above the actors, we zoom down on them then cut to a close-up of their entwined feet; a slow tracking shot, reflective of their languid poses, around them to the left so that the phone that has just started ringing comes into shot. The camera then zooms and tracks right to tighten on them as he answers the phone. Later, when Cartney dismisses Sara with his boot, he is shot dramatically from below, from Sara's point of view.

Darcy barks at Horace that he's going to his club. Horace offers to get his costume ready and Darcy retorts, "Not *that* club! My club in town!" There he meets Steed, who inveigles himself with Darcy, sensing the chink in Cartney's armour. They repair to Steed's flat where Darcy divulges his part in the plot – Willy changed the scissors, Darcy just got him inside – explaining that everyone in the club has to take part in a prank. Emboldened by Steed's support, Darcy says he knows now what he has to do and when Steed returns from preparing a hangover cure, Darcy is gone.

Mrs. Peel, meanwhile, has returned to Cartney's house and, much to Sara's annoyance, is invited to stay and see Cartney's recreation of the Hellfire Club. She's less than amused by the entertainment on offer, or by Cartney's misogynistic and elitist opinions:

Cartney: I try to recreate exactly the days of the original Hellfire Club...the same atmosphere and excitement and of course the same pleasures...a man controlled his destiny by the strength of his arm and the skill of his pen. And the divine right of his birth.
Emma: And women?
Cartney: Mmm. Mere vessels of pleasure.
Emma: I see.
Cartney: Do I detect a note of disapproval?

Women's rights are a frequent subtext of *The Avengers*, with Emma Peel and Cathy Gale embodying the thoroughly emancipated female of popular culture. It is this, perhaps, that sets *The Avengers* apart from other British television of its day most of all, especially in the action genre where Simon Templar and John Drake [1] are the debonair yet tough action heroes. Until the 1970s, only *The Champions* has a notable female lead to match those of *The Avengers*, and even there Sharron Macready frequently takes a back seat to the 'boys'. Those few strong female characters there were tend to be in science-fiction, where the apparently *outré* concept of a female lead is acceptable – the distant future is weird.

Darcy bursts in and demands a special meeting when Cartney tries to silence him; Darcy is angry now, rather than depressed, and is itching for a fight. Cartney concedes and a special meeting of the superior members is called. They assemble in the cellar, cloaked, masked and hooded like medieval acolytes. The symbolism here is obvious, with the hint of Satanic worship (another charge laid at the original Hellfire clubs). When Darcy is dispatched to the black abyss beneath the cellar in another dramatic top-down angle, the imagery is complete.

We next see Steed and Peel paying their respects to Darcy, lying in state in Cartney's house; Emma is sure the superior members murdered him and tells Steed briefly about the club. When Cartney appears, Steed claims Darcy was about to introduce him to the club and, with Emma's support, Cartney agrees he can present himself that evening for initiation. Steed is first put to the test of drinking a huge mug of ale, filled to the brim. He finishes it and makes the assembled members shout with laughter when he asks for more. "Do you mind? The drive down seems to have given me quite a thirst". Cartney is suspicious, however, and demands he undertake the "ultimate test": getting a dried pea off the block before Roger's axe can split it in two. Willy tried once for a bet and lost two fingers. Naturally, Steed wins by cheating, blowing the pea away rather than trying to grab it. Steed always cheats, it's part of his character. [2] He is granted membership, much to Cartney's chagrin, and invited to attend the Night of All Sins the following evening. Steed departs as the villains discuss their plot – the destabilisation of the government, culminating in a *coup* the next evening - but Cartney silences them when he hears a sound at the door. He creeps near it but then there is a knock – Steed, returning Cartney's snuff box.

He's all charm but Cartney is sure he was spying at the door (which, of course, he was).

Steed and Mrs. Peel prepare to attend the meeting together, arrayed in finest Rococo splendour. They find the party in full swing, with buxom wenches and free flowing ale. Steed goes to quiz the disenchanted Sara while Emma follows a suspicious sedan chair and evades Roger's advances. The plot enters another realm altogether. Historical figures Sir Francis Dashwood and Guy Fawkes are merged as we see the TNT inside the boxes. Emma rushes back and tells Steed there are enough explosives in the catacombs to sink a battleship. Cartney finds them; he murmurs that he had something different in mind for Mrs. Peel and two of the maidens whisk her away to change her wardrobe. Steed meanwhile presses his advantage with Sara, who is now both drunk and disenchanted, and reveals more than she ought. She confides that the Hellfire Club is "an exact replica of the original, in more ways than one" and when pressed explains that the original was politically powerful and for a time ran the country. "'Topple the government and then take over', that's what John says."

She reveals that the catacombs lead to Culverstone House, where the Cabinet is meeting that night. "Not for long... one big bang and they'll all be gone." Cartney returns and announces a drugged and provocatively clothed Mrs. Peel as their entertainment for the night, the Queen of Sin. Mrs. Peel is clad in black undergarments and fetish boots and collar; she has a chain from the collar to her wrist and is holding a writhing python in her hands. "She is yours. To do with what you will." This phrase is carefully chosen by Brian Clemens as it reflects the motto of Dashwood's club, *vide supra*.

At those words, Emma is swept off her feet and carried around the room by the men as she is showered with flower petals. This is the bone of contention for the episode – some fans find it annoying that the episode veers wildly into the overtly sexual, dispensing for once with the English restraint and flirtation. However, this is the 1960s and in truth the scenes are not that bawdy. Apart from the implication of drug use in her vapid stare and soft compliance, and the hint at sexual activity using the flower petal metaphor, there is little here; the Hellfire Clubs were known for their love of the erotic.

Diana Rigg, it is true, is dressed in fetish gear: the spiked leather collar and chain, the black corset, the tiny black underwear and the thigh-high lace-up patent leather ballet boots. Her hair has been pulled back into a bun and she has been made up with heavy, dramatic eye-shadow and mascara and a glass bindi on her forehead with two smaller ones on her eyelids. It has been widely reported that Diana Rigg designed the costume herself but I suspect this means she suggested the collar or some other detail, or helped choose items with the wardrobe mistress. Despite the *outré* nature of the costume, there is some modesty – the corset is not overly revealing, a sheer skirt on the hem of the corset disguises her underwear to a small extent, and the camera, except for the initial tilt up and long shots, is firmly fixed on her face and upper torso. There is none of the lurid voyeurism of Benny Hill.

There is one shot of the episode that doesn't quite work as intended. After the men carry Emma through the door, James Hill cuts to a large python writhing around the pillar of a grand fireplace. It's dramatic and symbolic, certainly, but so decontextualised that it always jars. Hill is clearly fond of the device as he cuts back to it several times as the action continues elsewhere. It's a phallic cliché, a sexual metaphor for the ardour of the men who have carried off Mrs. Peel and presumably suggests that they are indeed doing with her as they will. Is this, then, the issue to which people object? It is certainly a perverse turn of events, but not as foul as Hubert and Mickle's leering "I tell you what I got in mind" in *Murdersville* (another Brian Clemens script).

The plot has been accused of being weak and unlikely. It is certainly highly improbable but so are nearly all *Avengers* plots, that's the whole point. A department store as a massive nuclear bomb; the invasion of Britain, one village at a time; robotic killers instead of workers in factories – all of these are pointed to as highlights and yet are more outrageous than this plot.

The Club repair to their gymnasium to watch another bare knuckle fight, with Horace as one of the combatants. Midway through the fight he happens upon Steed and recognises him. Steed, unmasked as a spy, is ordered to duel Willy. He suggests feather dusters at four hundred yards but swords are the only weapons offered. Steed duels Willy, starting by throwing his coat over him and then gains the upper hand by butting him with his head and then kicking him out the door of the gym, which Steed locks behind him, trapping the club members. They fence their way through the house, Steed trying every trick in his repertoire. He disarms Willy, only to discover that Willy's prosthetic fingers have hooked blades inside, with which Willy now tries to slash him. Steed tears off the whole prosthetic and they recommence their fencing, Steed eventually knocking Willy out with a blow from his fist. Steed rarely tries to kill his enemies and prefers to render them insensible.

Emma descends to the cellars, pursued by Cartney (and watched by that writhing python). In the catacombs, she easily defeats the huge man unloading the explosives. The little man who fought him earlier appears, and she dispatches him after a balletic battle. She is unprepared, however, for Cartney who enters the room, bearing a whip and considerable malice.

Cartney: Very impressive. Now what are you like with the big boys?

Once again, the lighting and direction are superb, the catacombs brimming with unspoken malice and horrors, which is a great achievement for a studio set. In fact, Harry Pottle's art direction throughout the episode is superb – his sets are so good that you are easily led to believe it was all shot on location. The only standing set used is Steed's flat (a Pottle design); all the other sets are specially constructed: Darcy's flat, his club in town, the catacombs, gym, and other rooms of Cartney's house. It's true that these sets are constructed using scenery we see in many other episodes, but it's their use and combination here that sets them apart – the whole truly is greater than the parts. It's no wonder Pottle was snapped up to design sets for *James Bond*.

The soundscape of the episode is also notable. Laurie Johnson's score, specially written for the most part, is evocative of swashbuckling romances: harpsichord solos, orchestral and chamber pieces, drums rolling like thunder. The regular stings and themes that Johnson used for other episodes are there, often adapted to add a touch of harpsichord (much as he did for *Escape in Time* two years later). The action sequences have dramatic feature-film scores driving the action along. Mrs. Peel's parade by the members is accompanied by a joyous pastoral; the catacomb scenes and Steed's trial are accompanied by the ominously rolling drums. The raucous noise of the Hellfire Club bursts upon you every time, and the sudden silences after the scenes serve to accentuate the separation of normal life from the club. The sound editor often follows a loud action or wenching sequence with absolute silence to further dramatise the contrast. Mrs. Peel's fight with Cartney is the most dramatic of all, with the harsh cracking of the whip driven by Johnson's suspense sting and ever rolling drums.

Cartney lashes her several times – a scene supposedly edited for television executives who thought twelve lashes of a whip too much – as she tries to evade him around the vault. Diana Rigg is excellent here, effortlessly slipping from triumphant and proud to scared and desperate. By chance, his whip curls around the lever for the trapdoor and he is sent hurtling into the black abyss normally reserved for his victims. Justice is done and the villain is hoist on his own petard. Their task complete, Steed and Mrs. Peel depart, driving a coach and four down a familiar country lane, heading for a brighter horizon.

© Piers Johnson

1. *The Saint* and *Danger Man*.
2. Steed often plays 'dirty', it's true, but isn't this simply him using his initiative?! I also read Cartney's reaction here as jealousy as much as suspicion. Steed's ability in the drinking challenge, followed by showing off, is threatening to steal Cartney's thunder as the Hellfire number one.

Her desire to explore her own masochism diminished any fears of perverted damnation.
A brief allegiance with Hellfire's 60's Shades of Darkness
Offered the tempting pleasures of a bitter-sweet erotic fantasy

In May 1721 the Government Bill to 'Prevent Blasphemy and Profaneness' was designed to suppress a scandalous and immoral secret society of 'honourable' aristocratic Devil-worshippers who supposedly supped with Satan, Venus and Dionysus and who worshipped mythological Gods and Goddesses in ritual orgies of bizarre, erotic and profane perversions. The principal target of the King's/Government's legislation was the notorious Hellfire Club. 245 years later, in 1966, the Government, Steed and Emma Peel would be the principal targets of the notorious Hellfire Club.

"This is absolutely the most overtly erotic episode ever: with the most intense Emma-watching imaginable." (David K Smith, *The Avengers Forever!* - theavengers.tv/forever website)

"Fantastically wicked John Cartney delivers a debauched performance, culminating in Mrs. Peel being forcibly garbed as the Queen of Sin. Cracking plot delivered at a whip-snap pace... great sets and music... it doesn't get better than this." (Piers Johnson, *Mrs. Peel – We're Needed*: dissolute.com.au website)

"Rigg's striking physicality...the intentional titillation...the sensational whipping-scene...resulted in editorial censorship by the ITA." (Kathleen Tracy: *Diana Rigg: The Biography* – 2004)

PROLOGUE: This was extraordinarily audacious television for 1966. The most infamous, erotic and most-watched episode in *Avengers* history (8.4 million) has Mrs. Peel garbed in her kinkiest outfit ever: a sensational Diana Rigg personally designed dominatrix/submissive /SM fetish costume. *A Touch of Brimstone* has the most suavely smooth, sophisticated villain, brilliantly played by Peter Wyngarde;

an intriguing historical storyline, a compelling re-interpretation of the Hellfire Club/Gunpowder Plot with more than a dash of Hellfire's famous lust, debauchery and wanton-licentiousness; and a stunning triple-climax with Diana Rigg and Patrick Macnee at their very best. Brian Clemens' script is an ingeniously plotted, costume suspense-thriller, and *A Study in Terror* acclaimed director James Hill's stylish direction includes some splendid Hitchcockian moments: the charming villain, the 'impossible' pea-problem and the specifically targeted, spectacularly erotic heroine, Mrs. Peel, scantily-clad and in deadly jeopardy.

On 18th February 1966 *A Touch of Brimstone*, my favourite *Avengers* episode, was premiered by ITV/ABC Television. *The Evening Standard* sensationally headlined *A Touch of Brimstone*: 'What You Won't See on *The Avengers* Tonight' with a titillating article and risqué publicity-still of…"Miss Rigg semi-naked as the 'Queen of Sin'…stroking her leather-whip!" It was banned in the US and although the episode was transmitted in the UK the infamous whipping-scene was censored to just two whiplashes: 38 seconds were cut. In the uncut-version, Emma is whipped twelve times. Brian Clemens reflects, "When Peter menaces Di, we had to reduce the number of whip-cracks" and reminisces that *ABC-TV America* executives organised private viewings of the uncut version. The first uncut screening of *A Touch of Brimstone* was broadcast by *Channel 4* in spring 1985.

OPENING GAMBIT, AGE OF ELEGANCE: A series of apparently innocent trickster-jokes are, nevertheless, totally humiliating foreign dignitaries and endangering sensitive foreign relations. At their Queen's Theatre *rendez vous*, Steed informs Emma that an Honourable gentleman may be master-minding the mystifying, embarrassing events. Steed visits Lord Darcy while Emma investigates the Honourable gentleman whom she finds handsome, dynamic, very compelling and quite fascinating. Cartney, a cultured connoisseur of the arts, power-politics and attractive women, is highly stimulated by Mrs. Peel:

Emma: I've come here to appeal to you, Mr. Cartney.
Cartney: You certainly do that!

The Honourable John Cleverly Cartney is suave and arrogant, imperious and handsome, evil and charismatic, hedonistic and sadistic; a gentleman libertine and a diabolical mastermind. Mrs. Peel immediately receives an invitation to dinner at the George V Hotel in Paris and a donation of 1,000 guineas towards a home for 'wayward girls'. Laurie Johnson's elegant music-score harmonising the eloquent dialogue exchanges between Rigg and Wyngarde is spellbinding. When one of the trickster-jokes becomes shocking murder, Lord Darcy becomes hysterical; Steed calms him and gleans information.

Later, Cartney invites Emma to his "slightly unusual club" where she witnesses an '18th-century orgy'. Clemens' script evokes an extraordinary atmosphere of erotic suspense. He crafts a fabulous psychological and physical duel of wits, sexuality and power between Cartney and Mrs. Peel. Yet, Cartney is so sadistically dominant – riding-boot upon the shapely, scantily-clad, bosomy Sara – how can Emma possibly beat him?

Emma is introduced to champion swordsman-duellist Willy Frant/Lord Cartigan, Tubby Bun/Lord Ragslan and Roger Winthrop/Lord Lacon. Roger asks if Emma is "a new wench for our pleasure". Emma looks uncomfortable at being the focus of such bawdy exuberance. Cartney suggests to Mrs. Peel that women are "mere vessels of pleasure"; he has a penchant for beautiful, physical women.

HELLFIRE CLUB: "THAT FIRE, THAT HADES, THAT REALM OF PLUTO: GENTLEMEN! HELLFIRE!" Mrs. Peel appears particularly unsettled and uneasy in this episode; her enigmatic *joie-de-vivre* has vanished, perhaps a fearful foreboding of an especially dangerous assignment. It's as if she knows something evil is in store for her. Clemens' scripting is superb: he hypothesises the seduction of Mrs. Peel by ungodly wickedness. Viewers become similarly concerned for Emma, yet perhaps, secretly, also want our heroine to suffer. [1]

[The avenging heroine/hero] "should suffer something in return" said Ian Fleming in *Everything Or Nothing*, a James Bond documentary film. Cartney wants to seduce and inflame Emma to enter his web of sin, to spellbind her, to bewitch and induce Emma into submission, until she is lasciviously exhibited and suffers the kiss of his whip. Upon initiation examinations – drinking a huge goblet of ale; the ultimate-test of a speed-reaction pea-challenge, (with an ingenious solution) – Steed joins, whilst Emma uses her feminine wiles to infiltrate the notorious Hellfire Club.

Cartney's Hellfire Club is a pseudo-religious contemporary evocation of the *risqué* devil-worshipping rituals, bizarre black magic masses, satanic observances, wenching and banqueting of the real infamous Hellfire Club, or Knights of St. Francis of Wycombe, or the Masked-Monks/Friars of Medmenham Abbey whose motto was: 'Do What You Will'. The Hellfire Club was originally founded for elite noble and ignoble high-society by Philip, Duke of Wharton and the Honourable Sir Francis Dashwood circa-1719-1751. The President of Hellfire was the Devil himself. Clemens cleverly bases Cartney upon real-life 'trickster' Sir Francis Dashwood. The historically-based conspiracy plot symbolises Dashwood's diabolical Hellfire philosophy, as Emma, wearing an elegant, cleavage-exposing, green Regency gown, discovers, on her first reconnoitre of the catacombs.

NIGHT OF ALL SINS! HELLFIRE ORGY: GEORGIAN REGENCY: DEBAUCHERY AND DÉCOLLETAGE. Cartney plans an explosive coup, for there is an underground tunnel leading directly to Culverstone House and damning evidence of boxes of TNT high-explosives in the Hellfire catacombs. The Cabinet are meeting at Culverstone House that very night. Cartney admires Emma's Regency attire, but it's not quite right for what he has in mind for her. She is mysteriously smuggled away by two of Cartney's Ladies-in-Waiting. Emma disappears somewhere into the catacombs.

What happened next in the unseen-scene of sub-text is necessarily pure conjecture. Nevertheless, how is Mrs. Peel 'persuaded' to be transformed from her demure under-cover character in Regency dress, to become, and exemplify, the outrageously kinky and erotic dominatrix/submissive character of the Queen of Sin? Perhaps she was discreetly injected with an LSD-based hallucinogenic-aphrodisiac, dragged and driven through a hidden-tunnel, thrust into a secret-chamber, forcibly stripped, costumed, made-up and perfumed to the sinful specifications of Cartney. Characteristically, Cartney may have exploited and emphasised her costume-designed, enforced semi-nakedness, by cruelly caressing Mrs Peel's bare bottom-cheeks with his silver-topped cane, before cloaking her. Emma's reaction to her strict fetish costume? A hypothetical Mrs. Peel answer: "Beguiling, revealing, empowering and very, very kinky!"

Later, Cartney re-appears, cane in hand, to make an outrageous, 'Shakespearian' proclamation:

"Midnight approaches, the witching-hour, and as a sign of that hour, as a symbol of all that is evil, as the epitomy and purveyor of this Night of Sins, I give you the Queen of Sin...Mrs. Peel!"

QUEEN OF SIN: EXHIBITED! A black-cloaked Mrs. Peel is conducted by two women into Hellfire Hall. A roasting atmosphere of blistering sulphur, breathtaking suspense and lustful-wanting pervades the room. In front of an expectant audience, Cartney theatrically strips the cloak away, revealing the full, exquisitely kinky costume. He exhibits Mrs. Peel's highly eroticised, voluptuous, majestic figure and smouldering persona, upon the Hellfire 'stage' for the lascivious gratification of the spellbound members. Mrs. Peel has been erotically and wickedly garbed in a very tight, cleavage-exposing, black whalebone corset, tautly cross-laced at the back, covered with black decorative lace, descending to a translucent lace micro-skirt, only half- covering very tight, high-cut, black silk bikini-briefs. The black lace micro-skirt is only three inches in length and barely reaches the tops of her naked thighs. Her briefs exposure means that Emma is displaying much more cheek than usual! Further, she is wearing a spiked, thick leather choker-collar with silver chain-leash looped over her left gloved wrist. She is embellished in long, elegant, black elbow-gloves, an amethyst-jewelled bindi on her forehead, mauve eye-liner/eye-shadow, with tiny gems on eyelids, and knee-length, stiletto-high-heeled, black leather boots tightly laced up the back of her calves.

Director James Hill and photographer Alan Hume use an inspired, tight, close-up shot of high-heeled leather boots, then a slow, vertical camera panning-shot up her kinky boots, naked legs, thighs, tight briefs, over the tightly laced, breathtakingly cinched corset, thrusting cleavage, up to the spiked-collar, tight around her throat, and ultimately an extreme close-up of Mrs. Peel's smouldering eyes. Her 'special-look' is an incredible blazing fusion and embodiment of a statuesque submissive bondage-wench *and* an imperious Dominatrix: an Amazon-Queen. Rigg's performance and striking physique are simply magnificent. Macnee's Steed is perfectly mesmerised by the breathtaking vision before him. The scene is beautifully photographed by Hume, a sublimely focused illumination of Mrs. Peel's enchanting pose. The classical full-length Emma Peel 'Queen of Sin' pose was ingeniously 'photograph-still' captured and compiled using six separate screen-shots by David K Smith of *The Avengers Forever!* website.

Cartney offers Mrs. Peel to the Hellfire Club: "'She is yours...to do with...what you will...'"

The eroticised, semi-naked Emma is hoisted high, stretched-out, full-length, in near horizontal pose, displayed, showered in rose-petals and paraded around Hellfire Hall. In a teasing publicity-still Rigg poses in her rigorously kinky attire, with her director upon *her* leash! Cartney has transformed Mrs. Peel into his 'Goddess of Lust', 'Queen of Hellfire'! He wants absolute power over her, and her government. Cartney is obsessed *vis-à-vis* the power challenge the liberated Mrs. Peel represents. He wants her dishonour, obedience and surrender, which is why she has been so strictly uniformed in such provocative attire. Emma may see her role as the Dominatrix-Royale, but Cartney has also cleverly garbed her as the collared and leashed submissive. He wants to discipline her, enslave her, and possess her as Hellfire's own masochistic Queen of Sin.

Steed and Emma are exposed as spies. Steed is forced into a thrilling, frenziedly fast, duel-to-the-death sword-fight against champion swordsman, Willy (double-barrelled finger-blades) Frant. Upon her second reconnoitre of the catacombs, Mrs. Peel, wearing considerably less (Queen of Sin attire) than on her first exploration, descends into the atmospheric torch-lit Hellfire tunnels and chambers, a finely-crafted set-design by distinguished art director, Harry Pottle.

A QUEEN CAPTURED: ORDEAL BY WHIP. Mrs. Peel high-kicks Hellfire's Huge-Man fighter into oblivion, before being confronted by kickboxing tormentor, the diminutive, ballet-dancing Pierre. He arrogantly demonstrates his quicksilver, gymnastic *entrechat* jumps to an astonished Emma. Pierre neatly side-steps her high-kicking boot with effortless ease. He seems confident of tormenting her too. But Emma spectacularly accelerates her pounding martial-arts high-kicks and knife-hand karate-strikes. Pierre is overwhelmed by her furious, driving counter-attack, gets backed into a pillar, and receives a thumping high-kick, two pumping knee-strikes and three scything karate-chops. Pierre disintegrates. Emma poses, Cartney claps, whip in hand. He has trapped Emma, his prey. Upon the Hellfire Power-Octagon magic-witchcraft floor design, Cartney's gambit has captured a Queen, a Queen dressed for a whipping. Rigg's acting is extraordinary as she merges multiple passions of shocked dismay, absolute terror and concentrated steadfastness as she is lured, virtually hypnotised by the long snaking whip of the Honourable John Cleverly Cartney.

"Very impressive... now what are you like with the big boys?"

The snaking coils of Cartney's whip blaze forth, vicious stinging lashes repeatedly find their target. Rigg's Mrs. Peel exhibits a fantastic balletic and athletic virtuosity of pirouettes and pivots, feints and side-steps. Nevertheless, in a forty-three second whipping frenzy, she receives twelve ferocious whiplashes from the snarling, sadistic, lusting Cartney. Lash thirteen delivers the *coup de grâce*. Director James Hill's intelligent mixing of Ray Austin's dynamic fight choreography, Hume's incisive photography and Richard Best's superb, fast, jump-cut editing of the Pierre and Cartney fights – fabulous panoramic, medium and tight-in close-up shots, multiple flashing images, of Emma's stunning reactions, of her cleavage, thighs and bottom-cheeks – make for a most memorable finale.

END GAME: TRIPLE CHECKMATE. The dramatic effect of three thundering consecutive climax scenes – Steed's phenomenal swordfight, Emma's joyous ballet-karate fight with the dancing Pierre, culminating in the whip-lashing showdown with Cartney and Mrs. Peel's Queen of Sin balletic *tour-de-force* of magnificent *allegro-vivace* erotic athleticism – creates a staggering masterpiece, a truly extraordinary powerhouse end-game.

I believe that Clemens' outstanding storyline, Rigg's enchanting, fabulously sexy Queen of Sin and the thrilling triple-climax, directed, photographed, edited and choreographed with elegance and grace, *finesse* and *élan*, combine to make *A Touch of Brimstone* not only the most infamous and most watched, but also the finest episode in *Avengers* history.

© James Speirs

1. James Speirs' comments here (and, indeed, his entire essay) raise interesting and disturbing questions about the 'viewer'. Do 'we' enjoy seeing Mrs. Peel suffer? Some clearly do. Does the recurring, almost formulaic *Avengers* scene of her tied-up or captured contain a sexual element? Almost certainly, yes. Does our pleasure at watching the scenes make us part of the diabolical plot, as guilty as Cartney and the other masterminds throughout the season? If there is an element of sexual arousal from the male viewer, do heterosexual female viewers have a different approach to these scenes? Can we even generalise about the male/female viewer?

WHAT THE BUTLER SAW

Filmed: 26th December 1965 – 7th January 1966

Exterior Locations:
Lakeside
Grounds of country house
Deserted country lanes

Sets:
Butlers & Gentleman's Gentlemen Association: smoking room, training centre
Vice-Admiral Willows' house
Brigadier Ponsonby-Goddard's residence: living room,
Group Captain Miles' house: hall, conservatory, living room
Emma Peel's car
Three Services bar

WHAT THE BUTLER SAW

Main Character List:
Walters: valet
Sergeant Moran: barman, dishwasher, mastermind
Benson: butler
Barber: informer
Vice-Admiral Willows: naval commander
Reeves: brigadier's butler
Major-General Ponsonby-Goddard: ex-army, brigadier's father
Brigadier Percy Ponsonby-Goddard: army officer
Squadron Leader Hogg: RAF
Hemming: butler, trainer of butlers
Group Captain George Miles: RAF

The teaser of *What the Butler Saw* offers a perfect example of the playfulness in *The Avengers* at this point in the show's evolution. We arrive mid-speech as a valet (Walters) explains to his master that with his job becoming "more dangerous" by the day he merits a pay rise. He appears nervous, as if he has shocked himself by speaking out, reminiscent of Oliver Twist asking for 'more'. The master – sat in an armchair – remains unseen by us, save for a distinctive ring on the little finger of his right hand. He rings a bell, at which point his butler (Benson) arrives. The light-hearted music is at odds with the action which follows, as the master takes a silencer from the proffered silver tray and kills the valet. This inexplicable act is sandwiched by the butler clichés of "You rang, sir" and "Will that be all, sir?" Once again we have an uneasy mix of the mundane and the menacing, the routinely real and the strangely surreal. How can a valet's job be "dangerous"? Why is the obsequious butler not shocked by the sudden, cold-blooded murder? Who is the unseen murderer? There is a theatrical, almost Ortonesque [1] black humour at play.

This sense of incomprehensible, conflicting events continues into the post-teaser scenes. First, the dead valet is thrown overboard from a rowing boat by the same, unseen man. If he is a master, why is he performing this task himself? We are then shown a barber's shop. With another client – covered by a towel – present, Steed begins two intertwined conversations with the (double agent) barber: a dramatically loud, public one in which the weather is discussed; a private, whispered one in which the selling of defence secrets is mentioned. The scene is at once ridiculous yet also strangely dramatic, as we see the distinctive ring for a third time, the barber silenced by a stabbing blade and having a shaving brush pushed into his mouth like a cork. We are only four minutes in but already we have two bizarrely executed murders.

The barber's suggestion that there are three possible suspects selling state secrets warns us to expect a typical *Avengers* episode in terms of formulaic structure. Initially, this proves to be the case as Steed visits all three, in three different disguises. Vice-Admiral Willows' home is straight out of an *Avengerland* fantasy, his waterside house resembling a boat, down to the finer details such as a ship's steering wheel, gas lamps and portholes in the front door. Steed – as the bearded Commander Red – gets into the spirit, arriving by boat, accompanied by suitably nautical music and announcing his arrival with an "Ahoy there!" Despite the presence of Benson, as soon as we encounter Willows we know that he is not the villain, even before he laments the disappearance of his usual manservant, Walters. There is a clichéd, heavy irony as he describes him as going AWOL: "jumped ship, fell overboard." Interestingly, this was where the dumping of Walters' body was originally planned to be shown. One is left to wonder why it was brought forward; presumably to allow the irony to be apparent as the words are spoken.

As the anticipated triptych structure of the early plot reveals itself, Steed arrives at Brigadier Ponsonby-Goddard's house in a tank, the music still light-hearted but now recognisably military. Brian Clemens' script describes Steed's undercover character (Major White) as that of a caricature: "stiff upper lip, clipped speech and manner – rigid, 'proper' posture." As Steed waits to see Goddard, the scene becomes surreal, then absurd. First, his eyes are drawn to a life-size replica horse, with what appears to be a pale-faced male mannequin sat on it in an old-fashioned uniform. Having affectionately patted the horse, Steed is then astonished – as we are – to see that the figure is real. In true *Avengers* style, Steed is then encouraged by the Major-General to play some war games with him, the fireside representing the West Ridge.

Brigadier: Father, I've told you before about playing around in here.
Major-General: Playing! *Playing?*
Brigadier: Manoeuvres then. Kindly confine your activities to the garden. And don't blow up the roses again! All right then – off you go!

In this strangely eccentric *Avengerland* world, nothing is quite what it should be: butlers delivering silencers on silver trays, barbers acting as double agents, retired military men behaving like little boys. When the Major-General tells Steed that his son is a "traitor" we are left to wonder if there is any method in the madness; are they the ramblings of a senile old man? Is the Brigadier's early morning drinking the sign of nerves, or guilt? There are puzzling signs being playfully placed everywhere, daring us to interpret them. As Steed departs, he overhears another butler acting strangely, organising a nighttime *rendez-vous*. If Steed is baffled, then so are we; the opening ten minutes have been so odd that we doubt our ability to read between the lines.

The third and final part of the triptych opening almost inevitably sees Steed arrive at Group Captain Miles' residence in a helicopter. His undercover name is, of course, 'colourful' again: Squadron Leader Blue, taking the running joke into the genre of farce, in keeping with his giant moustache and the RAF marching music. Once again the house is decorated with themed props or toys, although this time Steed's over-the-top disguise is matched – quite literally – by the equally fruity-voiced, moustached Squadron Leader Hogg. The subsequent acronym-ridden conversation sees the slapstick reach an absurd crescendo, although the cycle has now been broken in that the randy Group Captain is absent.

The amusing sight of Steed hiding among the rose bushes while eavesdropping in the conservatory stylishly and seamlessly leads to the following scene in which it is a relief to find Emma Peel finally making her entrance, adding a more subtle touch to an episode which – it is already abundantly clear – will be 'played for laughs'.

Steed: Mrs. Peel, if a man's susceptibilities are to be strained to nerve-jangling breaking-point, if he's to be pushed to the very point of betraying Queen and Country, then who better than you to…
Emma: Vital you said?
Steed: It would not be exaggerating to say that the fate of…
Emma: The entire nation was in the balance?
Steed: That's just about it. Defence secrets are being sold to the…
Emma: Other side?
Steed: And it must be one of three people…an Admiral who gambles too much…a Brigadier who drinks too much…and a Group Captain who…A Group Captain.

The crisp dialogue offers us a knowing wink at the series' formulaic approach, while also demonstrating Mrs. Peel's weary or cynical attitude. The plot revels in the potential for red herrings, as well as its butcher/baker/candlestick maker structure. However, Emma Peel disrupts the formula, and adjusts Steed's sexist plan:

Steed: Shouldn't be too difficult to pick him up.
Emma: HE will come to ME.

Emma Peel is here living up to her carefully-created name, a woman with magnetic 'man-appeal'. Her carrying a rose cleverly connects to the previous scene. Has Steed offered her the flower in an attempt to win her over to his plan? It is a subtle touch amidst the less-refined humour.

Steed's moonlit arrival at the Brigadier's house offers us the first moment of genuine, (almost) straight drama. As he enters through the French windows, the toy horse is fore-grounded by the camera, offering us a playful warning before we see the mysterious ringed hand appearing on it. The scene is stylishly shot, the butler's dead body theatrically spread on the rug with a sword sticking out. The foregrounding of some spiked helmets again warns us that one will be used to attack Steed, allowing us to stay a split-second ahead of him while increasing the tension. After all, unlike Steed, we are powerless. The helmet fails to spear him but allows the villain to remain masked. The clever scene is completed by the odd sight of the Major-General in pyjamas and night cap playing the Last Post over the butler's corpse.

What the Butler Saw exemplifies the one-off, individual nature of each Season 4 episode. This is illustrated by the unnecessary but amusing short scene which follows, in which Emma Peel has driven out into "the middle of the countryside", in order to enjoy "a breath of fresh, country air" as she informs Steed on her car telephone. It is as if this mad caper itself needs a breather before galloping on. Her 'Operation Fascination' involves bombarding Miles with photographic images displaying her 'man appeal'. Laid low in his study with a hangover, her photos are everywhere. Moving on to the military bar, she even appears on his drink mat. The humour is heightened by the half-hidden Steed who is encouraging Mrs. Peel to speed up her romance campaign. The arrival of two female officers increases his concern, before Emma's wonderful, sexually-confident retort: "Competition? What competition?" The moment is a gently funny highlight of the season. As Mrs. Peel lowers her sunglasses, Miles is instantly smitten and Emma theatrically shuts the partition bar door, placing Steed outside the spectacle, a joke which will be reworked later on at Miles' love nest.

The noticeboard for the Butlers & Gentleman's Gentlemen Association is a forerunner of an *Avengers* tradition of amusingly snobbish organisations which runs throughout the colour filmed era, their motto typical of what will become a regular gag: 'BETTER BRIGHTER MORE BEAUTIFUL BUTLING'. Twenty minutes in and we are back in the elegant room of the teaser, a ringed hand tapping the arm of the same chair. The ringing of the bell and the subsequent arrival of Benson teases us, offering the (irrational) fear that Steed will be dealt with in the same way as Walters. (This works in much the same way, dramatically, as the twin aquarium scenes in *The Murder Market*.) To add an extra twist, the mastermind appears to have been finally revealed: surprisingly, it is the Group Captain's butler, Hemming. The subsequent conversation playfully sends up the language of domestic service, Hemming praising Steed for his "fine grasp of the vernacular". There is a delicious humour in the idea that Steed's "general demeanour" makes him a promising candidate for 'butling'.

The subsequent training fore-echoes that of the nannies in *Something Nasty in the Nursery* and the window cleaners of the Classy Glass Cleaning company in *Super Secret Cypher Snatch*. Indeed, from many points of view this episode has the comic-strip approach of the colour era, demonstrating how some of the late-season episodes were moving towards an increasingly bizarre *Avengerland*. The scenes involving shoe polishing, ironing and tray holding provide an echo of the early triptych structure, although they also represent amusing 'padding' at the halfway point of the episode. On another level, there is a clever self-referentiality at play as Hemming and Steed rehearse lines for a potential butler/master scene. On a final level, they should have us questioning whether Hemming really is the diabolical mastermind. After all, if he is the arch-villain then why is he bothering to train Steed in such a meticulous fashion?

What the Butler Saw is in a constant state of inner conflict, veering between silly and subtle, in common with a number of Brian Clemens episodes written towards the end of the monochrome era. The three high-ranking officers who were Steed's original suspects are seen discussing high security matters inside a zipped-up plastic bag, a new security ruling to foil bugging devices. Whether the image works or not is a matter of personal taste. Certainly, it tests the series' boundaries.

Hemming's murder takes us back to square one in terms of uncovering the identity of the mastermind. These scenes at the butler training academy are atmospherically shot by Bill Bain, with Hemming shadowed by Benson and, later, Steed's reappearance first indicated by the silhouette of his bowler, umbrella and upper body on a wall, before we see him adjusting his hat in an upturned, gleaming iron. If the storyline prefigures the cartoonish colour era then the more stylish touches remind us that we are still in the monochrome season. The sight of Hemming's corpse, seen through the glass porthole of the industrial washing machine, adds a chillingly surreal touch. Coupled with Benson's arrival, armed with a silencer, the dramatic tension rises but both Steed and the viewer are being teased. The discovery that his butler references are forgeries has allowed him into the villain's circle, rather than signing his death warrant. Benson's earlier remark that he will "attend to" Steed is a diabolically playful one, encouraging us to head down another false trail.

Steed's arrival as Miles' new butler allows the episode to return to its most natural tone, that of an almost slapstick, light-hearted humour, Steed rising above his new station to suggest that "Modom [Mrs. Peel] looks the cat's whiskers". Miles' 'master switch' instantly turns the room into a love nest: curtains drawn, soft lighting, smoochy music, chilled champagne at the ready. Even Miles himself has been transformed, wearing a silk lounging jacket. It is almost as if *The Avengers* has collided with a *Carry-On* film. The scene becomes manically absurd, as Emma desperately tries to avoid Miles' embraces by asking questions about his art collection and butler Steed regularly interrupts to demand if he should serve champagne, dinner etc. In a further twist it turns out that 'Casanova' Miles is a role he is tired of playing, relieved to enjoy a cup of tea, a chat and a board game instead. Like the retired Major-General, Miles is just a little boy at heart, offering a playful critique of the men running the modern day military.

When the plot is finally unravelled – miniature tape recorders stitched into the officers' uniforms; the bitter barman/dishwasher Sergeant Moran the unlikely mastermind – what we are left with is a strangely satisfying episode. Great credit should go to the strong guest actors: John Le Mesurier is wonderful as the obsequious, villainous butler – recalling his memorable role as the corrupt doctor in *Mandrake* – Thorley Walters plays the part of Hemming with style, Denis Quilley is hilarious as the Casanova officer, while Kynaston Reeves plays the batty, eccentric, retired Major-General with aplomb. As is so often the case, the strength of the supporting cast in this episode is a key element in the success.

At times, *What the Butler Saw* is subtly stylish, never more so than in the fight finale between Emma and Moran, a scene employing the butlers' doors – a wonderfully artificial set-within-a-set – but sometimes this subtlety makes way for farce, anticipating the comic-strip approach of many of the colour episodes. Brian

Clemens' story feels as if it is caught between two worlds: the noirishly fantastic monochrome world of Emma Peel and the colourful, cartoonish era which would replace it. It is a highly enjoyable, daring romp, but one which arguably lacks the dark, dramatic touches of earlier Clemens episodes. As the antithesis of – or antidote to – the disturbing *The House That Jack Built*, perhaps this doesn't matter; after all, *What the Butler Saw* adds yet more variety to this excitingly unique season. As the punch-line of the tag scene demonstrates – "the butler did it!" – it is happy to play with clichés, unwilling to take itself too seriously.

© Rodney Marshall

1. Joe Orton's final play was entitled *What the Butler Saw*, first performed in 1969 just months before his murder.

THE HOUSE THAT JACK BUILT

Filmed: 9th – 18th January 1966

Exterior Locations:
Woodland
Façade and grounds of country house
Deserted country lanes

Sets:
Country house: study, hallway, central 'hub', spiral staircase, box room, exhibition, control room, suicide box
Steed's apartment: kitchen, living room
Pennington's solicitors' office

THE HOUSE THAT JACK BUILT

Main Character List:
Burton: escaped prisoner
Emma Peel
John Steed
Pennington: Peel family solicitor
Pongo Withers: agent
Professor Keller: automation expert, deceased mastermind

Occasionally, the Emma Peel *Avengers* episodes drop the light-hearted, witty 'froth', allowing the dark, dramatic undercurrent to bubble to the surface. They retain the quirky, surreal elements, but the result is unsettlingly sinister, as is the case in *The Joker*, *Epic* and *Murdersville*. However, Brian Clemens' *The House That Jack Built* is (arguably) far more terrifying than any of these. A sadistically imaginative script, some experimental direction and a psychologically disturbing, psychedelic set combine to create a nightmarish episode. *The Avengers* frequently draws upon the gothic horror genre of the remote country house 'trap', but here the visual result is uniquely, creatively unpleasant.

The teaser, initially, offers us a realistic scenario as an escaped prisoner is pursued by guards and bloodhounds. Two stone lions – guarding the front door of a remote country house – offer us a playful example of delayed decoding. As the convict, Burton, breaks in, he/we are convinced that the house is empty, which, in a sense, it is. The stuffed owls provide the first unsettling image. However, it is the obviously artificial (film projection) lion attacking him which we close/freeze on as the title appears on the screen.

The isolated country house may be a popular *Avengers* location, but here it becomes a claustrophobic set-within-a-set, or rather a series of them. However, before this is revealed, we have the bizarre 'key' scenes. First, Steed's own film-developing ends up with his holiday snaps – realism – stamped with a surreal key image, offering us a fore-echo of later events. Then, as Mrs. Peel heads off along deserted country roads, the surreal sight of Withers/Pongo – dressed as an over-sized boy scout – adds a disconcerting, absurd humour as he races down the hillside before stepping out in front of her speeding sports car:

Emma: I might have killed you.
Pongo: The speed you were going – the stopping distance of this car is one hundred and forty-seven feet – allowing for average reflexes – I positioned myself one hundred and fifty feet away.
Emma: Very mathematical of you.
Pongo: I am a very mathematical person.
Emma: You are also very stupid.

During the subsequent car journey we are left to wonder about Emma Peel's last comment. Is Withers/Pongo simply a ridiculous, comic figure? As he stares at the dangling key, the camera focuses on his bare legs which he caresses. It is a potentially sexual image, and Emma Peel/we are understandably uncomfortable. His observation that this is "very pleasant countryside…so quiet, empty" is at odds with both his peculiar behaviour and the mechanically-changing road signs. The tension increases as a 'ROAD CLOSED' sign bangs down behind them; the music becomes disconcertingly strange as Emma Peel heads up the drive towards the house we saw in the teaser.

From now on, the film will move between the interior 'trap' of the house and Steed's journey along the country lanes, with the added problem of him having to read the road signs 'against the grain'. Steed is the knight – without shining armour – attempting to rescue the far from helpless damsel, *The Avengers* playing with the fairy tale genre as both Steed and Mrs. Peel acknowledge in the final minutes. The episode also undermines traditional gender stereotypes, with Emma Peel able to defeat the male diabolical mastermind without Steed's support.

Don Leaver's direction helps to create the dark, dramatic atmosphere inside the house. When Emma Peel sees the stuffed owls from the teaser, we now get a close-up of their dark, unreadable eyes: first both owls, then one, lastly just the one eye which almost takes up the entire screen. A bewildering range of sounds shatter the silence: a music box, a phone ringing, a lion growling. There is no sense of connection and it will be up to Emma Peel to decode the signs. As she answers the old-fashioned phone, her expression offers a weary, disbelieving, self-referentially theatrical look.

The surrealism takes full control once the clichéd hallway – suit of armour, portrait with seemingly moving eyes etc. – disappears, replaced by a psychedelic set. Brian Clemens' original script offers a detailed description:

"In the middle of this central area is a perpetual motion machine. This area is like the hub of a wheel – and the spokes are corridors running off to blackness…The corridors are painted black and white with a jagged crazy pattern… weird, distorted look."

What are we to make of this set? It is, in a sense, a visual tease, as it serves no purpose other than to test Emma Peel's ability to 'keep her head', as the sets shift and force her to question what is 'real' and what isn't, a question we are frequently forced to ask ourselves in *Avengers* episodes. The set may be visually striking but it is brought alive by the camera work: as Emma Peel heads down an almost *Alice in Wonderland* spiral staircase, we follow the floor's spiral pattern, both to indicate her movement and add a sense of an almost drug-induced trip. As rooms move and/or are replaced by sets of themselves – the windows now boarded up – the sets become psychedelically surreal, rather than simply nightmarishly odd.

The use of Emma Peel's 'thought voice' – or interior monologue – adds an effectively strange extra layer to the mind games played by the late Keller. Her stopping of the moving rooms reveals to her/us their artificiality as they become stuck mid-change. As Brian Clemens had hoped, the visual effect "is not unlike being behind a studio set or in the wings of a theatre." The artificiality increases the sense of surreal fear, rather than reducing it. What are we to make, for example, of Emma Peel cutting through her giant photographed face and then stepping through it, moments later coming back to take a double take? Clemens describes it as "a disturbing image". We might read it as the triumph of the 'real' over surreal, manufactured representation.

As in *The Joker*, the plot revolves around "a pitting of wits" between the house/mastermind and Emma Peel. However, the theme of 'perfect' automation versus 'imperfect' human reasoning recalls *The Cybernauts*:

Keller: The mind of a machine cannot reason. Therefore it cannot lose its reason...Its mind has no breaking point. But *your* mind...

The sadistic scheme has at its symbolic centre or core the 'suicide box', while the mad prisoner – who has, ironically, swapped one cell for another – offers living proof that the house trap can drive its victims insane. Emma Peel's victory is not simply an obligatory part of the show's formula. It represents the thinking, reasoning human's defeat of the unchangeable, programmed, soulless automaton, once again displaying *The Avengers*' unease with the 1960s technological revolution.

The maddening, psychedelic hub; Keller's preserved corpse sitting in its chair in a glass prism; the suicide box; the dark beady eyes of the owls; the 'late Emma Peel' exhibition; Burton's nursery rhyme singing, his mad eyes staring at Mrs. Peel/us, all connect to create a disturbing visual feast.

As Steed and Emma cycle away towards that bright horizon, the formulaic happy ending fails to lift the gloomy darkness we have been encased in. It is impossible to define/confine *The Avengers* as 'light entertainment' on viewing *The House That Jack Built*; particularly as this episode is almost devoid of humour and wit. If Keller's house represents an intellectual puzzle then so too does *The Avengers* in its 'classic' monochrome filmed episodes. Label it or attempt to place it within a specific genre at your peril.

© Rodney Marshall

A SENSE OF HISTORY

Filmed: 20th – 31th January 1966

Exterior Locations:
Country lane
Cloisters
Caravan area and woodland
St. Bodes University: façade
Country lanes

Sets:
Car
Garage
Lecture room
Duboys' room
University corridor
University archives

A SENSE OF HISTORY

Main Character List:
James Broom: economist
Emma Peel
John Steed
Richard Carlyon: economist
Dr. Gordon Henge: history lecturer at St. Bodes
Millerson: student
Pettit: student
Eric Duboys: student
Marianne Grey: student
Professor David Acheson: lecturer
D B Grindley: university archivist, mastermind

Writer Martin Woodhouse returned to the series for only one episode after it moved from videotape to film. He'd written six episodes during Seasons 2 and 3. His *Mr. Teddy Bear* was chosen to open Season 2 and introduce the radical new character of Mrs. Catherine Gale played by Honor Blackman. After Season 1 where John Steed and Dr. David Keel walked in a seedy world of drug dealers and commonplace espionage, Woodhouse's script featured a diabolical mastermind who chose to communicate through a teddy bear. It's debatable, without a fuller knowledge of the eccentricities of Season 1, but it seems that Woodhouse's script was the first time the series stepped into a fantastical world. Despite the fantastic notions in his scripts, the real world was always close at hand. Prior to Brian Clemens' involvement as lead writer, the writers allegedly had more freedom to follow their own interests. With the series becoming increasingly extravagant, Woodhouse's *A Sense of History* is the last hurrah of the old style. The characters in Woodhouse's script are still people rather than crazy eccentrics or generic ciphers. Woodhouse's characters have motivations and lives. Whilst there is a diabolical mastermind, his cohorts are not merely faceless stooges.

A Sense of History was actually Woodhouse's second submission for Season 4. His *Rip Van Winkle* script about suspended animation was allegedly rejected as being too 'science fiction fantasy'. Perhaps he decided to play safe with the more grounded *A Sense of History*. I'm sure a season later his first script would have been acceptable.

Another returning contributor to the series, also making his final mark, was director Peter Graham Scott. It seems that after failing to acquire the services of noted videotape era director Peter Hammond (allegedly the first director he asked following the move from Teddington TV Studios to Elstree film Studios), producer Brian Clemens turned to another Peter. Despite only working on Season 4 filmed episodes, Scott would have been just as able on the videotape episodes as he started his TV career with live drama productions. He had built up a solid reputation with film, handling feature films and cult dramas like *Danger Man*. Scott directed the original Emma Peel, Elizabeth Shepherd making her debut in *The Town of No Return*. Although the audience was deprived of seeing his full production following Shepherd's dismissal, Scott effectively created the new confident visual style for the film series due to being behind the camera for the first three episodes in front of it – *The Murder Market* and *The Master Minds* followed *The Town of No Return*. He then had a lengthy gap where many older film hands went behind the camera. During that time, the benefits of film were taken advantage of, allowing for more elaborate stunt sequences and scenes on location. It's therefore quite ironic that when Scott did return to the show, he was given an episode that could have so easily been made in a videotape studio, albeit after the intial scenes.

The first scene brings to mind the opening shots of the Scott directed episode *The Master Minds* from the start of the season. Where that had shots of Steed's car on fresh country roads, this has economist James Broom's Rolls Royce. Laurie Johnson's music is very pastoral and carefree as it accompanies shots of Broom's calm expression. It's lulling us into a false sense of security. Even when his journey is interrupted by grotesquely masked Rag Week students in Robin Hood costumes, the music is still playful and innocent, saying there is nothing to fear, it's just a prank. It's only when he is suddenly shot in the back by an arrow that the music and mood change to match the drama. The Johnny Dankworth stock music from the videotape era didn't allow for fine-tuned emphasis.

The caption card of the episode title is accompanied by rousing, heroic music that would have been familiar to UK viewers who'd grown up with Richard Greene in *The Adventures of Robin Hood* from the late 1950s.

Steed and Mrs. Peel then take part in a scene of pure exposition, to take the action from A to B. We discover why Broom was murdered – his revolutionary economic ideas to do away with poverty and unite Europe were fiercely opposed by a mysterious man connected with St. Bodes University. Being *The Avengers* this takes place with a man hidden in a car boot and Mrs. Peel wittily discovering she needs to further her education when unable to add two and two. It's witty shorthand in order to move the action along, played with a twinkle.

At this stage the episode has been entirely location based – a country road, a private road leading to an unseen destination and a garage. The music takes us on a journey to the noble courtyards of St. Bodes University suggesting a historic establishment through which many notable movers and shakers have passed. The shots of the university appear to come from stock as they lead us into footage from Elstree Studios representing the exterior courtyards. The stock footage is tracking left to right and the film studio footage is doing likewise. Director Scott was noted from his early days for clever imperceptible cutting from location film to studio videotape. Although this was with film, the cut is still done with expertise.

The noble quality is soon punctured by the rowdiness and arrogance of the students disregarding their History teacher Dr. Gordon Henge as he attempts to instruct them. It was very rare for the series to use young people. The most notable previous use was Season 3's *Build a Better Mousetrap*. There the young people, a biker gang, were seen with mistrust by the older characters and they weren't a faceless entity; they were individuals. *A Sense of History* uses the youths in a threatening way, cushioned by the suggestion of Rag Week high spirits but they still contain individuals. For all the intimidating behaviour it becomes clear that they are being misguided by an older character, they're not presented as just evil because they're young which in a show increasingly dealing with surface details you'd expect. It's interesting to note the change in Duboys when with his peers as opposed to being in the company of his leader; he becomes like an excitable, spoiled child. These are privileged students who likely come from wealthy backgrounds. They have an invested interest in the wealth of the economy staying where it is. It's an intelligent and logical reasoning behind their loyalty to the mastermind.

The first scene in the classroom and the two that follow, set in the courtyard and corridor outside Duboys' room, are a good example of lighting and the flexibility that filming allowed over 'live' videotaping. Director of photography, Gilbert Taylor, made his *Avengers* debut here; noted for his work previously with Stanley Kubrick. The classroom set is lit from overhead lamps very similar to the set up for multi-camera. It's an economical way to light, as all cameras share the same light. Despite the luxury of a single film camera setup, as with videotape it's a time saver. By this stage in production of Season 4 it's reasonable to suppose that time was running out so short cuts had to be made. Out in the bare courtyard, the lighting suggests directional sunlight. The scene then moves to an interior location yet it's the courtyard set. With careful redressing and creative work with floor lamps, though the set is merely open archways, the lighting suggests there are windows with strong sunlight shining through. The videotape era would have had to build two entirely different sets. Whereas one saves money on the continuous recorded action, the other can save on creative use of rearranging the same sets.

As the episode progresses the students are seen twice more wearing the grotesque masks from the opening scene. As the masks are connected with murder, they actually live up to their threatening look. On both occasions the rabble are pleasingly dealt with by Emma and Steed respectively. With Steed especially it's a joy to see them humiliated when fooled by his foppish demeanour. Steed was increasingly represented as the playful gentleman spy; it's refreshing to be reminded that his mask conceals a cold-hearted expert.

In retaliation, the students attack Steed and Carlyon (played by Nigel Stock) out in the forest near the university. In both scripting and visuals this is quite a scary scene as the masked students fire flaming arrows. Steed doesn't treat this as a bit of fun, as he would in stories like *Quick-Quick Slow Death* where you rarely see Steed without a smile on his face as he fights the baddies. No, this is serious. But the threatening reality is countered by Laurie Johnson's score which instead of accompanying the drama goes for the Robin Hood style heroic theme. This makes the action seem more light-hearted and pretend. After ABC executive Brian Tesler expressed a desire in memos to the production team about the show retaining a pre-10pm broadcast, favouring *The Saint*'s slot, and advising caution on how scripts like *A Touch of Brimstone* were handled, it wouldn't be surprising if Scott asked for the music to aid keeping the action for a family audience. [1]

Following the atmospheric death of student Pettit (Robin Philips) in the archives during a thunder storm, Steed and Mrs. Peel discuss the university tradition of "bury them quick, forget them quick". With writer Martin Woodhouse' own history as a student at

Cambridge, it's tempting to wonder if there was a bit of his own experience fed into the script. [2] The audience isn't given any sense of the glory days of school or "it's not as good as it was in our day". It's very unromantic in a series that quite often used nostalgia in the storytelling like *The Town of No Return* or *The Hour That Never Was* where Steed enjoys reliving memories of the past.

As the episode moves into its final act, a fancy dress party takes to the stage. This isn't a fun occasion for larks; the mean-spiritedness of the students is retained. There's an edge to their enjoyment. It comes at the expense of others. There are uncomfortable expressions and awkwardness. The last time we saw a party in the show was *A Touch of Brimstone* but there it was wild, carefree abandonment. This party has individuals with secrets and sadness. Marianne (played by a pre-*Blake's 7* Jacqueline Pearce), for example, has just lost her boyfriend, Pettit, at the hands of someone who her friends are in league with. It's a reminder of the old style of the show before *Brimstone*'s surface style began to take the lead.

But amidst the tensions at the party, there's still time for a panning shot to take in the full length of Mrs. Peel's feminine Robin Hood. Director Scott used a very similar shot for revealing her outfit in *The Master Minds*. It's interesting to compare Diana Rigg's expression in the two shots. In the former, she knows she is the sex interest in the show but is haughtily submitting, yet by *A Sense of History* she is more relaxed and just goes with the flow. The episode uses the Robin Hood aspect as mere set dressing. It's likely that had any future episode used the visual, it would have been the point of the whole episode.

The tag scene presents us with an ecstatic Steed, joyously expounding on "a freshness in the air" and the open road. Was this how Brian Clemens was feeling following the completion of this episode? For this episode marked the end of the old writers and he had the show to himself to guide into the direction he wanted. It was solely his vision now. "I wonder if history will be kind to him," says Mrs. Peel of the defeated mastermind.

With the film series enjoying frequent repeats throughout the world in the years that followed it, the videotape era – and those who made it – was a forgotten relic. Brian Clemens became the 'creator of *The Avengers*' according to a *Trivial Pursuits* question. Thankfully, with the advent of videos and DVDs, history has been allowed to be kind [3] as the fans can get the full picture of a series that developed thanks to the talents of many a creative input.

© Darren Burch

1. Alternatively, this might be another playful example of Laurie Johnson's music deliberately clashing with – rather than mirroring – the dramatic action, as *The Avengers* undermines traditional television conventions.
2. This is where I have a 'design' problem with the episode. Woodhouse, like Roger Marshall, was Cambridge-educated. In fact he was already a qualified medical doctor by the time he wrote for *The Avengers*. So why are we given the impression that this is a private preparatory school with tiny desks in a cramped classroom, rather than the traditional benches which universities provided in vast lecture halls? Is it a playful suggestion that these young students are more like rowdy schoolchildren? To me it creates a ridiculous sight.
3. ...and more truthful. The Clemens domination would become more intense in the colour era. Roger Marshall suggests: "The name of the fecund and indefatigable Brian Clemens is all over the show. No exaggeration to say that his influence pervades almost every scene. Lead writer,

associate producer and story editor. In my book that was at least one job too many...No longer was a writer able to write what he wanted and in the way he wanted. Wit and style were being squeezed out." (*The Avengers Forever!* November, 2007)

HOW TO SUCCEED... AT MURDER

Filmed: 1st – 15th February 1966

Exterior Locations:
Finlay's car
Office block
Urban road
Keep Fit building: façade
Bus stop
Graveyard
Deserted country lane

Sets:
Offices of Barton, Purbright, Morton, Rudge
Steed's apartment
Henry and Henrietta's drawing room
Hooter's offices (outer/inner)
Keep Fit school
Caravan

HOW TO SUCCEED... AT MURDER

Main Character List:
Barton: businessman
Liz Purbright: secretary
Henrietta Throgbottom: ventriloquist dummy
Henry Throgbottom: ballet/keep fit instructor
Sir George Morton: businessman
Mary Merryweather: secretary
Sara Penny: secretary
Joshua Rudge: chartered accountant
Jack Finlay: businessman
Gladys Murkle: secretary
JJ Hooter: perfumier
Annie: secretary

One of the most profound impacts of *The Avengers* is its contribution to feminism. The show was a pioneer in creating strong female characters. None of course more famous or enduring than Mrs. Emma Peel who *TV Guide* magazine declared one of the top fictional television characters of all time. Mrs. Peel exemplified true female empowerment at the highest level. She was a character that women could admire. More importantly, the male viewers did not feel threatened by her and therefore could respond to her with equal regard. Producer-writer Brian Clemens was key in the development of this character and, by extension, her effect on popular culture. It is curious then, that Clemens would go on to write the anomaly known as *How to Succeed...at Murder*. The episode is unusual for the time period in that it directly addresses the issues of women's liberation and sexism in the work place. It is an intriguing piece of work with many striking moments that unfortunately contains an incongruous mix of tones and ends up denigrating feminism as much as it sheds a spotlight on it.

Season 4 of *The Avengers* was a peak period of creativity. Narratively speaking, there was a tremendous degree of diversity and ongoing experimentation. By the end of the season the scripts were pushing boundaries to ambitious levels; none more extreme or dark than *How to Succeed....at Murder*. Presenting an episode in 1966 that features lethal female villains was nothing new for an action series. What made it groundbreaking, even brazenly so, was having the antagonists be a group of openly militant feminists striking out against male chauvinism. It would be amongst the earliest dramatic presentations on the subject and its broadcast would pre-date the official onset of the Women's Liberation movement in the United States.

Although dated, the premise of a group of frustrated secretaries (led by the enigmatic Henrietta Throgbottom) who resort to homicidal tactics to circumvent the 'glass ceiling', still manages to hold up fairly well today. This can be attributed in part to the still lingering presence of sexism today and to such recent programmes as *Mad Men* that successfully capture what life was like for women fifty years ago. Clemens gives a great deal of attention to who these women are and what they are all about. He does so to the point of abandoning his standard plot structure. Mrs. Peel doesn't appear in the episode until almost a third of the way through. We don't see our heroes working together out in the field until after the third on-screen murder has been committed. The focus early on is on the motivation of the women. They are shown to have a serious axe to grind with the male-dominated business world. All of them are exceptionally smart, capable and talented. But they live in a time where the prevailing belief is, that for women, having a job was a transient phase of their lives. They were still expected to ultimately get married and raise children. Running the world, whether in politics or business, was the province of men. Women who were more interested in a career than family were not 'normal' and needed to be set straight. If it were today, these secretaries would not only be able to attain the role of corporate leader but would be encouraged to aspire to such levels. But instead they are in an era where they are consigned to a role they see as unending servitude. It would not be an exaggerated statement to say each of them was a potential Emma Peel in the making. Alas none of them were lucky enough to have a father who could bequeath them a company to run.

One of the distinctive narrative elements of the story is the cultic nature underscoring the activities of our villains. The secretaries are presented in a way similar to a coven of witches with Henrietta serving both as their high priestess and their pagan idol. The murders evoke a sense of ritualistic sacrifice with the women donning their symbol of sisterhood prior to each act. And those acts rank amongst some of the most violent and unnerving moments of Season 4. The sight of Sara Penny strangling Sir George Morton or Gladys Murkle poisoning her boss, JJ Hooter, not only show how dangerous these women are but helps to create as unflattering a portrait of them as possible. It is no surprise that the group does not exactly come across as sympathetic. That's not unusual. However, Clemens writes with such extreme strokes that he makes it impossible for there to be anything remotely likable or even admirable about them. The women are not only cold-blooded killers; some of them clearly take great pleasure in the murders. The fanatical viciousness they exhibit prevents them garnering any positive feelings from the viewer even though it is clear they are formidable and very resourceful in enacting their agenda. It is poetically ironic that Miss Penny is able to execute so many men by using her looks to exploit their objectifying desires.

Alas, they are not just bristling against male bigotry. They exhibit a blatant contempt for men that crosses over into sexism. For them men are inferior and pointless and in that regard they are no less oppressive than those they rail against. Imbuing such attitudes in them supports a subtext that females of this kind are completely unnatural. They are not true women and therefore a threat to all that is decent and normal in society. They are more than the 20th century Amazons. They are modern day Maenads ready to unleash pain and suffering against any who cross their path. This idea of 'perversion' is further underscored with the suggestion of lesbianism. This can be inferred in the way one of their members, Mary Merryweather, takes a very special interest in Mrs. Peel. It is noteworthy that when Miss Merryweather discovers she's been duped by our heroine, she slaps Mrs. Peel across the face in the same domineering, backhanded way an enraged man would.

This would not be a major problem if not for the competing tones that Clemens and director Don Leaver create within the story. While the scenes with the villains maintain an eerie, dark feel, the scenes with Steed and Mrs. Peel carry the usual expected air of humorous spoof. The result is a schizophrenic atmosphere with the two worlds never quite coming together organically. That is a shame since director Leaver is able to create memorable individual moments within both styles. We get a classic example of the eccentric *Avengers* character with perfumier JJ Hooter. Actor Christopher Benjamin attacks the part with great skill and enthusiasm, manufacturing a truly lovable character. Such an endearing personality makes his murder all the more jarring. We get many great examples of Steed and Emma's enjoyable banter with just the right touch of intimacy. Conversely, there are a number of powerful and disturbing moments using the Henrietta doll. Particularly striking is the scene where her eyes follow Steed sneaking into her studio as well as the final moment of her and her husband Henry embraced in a kiss. In fairness, Leaver does manage in one scene to balance the dark violent side with the humour. The moment where the women reveal themselves to Steed, with each showing off a weapon more dangerous than the last, is handled quite deftly. The final cut with Gladys Murkle yielding a mace punctuates the scene with just enough levity to break the tension but not too much to upend the drama. It's a delicate balancing act that is not seen enough throughout the episode.

The story turns completely tragic when the true villain and motivation is unveiled. Henry is the real culprit and quite the mastermind, not the fumbling, dimwit that he has presented himself as. During the final minutes of the show the theme switches from fanatical feminism to psychotic revenge. The truth is disturbing and while Henry's (and Henrietta's) back-story is sadly moving, it completely undermines the original premise. More so, that revelation is indicative of what can be perceived by modern eyes as an underlying presence of misogyny courtesy of Brian Clemens. Whether Clemens did so consciously or not, he actually shows little respect for his villains. He spends the first half of the story establishing how formidable the women are, but spends the second half showing them as incredibly stupid. [1]

The revelation that the women have been taking orders from a crazed Henry all along isn't just a shocking twist. It is a humiliating one. It is rather incredulous that none of these women were ever suspicious of him, regardless of their own prejudices towards men. The episode even clues in the audience that Henry is not the buffoon he appears to be. During the exercise classes, Henry, as a former ballet master, is clearly a man who knows how to handle and exude authority. During those times, he is confident, strong and organised. Note how he had no qualms about that authority by physically touching Mrs. Peel. In retrospect, ignoring those signs makes the women seem inept. Adding to the disgrace that they have been pawns of a man is that the truth was unearthed by a man. Further, there is the issue of how Steed dispatches Sara Penny and Liz Purbright when they arrive to kill him. As an old world English gentleman, it is commendable that Steed would not knowingly hit a woman. But the actions he employs in place of his fists to subdue them are very demeaning: Steed overpowering Sara by tickling her as he sits on top of Liz reeks of condescension. The scene treats them as if they are merely two impudent children who daddy needs to properly put in their place. Steed has never treated a male adversary in such an ignoble way. [2]

However, the blunder that makes these secretaries appear most foolish is not knowing who Emma Peel is. How is that possible? In 1966, career opportunities for women were still limited. Emma Peel is the head of a successful shipping company; a company that she's been running since she was 21 years old. How can none of these women with their huge business aspirations be aware of her existence? By all rights, they should have a collection of articles and pictures of her, serving as a source of inspiration. What makes it worse is that Brian Clemens is the one who established this personal history of Mrs. Peel in the previously aired episode, *The House That Jack Built*. [3]

All of this brings up the question: how seriously was Clemens in tackling the issue of feminism? Was he merely using it as a MacGuffin plot device to distract from the real story he wanted to write? Or was he truly interested in exploring this subject? The unfortunate way he treats these characters may reflect an unconscious attitude he held at the time. As characters, Sara Penny, Liz Purbright, Gladys Murkle and the others are written as shallow, two-dimensional entities. Mary Merryweather has more depth but only in terms of how she relates to Mrs. Peel. Henry is the only one of the villains that is a clearly conceived and fleshed-out personality. As bold as the move is on his part to tackle this subject, Clemens falters with their characterisation. Alternatively it is possible in writing this script Clemens was faced with the same conundrum Shakespeare had with his play *Merchant of Venice* and the character of Shylock. Shylock is a Jew who is constantly demeaned in a society that is openly bigoted towards his ethnicity, nationality and religion. Frustration drives him to commit a reprehensible act in response to this prejudice. Audiences at the time had expectations as to how a Semitic villain would be portrayed and dealt with. Shakespeare accommodated those expectations while his own beliefs remained ambiguous. Clemens may have been in a similar situation where he felt he needed to take the prevailing attitudes of the times into account. This could also explain his portrayal and treatment of these women as disturbing aberrations. Regardless of the root causes, a golden opportunity was missed to create some truly fascinating in-depth adversaries that would have better explored the sexism that women experienced in the workplace.

© Frank Hui

1. Do we not have to question the intelligence of anyone taking orders from a ventriloquist's dummy?!
2. This is a difficult and contentious issue, as I find the scene amusing, which was clearly Clemens' intention. I guess this episode splits opinion depending on whether one sees it as a serious attempt to explore an important theme, or else an episode played simply 'for laughs'. Is it OK to use such an important gender/sexism topic for comedic purposes?
3. As stated previously, this opens up a fascinating debate about whether the 'personal history' of any one episode necessarily spills over into subsequent ones, or whether each film has to be treated as a one-off.

HONEY FOR THE PRINCE

Filmed: 20th February – 4th March 1966

Exterior Locations:
Bridge/Riverbank
Urban street

Sets:
Arabian Room (QQF)
Steed's apartment
Arkadi's health centre
George's flat
B. Bumble's honey shop
Barabian Embassy: grand reception hall, harem corridor

HONEY FOR THE PRINCE

Main Character List:
George Reed: agent
Ronny Westcott: agent
Vincent: assassin
Emma Peel
John Steed
Arkadi: diabolical mastermind
B Bumble: honey shop owner
Bernie: henchman
Ponsonby Hopkirk: QQF
Prince Ali: Barabian Embassy
Grand Vizier

In early March 1966 cameras were capturing the finishing touches to *Honey for the Prince*, the final *Avengers* episode filmed in black and white, broadcast in the UK only three weeks later. Crew members were waiting to film the first ever colour episode, *The Strange Case of the Missing Corpse*. 'Episode' is a cheat, of course, as David K Smith observes:

"What started out as a color film test to promote the new season to TV execs got transformed into an advertisement for the upcoming color episodes on American television, which was the only place to ever broadcast any part of it." (*The Avengers Forever!* website)

British viewers never saw this three minute film – which playfully advertises the show's reassuringly formulaic approach – yet the episode they tuned in to on 26th March 1966 in many ways gave them a fore-echo of what *The Avengers* would offer them 'in color'. *Honey for the Prince* represents a crossroads between the more subtle, witty world of Emma Peel in monochrome and the overtly comic strip, cartoonish colour *Avengerland*.

The teaser takes place on a set-within-a-set: Quite Quite Fantastic's *Arabian Nights*-inspired headquarters. Against an aural backdrop of an unsettling, exotic score, we immediately focus in on a series of objects such as a 'magic' lamp, vases and ornate doorways. *The Arabian Nights* is a fitting subject for *The Avengers*, given their hypnotic, charming ability to weave together the ordinary and the extraordinary, the real and the surreal into a single narrative. Here, two agents – George and Ronny – search the Arabian Room. The former, attracted to the lamp, rubs it as his colleague smiles, presumably amused by the child-like desire for magical fairy tales. The expectation – that nothing will happen – is undermined by a flash/bang – but the genie is simply a young machine-gun carrying hit-man. Already the story is playing with our pre-conceived ideas, threatening to provide us with something magically preposterous while ultimately maintaining the series' conventions and structure.

The teaser (inexplicably) closes on a giant, stuffed bear and this is playfully carried into the post-teaser scene where Emma Peel is carrying a teddy bear as she and Steed head home at dawn from an all-night party. From the fantasy world of ancient Arabic storytelling we have been plunged into the 'real', hedonistic, modern culture of the Swinging Sixties. Back at Steed's apartment, both Steed and Mrs. Peel are confused by Ronny's Arabian tale of a genie and honey, misinterpreting it as a story about a 'honey' called Jeannie. Their adventure will involve separating fantasy from reality.

The subsequent scene in the deceased George's flat shows *The Avengers* at the crossroads between the two Peel seasons. Steed and hit-man Vincent's fight ends with the villain thrown through the glass of an upper-storey window, only to land on a car roof and run off. Steed's comment – "Well I never" – sums up the increasingly bizarre make-believe world of *Avengerland*. This equally applies to B. Bumble's honey shop with its madly eccentric owner dressed in his bee sweater and talking nonsense about operating on one of his bees' knees. It is as if *The Avengers* has collided with *Alice in Wonderland*. The honey shop is a world away from the cracker store of *Mandrake* near the end of the video-tape era and prefigures those uncovered in the colour seasons such as the toy shop in *Something Nasty in the Nursery* or the jigsaw store in *Game*.

Ponsonby Hopkirk's QQF company mirrors *The Avengers* itself, offering a wide range of adventures or fantasies which allow clients to leave the drudgery of real life for a short spell of escapism, just as the television series allows viewers to seek refuge and entertainment in their weekly fix of 'light drama'.

"We will create your fantasies and allow you to live them...A matter of the right décor, the right atmosphere, a few tricks."

The self-referential connections between *Avengerland* and the QQF corporation are then taken a step further as Hopkirk recommends a fantasy for Steed:

"...a secret agent? Yes, indeed, ideal for you. Licensed to kill, pitting your wits against a diabolical mastermind. Make a change from your everyday humdrum existence, wouldn't it?"

The playfulness of the script offers a fore-echo of Brian Clemens' colour vision: to take *The Avengers* into more extreme, artificial plots divorced from realistic drama; there would often be two feet firmly planted in *Avengerland* in Season 5. The telephone conversation between Steed and an angry Colonel Robertson also illustrates the gradual move from a subtle, witty humour towards a more slapstick approach. When Hopkirk later asks Mrs. Peel if she is interested in a fantasy she informs him that she hasn't "yet exhausted reality"; the script suggests otherwise: surrealism and comic strip adventure are beginning to dominate as *Honey for the Prince* brings the curtain down on the monochrome era.

Nevertheless, *Honey for the Prince* retains some of the charm of the monochrome era, such as the fawning Vizier, the delightful improvised cricket match at the Barabian embassy and the wonderfully diabolical character of Arkadi who enjoys a foot massage with a difference. It also revels in the playfully sadistic elements which Clemens scripts often contain. The best example of this is when Hopkirk is helping Vincent to prepare for his murder fantasy, blissfully unaware that he is about to be killed:

"No, no, man. You're not putting enough into it...Think murderously. Your expression, your whole attitude is too bland, too unconvincing...Much better, much more...realistic!"

The dark humour is cleverly played, particularly between the attractively camp assassin Vincent and his boss:

Arkadi: Hopkirk certainly knows his business.
Vincent: *Knew* his business.

Vincent is a typical *Avengers* hit-man: young, handsome, urbane, smartly dressed yet also chillingly cold. He prefigures the type we will often encounter in the colour seasons where they add an amusingly disturbing element to the spectacle.

If *The Avengers* retains a 'timeless' charm then the scenes at the Barabian Embassy might now seem faintly racist or stereotypical, with the humour surrounding the Prince's three hundred and twenty wives, mothers-in-law, buying women in exchange for bags of salt and goats, and his comments about chopping off his wives' toes – "gingers them up no end". The scenes would probably be criticised in today's multi-ethnic culture; in particular after Emma Peel's dance of the seven veils when Steed describes her as "retarded" and offers her as a present to the Prince: wife number three hundred and twenty-one. As the Prince – "renowned for his ardour" – searches his harem for Emma Peel it potentially leaves the viewer feeling uncomfortable. Should we accept the Barabian scenes as simply escapist, amusing, light entertainment, or is there a distasteful element to both Steed's actions and the script's narrative? Does *The Avengers* display a patronisingly colonial stance? [1] Or are we in danger of placing 21st century value judgements on a light-hearted mid-1960s television series which was playfully connecting with an *Arabian Nights* fantasy? [2]

Certainly, the sets are wonderful, none better than the atmospheric harem corridor with its giant honey pots, each one a potential hiding place for the deadly Vincent. The dramatic finale cleverly intertwines the Prince's (comic?) sexual pursuit of Emma Peel with Vincent's attempt at assassinating him. The Steed genie and magic carpet add final fantastic flourishes, counterbalanced by the reality checks: our knowledge that the vanishing act is a trick of QQF's trade and the sight of a perfectly ordinary vehicle carrying Emma, Steed and the carpet as they head off for a final time towards that bright horizon.

Honey for the Prince has plenty of charm and style, helped by an excellent support cast including Ron Moody (Hopkirk), Zia Mohyeddin (Prince), George Pastell (Arkadi) and Roland Curram (Vincent). The quality of the guest actors is first class throughout the monochrome filmed season, as it would continue to be in colour. The final episode of the season is not a classic 'film' of this era and lacks the disturbing, darker edge of some of the earlier ones. Nevertheless, it demonstrates where *The Avengers* had reached on its extraordinary, evolutionary journey between the noirish realism of Season 1 and the comic strip adventure of *Avengerland* in colour.

© Rodney Marshall

1. In *Small Game for Big Hunters* Levene's script satirises the white British male who is either murderously vengeful – Professor Swain or Simon Trent – or blissfully unaware that the Empire is a fading memory, with former colonies becoming independent from British rule: Colonel Rawlings is living in the past, both mentally and physically. The Kalayan agent, by contrast, is polite, articulate and ready to move with the times. Here, in *Honey for the Prince*, racial stereotypes and clichés are reinforced, rather than questioned. It is hard to generalise about the series' 'stance' because, for the most part, ethnic minorities are simply absent.

2. It is unhelpful to look back at a 1966 text from a 2014 viewpoint. The world has changed so much in half a century that exploring the episodes with 'moralistic' hindsight is the equivalent of criticising the back projections in the countless car scenes. *The Avengers* was a product of its time; context-dependent rather than timeless and free-floating. In addition, *Avengerland* is a fantasy world, rather than a reflection of contemporary society. This does not, of course, excuse racial stereotyping but does explain the absence or lack of working-class and ethnic minority figures in most of the episodes.

AFTERWORD

Every fan and critic has his or her favourite episodes from this remarkable, chameleon-like television series which was constantly changing and evolving in terms of style and content. However, there is a popular belief that Season 4 represents the artistic pinnacle of the show. Why?

The black and white Emma Peel era did not appear suddenly, as if by magic. Ever since the arrival of Honor Blackman/Mrs. Gale at the beginning of Season 2, *The Avengers* began to experiment, defying genre as it playfully shifted – often seamlessly – between realism/surrealism, combining light-hearted wit and charm with something darker and more dramatically disturbing. It cannot be easily labelled in terms of traditional genres of television fiction. There are some wonderful scripts in the Gale era but the main drawback is the limitations of 'live' videotape. Almost like recording a stage play, it was exciting to make but was essentially studio-bound with sound problems, fluffed lines and set wobbles all part of the mix. The three main sets/three corner sets structure was more like stricture. Film liberated the series and provided a visual feast unavailable in the previous seasons.

Colour offered an extra dimension in the following seasons but encouraged the show's increasingly comic strip, cartoonish tendencies. Seasons 5 and 6 look fantastic but sometimes the scripts demonstrate 'formulaic fatigue'. By contrast, the 26 monochrome filmed episodes have an individual, *film noir* quality to them. The subtlety of the lighting and camera work match the charm of the stories themselves. It is worth recalling the dialogue between Robert Banks Stewart and Jaz Wiseman which I used as one of my epigraphs in the front of this book:

RBS: Colour makes you more 'showbusy entertainy'. Black and white *invested*.
JW: There's a real depth in terms of the quality; the contrast, and the lighting has to be great…The black and white Emma Peel is the peak of the show.
RBS: If you are going to film in colour you want to be 'colourful' and you're maybe sometimes drawn into filming locations for location sake.
JW: This retains a certain *noir* quality in terms of the directing and the acting. There are shots where it's very black and then suddenly you get a face coming out. The black and white adds to the storylines and plot. And the enjoyment.
RBS: It adds to the *menace*.

(Jaz Wiseman and Robert Banks Stewart discussing the advantages of filming in black and white on the *Optimum Classic/Studio Canal* DVD commentary of *The Master Minds*)

That 'menace' – so apparent in the opening episode, and yet almost entirely absent in the final one – is a key element in the series/season, adding substance and dramatic depth to the witty froth. It comes from the scripts, the direction, the sets/locations, actors/characters, but also from the monochrome imagery. The sight of Saul (the fake fisherman) standing fore-grounded in the fading light of the cemetery and, later, silhouetted on the horizon with his bloodhounds as he hunts Smallwood on the coastline in *The Town of No Return* are atmospheric in a visually pure way which simply cannot be captured in colour. Even Brian Clemens – upset that the green light for colour film was withheld for financial reasons – has since admitted that it was far more "real" in black and white. [1]

The social or cultural context was also a key element to Season 4's appeal. If Season 1 still evokes the aftermath of a 1950s post-war austerity and Season 6 offers a fore-echo of the 1970s louder, punkish fashions, the monochrome film season captures that mid-decade 'Swinging Sixties' style in terms of fashion, music and a countercultural confidence. The photographer scene in *The Murder Market* offers a delightful microcosm of the mid-1960s vibrant pop subculture. Each episode in the season – even the few vaguely disappointing ones – have a charm and individual 'film' feel to them. Laurie Johnson's *Avengers* main titles theme and his incidental scores are also vital, providing – or sometimes provocatively clashing with – the tone, be it comedic, dramatic, bizarre or disturbing. The sets are almost always works of art, capturing the claustrophobic feel of a lift shaft, department store, sinister house or pub, jungle or dream, while the exterior locations liberate the series, adding an agoraphobic feel in episodes such as *The Hour That Never Was* and *Silent Dust*. Set or location, an alternative world – *Avengerland* – is created with the right music, lighting, direction and unsettling details: a spinning bicycle wheel, nodding dog or whine of a milk float. Even an empty street or warehouse can create (or reflect) an atmosphere or state of mind.

In terms of the scripts, precisely half the season was written by just two men: Brian Clemens and Roger Marshall. As a broad generalisation, Marshall's scripts tend to have one foot in the real world and one in *Avengerland*. While I, personally, love *Silent Dust* and *The Danger Makers*, there is no doubt that it is his formula-bending, disturbingly atmospheric *The Hour That Never Was* that he is most fondly remembered for. Roger's foreword to *Bright Horizons* sheds new light on the serendipity required in order to write such an iconic *Avengers* script.

While Clemens' initial scripts also offer a fine balance between the real/surreal, the later ones are more extreme and sometimes sadistically surreal. This offers us a fore-echo of what a Clemens-inspired *Avengerland* would be like in colour. There is no doubt that he was the most influential figure in Season 4 (and beyond). *The Town of No Return* and *Death at Bargain Prices* are two of the most memorable episodes; the former is arguably as good as any in the 26 'film' run. Conversely, there are times when his scripts lack subtlety and lead us to wonder whether Frank Hui has a point when he suggests that "Clemens writes with such extreme strokes that he makes it impossible for there to be anything remotely likeable or even admirable about [his guest characters]." Hui was talking about the female secretaries in *How to Succeed...at Murder* but I think that 'extreme strokes' is an excellent description of Clemens' creative approach in general. (This is intended as an observation rather than a criticism, as I admire much of what he brought to *The Avengers*' creative table. At the same time there is no doubt that with the move from videotape to film, Clemens wanted his own particular vision of *Avengerland* to dominate, sometimes at the expense of creative freedom.)

As for the two other main writers, Philip Levene offers a number of delightful, clever scripts including the far-more-subtle-than-people-remember sci-fi 'classic', *The Cybernauts*. Tony Williamson is arguably harder to label or pigeon-hole than the others, and his *The Murder Market* and *Too Many Christmas Trees* are two of the very best Season 4 offerings. Colin Finbow may only have contributed a single episode, yet his wonderfully off-beat *A Surfeit of H$_2$O* is a highlight. In terms of atmospheric charm it is hard to find a better episode than John Lucarotti's *Castle De'ath*. The fact that nine writers provided (memorable) scripts helps to explain the magical, dazzling variety, as does the use of nine directors, each bringing with him an individual filmic style.

I referred, in my introduction, to the painstaking time and thought which went into 'casting' each episode. Not just the guest actors, but also the set designs, music and costumes. The same applies to the title of each episode, with some being re-named a number of times before filming commenced. They are as stylish as the visual content, ranging from the mysterious – *The Town of No Return* and *The Hour That Never Was* – to the poetic – *Silent Dust* – the devilishly clever – *Death at Bargain Prices* – and the alliteratively memorable – *The Murder Market* and *Dial A Deadly Number*. Can any other television drama series rival *The Avengers* in terms of episode titles which tease us and/or reflect the mood and style of the 'hour'? As Brian Clemens observes, the production team treated each one as an individual film and the attention to every detail shines through half a century later.

It would be ridiculous to close without commenting on the importance of Patrick Macnee/John Steed and Diana Rigg/Emma Peel. Rigg brought comic timing, dramatic ability and sophisticated sex appeal to her role. Her on-screen chemistry with Macnee is breathtakingly tangible in episodes such as *Too Many Christmas Trees*. There are moments in the following colour season when she looks bored or stale but in the monochrome season she brings a fresh, 'cool warmth' and a cutting edge to the series. Honor Blackman/Cathy Gale paved the way and both Linda Thorson/Tara King and Joanna Lumley/Purdey would later bring their own individual qualities to the ever-evolving *Avengers*. However, I am willing to publically proclaim what many others privately believe: Rigg/Peel was the best *Avengers* actress/character in the entire run. The series was incredibly fortunate to have her on board for two seasons and her innate ability brought out the best in Patrick Macnee.

Macnee's Steed is caught here between the sometimes callous figure of the videotape era and the softer Steed of the colour seasons. He is, as I described him in an earlier chapter, a salesman of adventures. We are always delighted to head off with him; Emma

Peel is sometimes – understandably – more reluctant. Here, he maintains a 'suave edge' but has a delightful rapport with Emma Peel. Their verbal fencing is as important as the surrealism, the darker, dramatic depths, the sets, music and innovative writers and directors.

Emma Peel and John Steed's apartments offer us a microcosm of their contrasting, complimenting personalities. Peel's traditional-looking (and sounding) doorbell is a misleading initial 'sign'. Above it is a far more intriguing object: an odd cyclops eye (with lashes) which opens as a post-modernist peephole. It suggests that its owner will be stylishly *avant-garde*. [2] Inside, there is a fashionable three-sided bench seat with ornaments on its backshelf, a hard-looking sofa, small desk and, in the centre of this living area, another eye-catching object: a modern, circular, free-standing fireplace. The room is flooded with light from the expansive windows which offer a panoramic view of London. (We know from *The Girl From Auntie* that the flat is housed in a modern highrise block.) Various ethnic *objets d'art* suggest that she is well-travelled and open-minded. French windows lead out to a patio or roof terrace with a Henry Moore-style sculpture. A sliding door leads to the kitchenette which, ironically, we only properly view when Georgie, the fake Mrs. Peel, is living there. It looks like the type of flat which is used for work but rarely for play. The owner is young, vibrant and probably eats out a lot.

Steed's apartment is far more traditional, with a darker, warmer feel to it and furniture to match. Victorian Gothic-style French windows lead out to a balcony/terrace, again with city views. It is a bachelor pad for a well-heeled, middle-aged man who definitely hosts parties, with a comfy sofa and armchairs, full of military, naval and hunting paintings and ornaments. It is almost like a miniature gentlemen's club. Both the internal staircase from the front door and the fireplace are ornate. His kitchen is a proper cook's one, with room for intimate meals. The tuba and hanging swords add quirky details, suggesting that Steed is capable of surprising us.

It is no surprise, however, that when Steed and Emma socialise together it is usually at Steed's home. The two apartments counterbalance each other perfectly, just as John Steed and Emma Peel do. Their homes offer fascinating clues and intriguing insights into their characters. One could argue that the two apartments are more than simply 'permanent' sets; they are personalities or characters in their own right with important roles to play throughout the season.

In closing *Bright Horizons*, it seems appropriate to leave the final word to Patrick Macnee, the one constant throughout *The Avengers*' history.

"We were a bunch of merry men and women, some of the finest craftsmen, creators and curators of a place that existed somewhere in our imaginations...I understood, as I started reading the script for each new episode, that I would be given the key to a new world. Surrounding me was a host of writers, directors, set designers and actors, as well as wardrobe, sound, and lighting people, all with inspired shooting and editing skills. All were at the top of their game, at the right place, and at an extraordinary moment in time. What a privilege it was. What an amazing confluence of good luck, good timing and grace...I leave it to historians to figure out whether *The Avengers* 'mattered', to anthropologists, to experts of every kind. All I know is that we did it." (Patrick Macnee, Foreword to *The Avengers: A Celebration*, Titan Books: 2010, p. 6)

Bright Horizons reflects the fact that a lot of people believe that *The Avengers* was an extraordinary series, that the monochrome filmed season was a groundbreaking moment in television drama's history and that it certainly did – and still does – 'matter'. As I suggested in my preface, with 2014 representing the 50th anniversary of *The Avengers* on film there is no better moment to celebrate this magical series.

© Rodney Marshall

1. I reproduce here the note used in my introduction: *film noir* is a term used to refer to the monochrome episodes by a number of critics/writers including Jaz and myself. Hitchcock's *Psycho* is often viewed as the ultimate *film noir*. It is easy to see how *The Avengers* makes use of a number of the techniques and styles of this cinematic genre: shadow, low-lighting, quirky camera angles etc. These characteristics give an episode such as *The Town of No Return* a psychological thriller element. Some might even argue that *neo-noir* is a term better suited to *The Avengers* given both the decade and the series' increasingly self-referential approach.
2. There is, I would imagine, a visual reference here to Fritz Lang's *film noir Ministry of Fear*.

CONTRIBUTORS

Darren Burch became a fan of *The Avengers* through the 1980s Channel 4 repeats. He lives in East London. His interests include cult 1960s TV, swimming, running, composing music, graphic design, and photography. He is currently a youth worker and caretaker of a church. He has contributed the chapter on *A Sense of History*.

Denis Chauvet teaches English and lives 30 kilometres south of Paris. He is one of the webmasters of *Le Monde des Avengers*, the French website dedicated to *The Avengers*. His interests include travelling and 'vintage series'. He likes the Emma Peel monochrome season because of "its pure Britishness". He has contributed the chapter on *Silent Dust*.

Richard Cogzell lives in Birmingham, England. He is a self-employed hairdresser and chiropodist. His main interest is amateur dramatics. He won a best actor award in 2013. His all time favourite role was Richard Hannay in *The 39 Steps* in 2012. He also loves reading, and would like to get a novel or a play of his own published one day. He has contributed the chapter on *The Cybernauts*.

Sam Denham is a professional writer who first encountered *The Avengers* through the pages of a 1960s Corgi toys catalogue, and when he was allowed to stay up late enough caught the tail end of the Tara King series on TV. The arrival of *The New Avengers* piqued his interest in seeing more of the original and with the Scala cinema and Channel 4 screenings of the early 1980s the "wonderfully written and stylishly visualised world of *Avengerland* was opened up" to him. Since then he has helped others revisit the 'real' world of *The Avengers* through his contributions to the *Avengerland* locations guides and websites, and is never happier than when "tootling through the leafy lanes of its quintessentially English landscape". He has contributed the chapter on *The Murder Market*.

J.Z. Ferguson is interested in all aspects of British and Canadian popular culture, but has a particular love for television. She resides in her native Canada, where she studies an eclectic array of subjects. She has contributed chapters on *The Thirteenth Hole* and *Quick-Quick Slow Death*.

Bernard Ginez lives in the south of Paris. He is one of the webmasters of *Le Monde des Avengers*, the French website dedicated to *The Avengers*. He enjoys science fiction and fantasy television series, particularly *The Avengers* and *Doctor Who*. He has contributed the chapter on *Too Many Christmas Trees*.

Margaret J Gordon MD is a practising psychiatrist in Northern California where she lives with her family. "I grew up watching the Emma Peel era with my dad, simply for the entertainment value. She was a young girl's role model. I never realised the full psychological power of these episodes until I sat down and analysed them. There are megalomaniacs and phallic symbols at every turn." Her other passions include jazz piano, her family and a terrier dog called Purdey. She has contributed chapters on *The Girl From Auntie*, *Death at Bargain Prices* and *Dial A Deadly Number*.

Frank Hui is a molecular biologist in Austin, Texas. His interests include comic books and photography. He has been a fan of *The Avengers* since the early 1970s and has contributed the chapter on *How to Succeed...at Murder*.

Piers Johnson was born in England but has spent almost his entire life in Australia. He holds degrees in History and Computing Science and lives in Sydney with his wife and three children where he builds websites. His *Mrs Peel, We're Needed!* site has been constantly updated since 1993. He has contributed one of the essays on *A Touch of Brimstone*.

Rodney Marshall is a teacher and writer in Suffolk, UK and Poitou-Charentes, France. His main passions are *Rebus*, *The Avengers* and Chamois Niortais FC. He has contributed the chapters on *The Town of No Return*, *The Master Minds*, *Room Without A View*, *Man-Eater of Surrey Green*, *A Surfeit of H_2O*, *Castle De'ath*, *What the Butler Saw*, *The House That Jack Built* and *Honey for the Prince*.

Roger Marshall has enjoyed a long, distinguished career as a television and film scriptwriter. He created the private detective series *Public Eye*, writing twenty-one of the episodes. He created/wrote *Missing From Home*, *Mitch*, *Travelling Man* and *Floodtide*. He provided scripts for *The Sweeney*, *The Professionals* and *Lovejoy* among many others. His films include the critically-acclaimed science fiction-based *Invasion* (1966), and the horror film *And Now the Screaming Starts* (1973), starring Peter Cushing and directed by Roy Ward Baker. He worked on *The Avengers* from the videotape era until the colour Emma Peel season, penning fifteen episodes, fourteen of which carry his name. His *The Hour That Never Was* remains arguably the series' most iconic 'film'. His favourite *Avengers* vintages are the late-Gale and early-Peel periods; his favourite scripts: *Mandrake* and *The Hour That Never Was*.

Dan O'Shea, after spending 35 years in the corporate world, has retired along with his wife to live on a ranch in Arkansas, USA, and raises Arabian horses. He first saw an *Avengers* episode (*Murdersville*) when he was in college and has been hooked on *The Avengers* ever since. He has contributed the chapters on *The Gravediggers* and *The Danger Makers*.

James Speirs is a retired researcher and writer, living in the North East of England. His interests include graphic art, theatre and cinema, most notably the films of Alfred Hitchcock. A fan of Newcastle United FC, his passion for *The Avengers* stems from "the show's acting, inspired, thrilling story lines and Diana Rigg's catsuits!" He has contributed an essay on *A Touch of Brimstone*.

Frank Shailes started watching *The Avengers* because he loved *The Prisoner* and "it seemed just as fun, stylish, wacky and intelligent." The Cathy Gale era is his favourite vintage. He has contributed the chapters on *Two's A Crowd* and *Small Game for Big Hunters*.

Jaz Wiseman is an *Avengers* stalwart. His work on the Optimum/Canal digitally-restored DVD collection – in particular his moderated commentaries with key *Avengers* writers, directors, cast and crew – has ensured that the series' history has been retrieved, captured, protected and attractively packaged for future generations. He has contributed the chapter on *The Hour That Never Was*.

SEASON 4 PRODUCTION ORDER

December 1964-March 1966

The Town of No Return *

The Murder Market

The Master Minds

Dial A Deadly Number

Death at Bargain Prices

Too Many Christmas Trees

The Cybernauts

The Gravediggers

Room Without A View

A Surfeit of H$_2$0

Two's a Crowd

Man-Eater of Surrey Green

Silent Dust

The Hour That Never Was

Castle De'ath

PRODUCTION ORDER (continued)

December 1964-March 1966

The Thirteenth Hole

Small Game for Big Hunters

The Girl From Auntie

Quick-Quick Slow Death

The Danger Makers

A Touch of Brimstone

What the Butler Saw

The House That Jack Built

A Sense of History

How to Succeed...At Murder

Honey for the Prince

(* Filmed first, but later re-filmed with Diana Rigg)

BIBLIOGRAPHY OF WORKS CONSULTED

The Avengers: Digitally Restored Special Edition: The Complete Series 2 (Optimum Classic/Studio Canal, 2010)

The Avengers: Digitally Restored Special Edition: The Complete Series 3 (Optimum Classic/Studio Canal, 2010)

The Avengers: Digitally Restored Special Edition: The Complete Series 4 (Optimum Classic/Studio Canal, 2010)

The Avengers: Digitally Restored Special Edition: The Complete Series 5 (Optimum Classic/Studio Canal, 2010)

The Avengers: Digitally Restored Special Edition: The Complete Series 6 (Optimum Classic/Studio Canal, 2010)

The Avengers Dossier: The Definitive Unauthorised Guide (Paul Cornell, Martin Day and Keith Topping, Virgin: 1998)

The Avengers: A Celebration (Marcus Hearn, Titan Books/Studio Canal, 2010)

Subversive Champagne: Beyond Genre in The Avengers: the Emma Peel Era (Rodney Marshall, Amazon, 2013)

The Avengers Forever! (David K Smith, copyright 1996-2008) theavengers.tv/forever

Le Monde des Avengers (theavengers.fr)

Mrs. Peel – We're Needed! The Avengers 1961-1977 (Piers Johnson) dissolute.com.au/the-avengers-tv-series/

Delightful, diabolical debate with fellow *Avengers* can be found at:
avengersfanforum.s2.bizhat.com

Any questions, feedback or criticism about this book can be directed to me at:
rodneymarshall628@btinternet.com

Printed in Great Britain
by Amazon.co.uk, Ltd.,
Marston Gate.